高等学校试用教材

建筑类专业英语
暖通与燃气

第二册

向　阳		主编
钱申贤	夏　岩	编
陈素红	胡　昱	
钱申贤		主审

中国建筑工业出版社

前　言

　　经过几十年的探索，外语教学界许多人认为，工科院校外语教学的主要目的，应该是："使学生能够利用外语这个工具，通过阅读去获取国外的与本专业有关的科技信息。"这既是我们建设有中国特色的社会主义的客观需要，也是在当前条件下工科院校外语教学可能完成的最高目标。事实上，教学大纲规定要使学生具有"较强"的阅读能力，而对其他方面的能力只有"一般"要求，就是这个意思。

　　大学本科的一、二年级，为外语教学的基础阶段。就英语来说，这个阶段要求掌握的词汇量为 2400 个（去掉遗忘，平均每个课时 10 个单词）。加上中学阶段已经学会的 1600 个单词，基础阶段结束时应掌握的词汇量为 4000 个。仅仅掌握 4000 个单词，能否看懂专业英文书刊呢？还不能。据统计，掌握 4000 个单词，阅读一般的英文科技文献，生词量仍将有 6％左右，即平均每百词有六个生词，还不能自由阅读。国外的外语教学专家认为，生词量在 3％以下，才能不借助词典，自由阅读。此时可以通过上下文的联系，把不认识的生词猜出来。那么，怎么样才能把 6％的生词量降低到 3％以下呢？自然，需要让学生增加一部分词汇积累。问题是，要增加多少单词？要增加哪一些单词？统计资料表明，在每一个专业的科技文献中，本专业最常用的科技术语大约只有几百个，而且它们在文献中重复出现的频率很高。因此，在已经掌握 4000 单词的基础上，在专业阅读阶段中，有针对性地通过大量阅读，扩充大约 1000 个与本专业密切有关的科技词汇，便可以逐步达到自由阅读本专业科技文献的目的。

　　早在八十年代中期，建设部系统院校外语教学研究会就组织编写了一套《土木建筑系列英语》，分八个专业，共 12 册。每个专业可选读其中的三、四册。那套教材在有关院校相应的专业使用多年，学生和任课教师反映良好。但是，根据当时的情况，那套教材定的起点较低（1000 词起点），已不适合今天学生的情况。为此，在得到建设部人事教育劳动司的大力支持，并征得五个相关专业指导委员会同意之后，由建设部系统十几所院校一百余名外语教师和专业课教师按照统一的编写规划和要求，编写了这一套《建筑类专业英语》教材。

　　《建筑类专业英语》是根据国家教委颁发的《大学英语专业阅读阶段教学基本要求》编写的专业阅读教材，按照建筑类院校共同设置的五个较大的专业类别对口编写。五个专业类别为：建筑学与城市规划；建筑工程（即工业与民用建筑）；给水排水与环境保护；暖通、空调与燃气；建筑管理与财务会计。每个专业类别分别编写三册专业英语阅读教材，供该专业类别的学生在修完基础阶段英语后，在第五至第七学期专业阅读阶段使用，每学期一册。

　　上述五种专业英语教材语言规范，题材广泛，覆盖相关专业各自的主要内容：包括专业基础课，专业主干课及主要专业选修课，语言材料的难易度切合学生的实际水平；词汇以大学英语"通用词汇表"的 4000 个单词为起点,每个专业类别的三册书将增加 1000~1200 个阅读本专业必需掌握的词汇。本教材重视语言技能训练,突出对阅读、翻译和写作能力的培养,以求达到《大学英语专业阅读阶段教学基本要求》所提出的教学目标:"通过指导学生阅读有关专业的英语书刊和文献,使他们进一步提高阅读和翻译科技资料的能力,并能以英语为工具获取专业所需的信息。"

《建筑类专业英语》每册 16 个单元,每个单元一篇正课文(TEXT),两篇副课文(Reading Material A&B),每个单元平均 2000 个词,三册 48 个单元,总共约有十万个词,相当于原版书三百多页。要培养较强的阅读能力,读十万词的文献,是起码的要求。如果专业课教师在第六和第七学期,在学生通过学习本教材已经掌握了数百个专业科技词汇的基础上,配合专业课程的学习,再指定学生看一部分相应的专业英语科技文献,那将会既促进专业课的学习,又提高英语阅读能力,实为两得之举。

本教材不仅适用于在校学生,对于有志提高专业英语阅读能力的建筑行业广大在职工程技术人员,也是一套适用的自学教材。

建设部人事教育劳动司高教处和中国建设教育协会对这套教材的编写自始至终给予关注和支持;中国建筑工业出版社第五编辑室密切配合,参与从制定编写方案到审稿各个阶段的重要会议,给了我们很多帮助;在编写过程中,各参编学校相关专业的许多专家、教授对材料的选取、译文的审定都提出了许多宝贵意见,谨此致谢。

《建筑类专业英语》 是我们编写对口专业阅读教材的又一次尝试,由于编写者水平及经验有限,教材中不妥之处在所难免,敬请广大读者批评指正。

《建筑类专业英语》

编审委员会

Contents

UNIT ONE

Text   New Areas of Gas Consumption

[1]   New technologies introduce the possibility of whole new areas of gas consumption. In the history of gas industry, technical change has from time to time led to important shifts inthe main sectors of consumption-the most obvious of which have been the changes in the principal uses of gas from lighting to cooking and from cooking to heating. Over a 25 year period, such as the one covered in this study, it is possible that some new use of natural gas, based on a novel technical development, could have an appreciable impact on the demand for gas. [1]It is difficult or impossible to predict with any degree of certainty how changing economic, technical and social needs might evolve to create new areas of demand. [2]It is possible, however, to identify areas of current research and technical interest which may offer some potential for the future.

[2]   Four technologies may be of primary interest over the next twenty five years-fuel cells, combined cycle power generation, compressed natural gas (CNG) as a vehicle fuel and gas-to-gasoline or gas-to-middle distillates conversion processes. Fuel cells and combined cycle power generation offer efficient and environmentally attractive means of producing electricity. CNG and gas-to-synthesis fuels conversion processes may offer natural gas a significant niche in the transportation sector energy demand in some countries.

[3]   Fuel cell technology is, in the mid 1980s, still at the research and demonstration stage. In simple terms, a fuel cell can use natural gas as a feedstock to generate electricity (without burning the gas) by a sort of electrolysis-in-reverse; the hydrogen in natural gas is electrochemically combined with oxygen to yield electricity and usable heat. The advantages of fuel cells include an ability to run up and down to follow load requirements, cleanliness, and energy efficiencies of about 50% (compared with about 40% for state-of-the-art conventional power generating) Research work is continuing in Germany, Japan and the United States, and performance is considered by some major engineering manufacturers to be sufficiently reliable to warrant engineering development for utility sized cells. Small-scale, on-site use of fuel cells by industrial or commercial users is considered the most likely path for development.

[4]   Combined cycle power generation using natural gas is at a much more advanced stage of development and commercialisation. A gas-driven turbine can be combined with a steam-driven turbine using heat recovered from the flue gases to give conversion efficiency gains in the generation of electricity. This may prove economically attractive to quite a wide range of users. In the United States, gas in combined cycle use has become an attractive fuel for industrial co-generation; the economics depend partly on relative gas and electricity prices to industry, but also on the level of prices paid for surplus power delivered to

the public grid by co-generating plant. As with all new technologies, it is difficult to quantify how widely combined cycle will spread and to what extent, if at all, it may cause gas to displace other fuels in the power generation sector. ③

[5]   Compressed natural gas as a vehicle fuel is not a new technology—it was established in Italy in the 1930s and CNG vehicles are in operation in Italy and New Zealand as well as in experimental fleets in the Netherlands, Canada and the United States. Worldwide there are between 300,000 and 400,000 natural gas vehicles powered by CNG. The economic attractiveness of CNG as a vehicle fuel is mainly dependent on relative fuel prices and fuel taxation policies and it is these rather than technical innovations which will probably determine the ultimate size of the market. Substantial growth is not anticipated under existing taxation policies and with the fuel price assumptions used in this study.

[6]   Production of synthetic liquid fuels (gasoline, kerosene or gas oil) from natural gas is now technically feasible under processes patented by two major multinational oil companies. There are no short term prospects for further commercialisation of these technologies in the OECD world, but there is a proposal for a gas-to-gas oil conversion project in Malaysia. ④In general, these technologies are likely to be of most interest as a means of obtaining value from remote gas reserves which may otherwise lie dormant. ⑤They may be even more attractive where the foreign exchange component of petroleum-based fuels is high. In most OECD countries, with the clear exception of New Zealand, the relative proximity of well developed or potential markets to gas reserves means that alternative outlets are readily available for gas. This may limit the potential for projects based on these technologies in the OECD area. They may represent an interesting opportunity for both resource development and technology transfer, however, in the developing world.

New Words and Expressions

sector ['sektə]	n.	部门
appreciable ['əpriʃiəbl]	a.	明显的，可观的
distillate * ['distilit]	n.	蒸馏液
synthesis * ['sinθisis]	n.	合成
niche [nitʃ]	n.	地位，作用
demonstration [ˌdeməns'treiʃən]	n.	示范，演示
in simple terms	n.	简单地说
feedstock * ['fiːdstɔk]	n.	原料
electrolysis-in-reverse	n.	逆向电解
electrochemically * [iˌlektrəu'kemikəli]	ad.	用电化学方法
state-of-the-art	a.	现代水平的
warrant ['wɔrənt]	vt.	保证
on-site	a.	现场的，就地的

commercialisation [kəˈməːʃəlizeiʃən]	n.	商业化
turbine * [ˈtəːbin]	n.	涡轮机
flue gas [fluː]	n.	排烟气
surplus [ˈsəːpləs]	a.	过剩的
public grid [grid]	n.	电网
quantify * [ˈkwɔntifai]	vt.	确定数量，量化
displace [disˈpleis]	vt.	顶替，取代
fleet [fliːt]	n.	汽车队
in operation		起作用，运转
taxation [tækˈseiʃən]	n.	税收
innovation [ˌinəuˈveiʃən]	n.	革新
assumption * [əˈsʌmpʃən]	n.	假定，设想
kerosene [ˈkerəsiːn]	n.	煤油
multinational [ˌmʌltiˈnæʃənl]	a.	多国的，跨国的
gas oil	n.	粗柴油
patent [ˈpeitənt]	v.	获专利权
dormant [ˈdɔːmənt]	a.	没有利用的
proximity * [prɔkˈsimiti]	n.	接近，近似

Notes

①such as the one covered in this study＝such as the period which has been covered in the study of natural gas。

②to predict with any degree of certainty how… with any degree of certainty 作状语插入，引起动词（predict）和它的宾语从句（how 引出）的分离。

③if at all 惯用结构，意为"不管在任何程度上（或范围内）。"

④OECD ＝ Organization for Economic Cooperation and Development 经济合作和发展组织。

⑤which may otherwise lie dormant，otherwise 为副词，意为"不然的话"，修饰谓语 may lie dormant。

Exercises

Reading Comprehension

Ⅰ. Choose the best answer for each of the following.

1. The most obvious of the important shifts in the main sectors of gas consumption may be _____ .

A. the change from cooking to lighting

B. the change from heating to cooking

C. the change from lighting to heating

D. the changes from lighting to cooking and from cooking to heating

2. According to the author, it is impossible to _____ .

A. identify areas of current research and technical interest

B. have some new use of natural gas which may have an appreciable impact on the demand for gas

C. predict how changing economic, technical and social needs might evolve to create new areas of demand

D. quantify how much combined cycle will spread

3. It is said that fuel cells, combined cycle power generation, compressed natural gas as a vehicle fuel and gas-to-gasoline or gas-to-middle distillates conversion processes _____ .

A. were widely used 25 years ago

B. have been successfully employed in the past 25 years

C. may be of primary interest over the next 25 years

D. may be of no use in the future

4. Which of the following is not related to the determination of the ultimate size of CNG market?

A. relative fuel price

B. fuel taxation

C. relative fuel price and fuel taxation

D. technical innovation

5. The technologies of production of synthetic liquid fuels may be more attractive in _____ .

A. the areas where the foreign exchange component of petroleum-based fuels is high

B. most OECD countries

C. New Zealand

D. Malaysia

Ⅱ. Are the following statements true or false?

1. Fuel cell has the ability to run up and down to follow load requirements, cleanliness, and energy efficiencies.　　　　　　( )

2. Combined cycle power generation can not cause gas to displace other fuels in the power generation.　　　　　　( )

3. Compressed natural gas as a vehicle fuel will have substantial increase under existing taxation policies.　　　　　　( )

4. Synthetic liquid fuels from natural gas have successfully been produced by two major multinational oil companies.　　　　　　( )

4

5. The potential for projects based on these technologies for production of synthetic liquid fuels may be limited if alternative outlets are readily available for gas in the OECD countries. ( )

Vocabulary

I . Fill in the blanks with some of the words listed below, changing the form where necessary.

warrant	feedstock	operation	dormant
impact	quantify	patent	displace

1. It is possible to predict that some new use of natural gas will have an appreciable on the demand for gas.
2. Natural gas can be used as a _____ to generate electricity in a fuel cell.
3. Fuel cells are sufficiently reliable to _____ the ability to run up and down to follow load requirement.
4. Although it is difficult to _____ how much combined cycle will spread, gas is believed to displace other fuels in the power generation in future.
5. It is estimated that over 40,000 CNG vehicles are in _____ in the world.

II . Complete each of the following statements with one of the four choices given below.

1. A major programme of extension of the nation-wide gas distribution _____ to more remote areas is expected to enable natural gas to increase its share of the residential and commercial sector energy market.

   A. system   B. grid   C. network   D. framework

2. The major use of natural gas is as a feedstock to city gas works, _____ as a directly piped fuel as in other parts of the world.

   A. would rather   B. rather than   C. as well   D. just the same

3. The possibility of new areas of gas consumption is introduced by some _____ tech- nologies.

   A. state-of-the-art   B. good-for-nothing

   C. out-of-date   D. non-self-governing

4. Remote gas reserves will probably lie _____ until these new technologies are used to produce fuel cells and CNG.

   A. operative   B. active   C. dormant   D. useful

5. _____ can be used to generate electricity without burning the gas in a fuel cell.

   A. Electrolysis   B. Electrolyzer

   C. Electromoter   D. Electrolysis-in-reverse

Translation 词义选择

　　英语词汇有一词多类和一词多义的现象，因而在翻译时要正确选择词义。通常选择词义要根据 1）词在句中的词类；2）词与上、下文的联系；3）词的搭配习惯。

例 1. 1）Structures built on strong rock generally need no foundation since rock is usually as strong as concrete.

　　　由于岩石通常象混凝土一样坚固,因此建造在坚硬岩石上的结构一般不需要基础。

　　2）A continuous foundation is cheap to dig and to concrete.

　　　连续基础的土方开挖和混凝土浇灌费用低廉。

例 2. 1）Power can be transmitted over a long distance.

　　　电可远距离输送。

　　2）Friction causes a loss of power in every machine.

　　　摩擦引起机器功率的损耗。

例 3. 1）The gas industry is broken down into several areas.（习惯搭配）燃气工业分为若干部门。

　　2）The experiment is at once interesting and instructive.（惯用法）

　　　该实验既有趣又有教益。

Directions：

I. Translate the following sentences into Chinese, paying attention to the underlined words.

1. The fuel for the lamps was animal fat.

2. The amount of work is equal to the product of the force by the distance.

3. Structures that fit in with nature are more popular.

4. Civil engineers can not be excused from the oral examination.

5. I shall be only too pleased to do my best in that line of work.

II. Give the Chinese equivalents to the following technical terms.

1. heat delivery surface

2. mass concrete heat rise   3. water-proof membrane

4. water-cement ratio strength law

5. air-exhaust ventilator

6. ventilation conditioner

7. vent condenser

8. vented gas heater

9. approximate treatment

10. waste-water treatment

Reading Material A

Liquefied Petroleum Gas（LPG）

The mixture of C3 and C4 hydrocarbons which are extracted from "wet" natural gases (and alsoobtained from crude oil refining operations) are mainly composed of propane (C_3H_8) with somepropylene (C_3H_6); and butane (C_4H_{10}) with some butylene (C_4H_8). Small proportions of ethane, ethylene, iso-butane and iso-pentane may also occur in the mixture, and an odorant is usually added for safety reasons. The term " LPG" is a rather unsatisfactory general description of a variable product, whose overall properties, however, are usually determined by appropriate national standards specifications.

Commercial liquefied "butane" has a boiling point of-0.5℃, a calorific value of 3,390 btu/cf(after vaporisation)and a gaseous volume of about 240 times its liquid form. It isusually distributed for large-scale applications (e. g. factory heating and direct-firing industrial operations) in the form of a vaporised butane/air mixture, the composition of the mixture being selected so as to depress the dewpoint to an acceptable level[1]. Suitablemixtures have frequently been used(particularly where LNG is not yet available)in "peak-shaving" operations, to provide additional gaseous fuel at peak periods where the local supply of natural gas is inadequate to meet demand, or as a source of SNG in rural areas.

Commercial liquefied "propane" has a boiling point of 42.1℃, a calorific value of 2, 563 btu/cf,and a higher degree of volatility than "butane",with 275 times its liquid volume in the gaseous state. Because of its relatively low boiling-point, propane does not normally require external vaporizers. It is commonly used for special applications-e. g. the production of protective atmospheres in metal treatment operations, or in the glass industry, propane-air SNG plants are used to supplement natural gas supplies at times of high demand or during conversion operations.[2] In the United States, there are currently nearly 500 such plants, witha combined deliverability of over 5 Bcf/d, which are used for peak-shaving operations. The properties of commercial LPG mixtures vary according to the proportions of the differentcomponents present. LPG in cylinders forms a convenient and highly portable source of heat and light for domestic and commercial applications, particularly where supplies of piped gas are not available. LPG is also widely used in industry wherever a consistent, sulphur-free,non-toxic fuel gas is of special value,as in food manufacturing and poultry breeding.

Its use as an automobile engine fuel has developed more recently, particularly for heavy lorries, public vehicles and urban bus and taxi services.

Existing automotive equipment designed for fuels other than LPG can be converted to operate success fully using the battery. In addition to conversion however, there are on the market engines designed specifically to operate on LPG, particularly smaller engines suitable for indoor use, where their clean exhaust makes it possible to use an internal combustion engine without excessive ventilation. Instances which come to mind are lift trucks for warehouses or ship-hold use, cement mixers. Coal and iron-ore mining equipment and other forms of indoor or underground transport and mechanical power generation. Similarly, certain agricultural tractors and other forming machinery have been designed from the start to operate on LPG.

Notes

①通常将液态丁烷以蒸气丁烷—空气混合气的形式输配给大型用户，混合气组分的选择要使露点减低到容许程度。

②It is commonly used…in metal freatment operations,丙烷-空气代用天然气装置在高需用量或转换运行期间用于补充天然气供应。

Reading Material B

Coal-related Gases

Combustible gases have traditionally been obtained by heating coal in various types of retortin the absence of air; in fact, the coal-gas industry predated the natural gas industry in mostof the world where both types of fuel have been found. The principal components are methane and hydrogen, with smaller proportions of carbon monoxide, ethylene and nitrogen. The dry distillation of coal takes place at temperatures of around 1,000°to 1,150℃, although in the "low temperature carbonization process" somewhat lower temperatures of 500°-750℃ are used.

It has more recently been appreciated that the gentler and long-sustained heating involved in the formation and maturation of coal beds must have produced enormous volumes of methane and other gases in the geologic past, and that a proportion of these gases is likely to have been trapped in the subsurface. Early biogenic and subsequent geochemical transformation processes were probably involved. First, the bacterial degradation of relatively massive terrestrial vegetable material, growing and decaying in a deltaic environment, formed peats and lignites, with the accompanying evolution of carbon dioxide, nitrogen and small volumes of methane. As the delta floor subsided, a process of "coalification" would have set in as a consequence of the increasing heat and pressure resulting from the growth of sedimentary overburden. ①Peats and lignites would thus gradually have been converted into coals by a reaction.

Further volumes of methane and carbon dioxide would then have been evolved; with increasing depth of burial and a sufficient level of temperature, the coalification process would have continued to produce coals of increasing maturity or "rank". The moisture content of the coals would have become progressively less while the proportions of fixed carbon remaining increased. Thus, brown coals, sub-bituminous coals, bituminous coals and eventually anthracites would have been formed.

During the period of geochemical evolution, it is believed that carbon monoxide and carbon dioxide (with considerable amounts of water) were first evolved; then the main stage of methane evolution began when the proportion of fixed carbon approached 75%, i. e. when a temperature of about 140℃ had been reached, corresponding to a depth of burial of perhaps 3,000m; at this stage, medium volatile bituminous coals would have begun to be formed. At about this time also, some of the maceral components (liptinites and vitrinites) of the coals were probably converted into bituminous, oily liquids, which for the most part were subsequently gasified to CO_2 and CH_4. Thereafter, these gases continued to be evolved, with smaller volumes of carbon monoxide and nitrogen, until the final postmature anthracite stage, with perhaps 95% of fixed carbon, was reached.

Some of the gases generated in these processes were adsorbed on and near the coal so that today methane is commonly exuded from freshly-cut coal faces and also occurs (usually with nitrogen, carbon dioxide and some carbon monoxide) in highpressure pockets and fissures in the coal seams, from which dangerous "blowers" of gas may be released. In some modern mines, sufficient methane can be produced by drilling bore-holes from the surface into coal beds to form a useful local fuel source; while it has been estimated that the volume of potentially usable methane contained in US coalfields may amount to as much as 325 Tcf of gas.

Enormous volumes of coal-derived gas must have been generated in this way during the formation and evolution of the roughly 9 trillion tons of the world's known coal resources, and clearly only a very small proportion of this gas could have been retained in the coal-beds, which are generally too dense and impervious to allow much gas to accumulate within them. No doubt, most of the methane was lost to the atmosphere or dissolved in circulating ground waters and in this way removed.

Notes

①随着三角形底层沉降，由于沉积覆盖层增长而引起热和压力升高的结果而进入"煤化"过程。

②显然，只有一小部分的这种气体可能残留在煤层中，通常煤层很密实和不渗透，可使很多气体积存于其中。

UNIT TWO

Text   Reaction Kinetics

[1]   Thermodynamic equilibrium constants, K, indicate the extent to which a given reaction will proceed toward the right under given conditions if enough time is allowed for e-quilibrium to beestablished. A small K implies little conversion to products; a large K indicates large equilibrium conversion. Exothermic reactions have a tendency to spontaneity. Thus carbon in an oxygen bearing atmosphere should be expected to oxidize spontaneously, as, indeed, it does. But the rate of oxidation is normally so slow that we consider it zero at ambient conditions. At higher temperatures the rate of oxidation is increased, and the heat evolved tends to raise the temperature further, thus further increasing the rate of oxidation. Temperature ultimately is stabilized at a value fixed by the rate of heat loss from the oxidizing system and the rateat which oxygen is brought to the carbon for reaction.

[2]   Endothermic reactions, on the other hand, proceed at a faster rate, as temperature is raised only if the endothermic heat of reaction is supplied from a source exterior to the reaction. An endothermic reaction cannot, on this account, be considered spontaneous and is incapable of an autothermic reaction of the kind described above. [1] A good example is shown in the steam gasification of graphite, in which the reaction is highly endothermic and shows an equilibrium constant so small at room temperature as to make equilibrium conversion of carbon to carbon monoxide essentially zero at this temperature. However, as temperature is increased, the thermodynamic equilibrium constant increases rapidly, but the endothermic heat of reaction remains nearly unchanged. Conversion of carbon to CO is clearly facilitated by an increase in temperature in at least two ways: greater equilibrium-conversion is favored, and the rate of conversion is increased with increasing temperature.

[3]   This discussion inevitably leads to the conclusion that the thermodynamic equilibrium constant is related to the kinetics of a given reaction. Furthermore, since we are dealing largely with interactions between gaseous and solid phases, diffusion effects must be taken into consideration. Thus, in the case of carbon burning in an oxygen bearing atmosphere, diffusion of oxygen to the carbon interface must occur before oxidation of carbon can take place. [2]In the process of diffusing oxygen from air to such an interface, the tendency is to accumulate nitrogen near the interface on account of the depletion of oxygen from the interfacial gas mixture. Thus the oxygen diffusing to the interface and the product CO or CO_2 diffusing from the interface must find their way through the film of nonreacting and "stagnant" nitrogen molecules. The stationary film offers a resistance to the diffusion of reactants and products which can be reduced by higher relative velocities between gas and solids. [3] In the limit, high relative gas velocity erodes the thickness (hence resistance) of the stagnant film to nearly zero at topographical surfaces, but is unable to affect similar

film resistances encountered in the pore structures of reacting solids.

[4]   Numerous kinetic investigations have been conducted to study the various reactions involved in the steam and hydrogen gasification of coal and other hydrocarbons. A substantial body of literature has developed. Most authors agree that the initial reaction rates in steam and hydrogen gasification of coal are substantially more rapid than the later rates of conversion of residual chars. Johnson postulates that overall gasification occurs in three consecutive stages: (1) devolatilization, (2) rapid rate methane formation, and (3) low rate gasification. The reactions in these stages are independent. He further postulates that carbon occurs in two forms; one is called "base" carbon, and the other is the carbon in volatile matter. Volatile carbon can be evolved only by thermal pyrolysis, independently of the gaseous medium in which the reaction occurs. Base carbon remains in the coal char after devolatilization is complete. This carbon can subsequently be gasified in either the rapid rate methane formation stage or the low rate gasification stage.

[5]   When devolatilization occurs in the presence of a gas containing hydrogen at an elevated pressure, coals or coal chars containing volatile matter also exhibit a high (although transient) reactivity for methane formation in addition to thermal pyrolysis reactions. Studies performed with good time resolution indicate that this rapid rate methane formation occurs at a rate which is at least an order of magnitude slower than devolatilization.④ This can be interpreted to mean that rapid rate methane formation occurs after devolatilization.

[6]   The amount of carbon gassified to methane during transient high reactivity increases significantly with increased hydrogen partial pressure. Evidence indicates that at sufficiently high hydrogen partial pressures virtually all of the carbon not evolved during devolatilization can be gasified quickly to methane by this process.

[7]   Devolatilization reactions begin at about 700 ° F, and the rate of devolatilization increases continuously with temperature up to 1300 ° F, at which temperature rates are considered to be essentially instantaneous. These rates are actually determined by the temperature, pressure, and gas composition existing during devolatilization. After the devolatilization and rapid rate methane formation stages are completed, char gasification occurs at a very much reduced rate. The new slow rates for residual chars are determined by temperature, pressure, gas composition, carbon conversion, and prior history, particularly with respect to temperature.

New Words and Expressions

kinetics [kai'netik]	n.	动力学
thermodynamic * [θə:məudai'næmik]	a.	热力学
equilibrium * [i:kwi'libriəm]	n.	平衡，均衡
constant * ['kɔnstənt]	n.	常数，恒量

exothermic *	[eksəu'θə:mik]	a.	放热的
spontaneity *	[ˌspɔntə'ni:iti]	n.	自发性，自生
oxidize *	['ɔksidaiz]	vt.	使氧化
oxidation	[ɔksidai'zeiʃən]	n.	氧化
endothermic *	[endəu'θə:mik]	a.	吸热的
ambient	['æmbiənt]	a.	周围的
evolve *	[i'vɔlv]	v.	放出，离析
autothermic	[ɔ:təu'θə:mik]	a.	自供热的
monoxide	[mɔ'nɔksid]	n.	一氧化物
facilitate *	[fə'siliteit]	vt.	便于，促进
favor	['feivə]	vt.	给予
graphite	[græfait]	n.	石墨
interface	['intə:feis]	n.	交界面
nitrogen	['naitrədʒən]	n.	氮
depletion *	[di'pli:ʃən]	n.	耗尽
erode *	[i'rəud]	v.	浸蚀，冲刷
stagnant *	[stægnənt]	a.	滞止的
stationary	[steiʃənəri]	a.	稳定的
reactant *	[ri:'æktənt]	n.	反应剂，反应物
pore	[pɔ:]	n.	气孔
hydrocarbon	[haidrəu'kɑ:bən]	n.	碳氢化合物
char	[tʃɑ:]	n.	炭
postulate *	['pɔstjuleit]	v.	主张，假定
consecutive	[kən'sekjutiv]	a.	连续的
devolatilization *	[di:vaitəlai'zeiʃən]	n.	脱去挥发成份
methane	['meθein]	n.	甲烷
volatile	['vɔlatəil]	a.	挥发性的，挥发的，n. 挥发物
phrolysis *	[pai'rɔlisis]	n.	高温分解，热解（作用）
elevate *	['eliveit]	v.	增加，提高
transient *	['trænziənt]	a.	暂时的，瞬态的，过渡的
magnitude *	['mægnitju:d]	n.	数量
instantaneous	[insten'teinjəs]	a.	瞬时的，即时的
only if			只有当…的时候
on this account			由于这个缘故，于是
on account of			由于……
in the limit			在极限范围内
a substantial body of			大量的……
independently of			与……无关，不取决于……
in the presence of			在有……的情况下

12

Notes

①the kind：this kind。

②in the case of carbon burning in an oxygen bearing atmosphere 当碳在含氧气氛中燃烧时。carbon burning in an oxygen bearing atmosphere 为动名词复合式作介词 of 的宾语。

③which 引起的定语从句修饰 diffusion。

④with good time resolution 用高时间分辨率；an order of magnitude 一个数量级。

Exercises

Reading Comprehension

Ⅰ. Choose the best answer for each of the following.

1. Which of the following statements is not true?

A. The rate of oxidation is usually considered zero at ambient conditions.

B. A given reaction will proceed toward the right to the extent indicated by thermo-dynamic equilibrium constants，K under any conditions.

C. A small K shows little conversion to products.

D. A large K implies large equilibrium conversion.

2. The value at which temperature finally is stabilized is fixed by _____ .

A. the rate of heat loss from the oxidizing system

B. the rate at which oxygen is brought to carbon for reaction

C. the rate of oxidation

D. both a and b

3. Exothermic reactions are different from endothermic reactions in that _____ .

A. the former proceeds at a faster rate

B. the latter can be considered as spontaneity

C. the former tends to be spontaneous

D. the latter is capable of an autothermic reaction

4. The steam gasification of graphite is a good example to show _____ .

A. an exothermic reaction

B. an endothermic reaction

C. a large equilibrium constant

D. a equilibrium conversion of carbon to carbon monoxide

5. It is possible to help conversion of carbon to CO by _____ .

A. offering greater equilibrium-conversion or increasing temperature

B. both greater equilibrium-conversion and continuous increase of temperature

C. supplying endothermic heat of reaction

D. the increased rate of oxidation

II. Are the following statements true or false?

1. In the case of carbon burning in an oxygen bearing atmosphere, oxidation of carbon can occur after diffusion of oxygen to the carbon interface takes place.　　( )

2. The diffusion of reactants and products can be reduced by film resistance.　　( )

3. Base carbon can be gasified in the rapid rate methane formation stage or the low rate gasification stage.　　( )

4. The result of research that rapid rate methane formation occurs at a slower rate than devolatilization shows that rapid rate methane formation takes place after devolatilization.　　( )

5. Char gasification occurs at a rapid rate after the devolatilization is completed.　　( )

Vocabulary

I. Fill in the blanks with some of the words listed below, changing the form where necessary.

> conversion facilitate evolve gasification
> oxidize diffuse constant devolatilization

1. Since exothermic reactions have a tendency to spontaneity, carbon in an oxygen bearing atmosphere should _____ spontaneously.

2. In the steam _____ of graphite the reaction is endothermic.

3. When oxygen _____ from air to an interface, it is likely to accumulate nitrogen near the interface.

4. Thermal pyrolysis can _____ volatile carbon.

5. An increase in temperature can _____ conversion of carbon to CO.

II. Complete each of the following statements with one of the four choices given below.

1. It is believed that the thermodynamic equilibrium constant is _____ the kinetics of a given reaction.

   A. related to　　B. linked to　　C. connected with　　D. referred to

2. All of the carbons which are not evolved during _____ can be gasified quickly to methane.

   A. oxidation　　B. carbonization　　C. devolatilization　　D. ventilation

3. An equilibrium constant is so small at room temperature that equilibrium _____ of carbon to carbon monoxide is zero.

   A. constant　　B. conversion　　C. point　　D. potential

4. The thermodynamic equilibrium constant increases rapidly with the increase of

   _____.

   A. humidity　　B. condensity　　C. condensation　　D. temperature

5. A resistance to the diffusion of _____ and products is offered by the stationary film.

    A. reactor   B. reactants   C. reactance   D. reaction

Translation   **词义引伸**

在汉译时，有时会遇到某个词在上下文的词义不同于英汉词典所给出的意思，这时就需要从词的基本含义出发，根据上、下文作词义引伸，切忌搬词典中的汉语释义作直译。

例 1. On the horizontal axis is the strain and on the vertical axis is the stress.

    水平轴表示应变，而纵轴表示应力。

例 2. All these things _____ axes, circles, right angles _____ are geometrical truths.

    所有这些图型_____轴、园、直角_____都是几何图形。

Directions: Translate the following sentences into Chinese, paying attention to the underlined words.

    1. How does the magnet tell us direction?

    2. Where strength is important, and the cement at the site is old, it should be tested.

    3. Eyes are made to see forms in light; light and shade reveal these forms.

    4. The dynamic aspects of life combine with other experiences to become part of the artist's expressive pallet.

    5. As related to any product, high quality is seldom associated with low first cost and the client must always think twice before accepting the cheapest tender.

    6. There is nothing like home.

Reading Material A

Prospects for Coal Gasification

Production of high Btu gas from coal is indeed a complex and expensive prospect. Obstaclesto commercial coal gasification range from technical to economic to political in nature.① Ampleprovision must be scheduled for procurement of permits from governmental bodies such as the Federal Power Commission and multilevels of local, state, and federal regulatory, environmental, and other affected agencies. Further delays can arise from actions of various citizens' groupsconcerned with environment and local ways of life, as well as from landowners in the affectedregion.

If all political resistance could be resolved, commercial coal gasification would still facethe inherent deterrent of cost, which follows directly from the common nature of nearly allknown processes. Readers should note that SNG processes carry out a highly endothermic reaction (gasification) at high temperature, purify the product gas after cooling, and then carry out ahighly exothermic reaction (methanation) at intermediate temperature levels. Because real-worldeconomics requires it, methanation heat must be recovered and in effect pumped uphill for usein the process. This is analogous to a refrigerator operating at enormous scale and at veryhigh temperature.

Since all processes employ this concept in one way or another, all must suffer its economicconsequences. These are embodied in the large amount of expensive capital equipment required and the associated operating expense implied. Analysis of coal gasification capital cost distribution shows less than 10% of total capital cost in any one part of the process except gas purification (16%). General facilities and steam and utility systems taken together account for about 30% of total capital cost. [2] It is evident that even total elimination of the cost ofany process element is incapable of making large reductions in product cost.

Projections of U. S. requirements for natural gas produced by various agencies, including the Institute of Gas Technology, indicate a deficiency of supply growing approximately linearly from 1975 to 2000 if no SNG plants are built. The deficit would grow to about 20 trillion scf per year by 2000, creating a demand for SNG of, say, 1 trillion scf of new capacity each year beginning in 1980. [3] One plant producing 250 million scf/day and on-stream 90% of the time would produce 0. 082 trillion scf/year. It thus would take 12 new plants per year to satisfy thedemand.

Could it be done? Probably not, starting before about 1986, even with a proven, commercially accepted process because lead time for engineering design, procurement, construction, mine development, and water supply development dictates an interval of 8-10 years from commitment to production. Other factors can further limit the attainable rate of construction of U. S. coal gasification facilities. Some examples are the national ability to finance at this rate, the national steel making capacity in the face of competing demands, the national metal fabricationcapacity, and the national availability of managerial, operator, and maintenance skill of allkinds at all levels. There are many more possible bottlenecks, making it appear improbable thatthe United States will build 12 SNG coal gasification plants per year. An analysis of thenation's capacity to meet its natural gas and other energy requirements to the year 2000 wouldbe very interesting indeed.

While these speculations cast suspicion on the suitability of currently known processes for the future needs of the country, they also suggest the strong incentive that exists for innovative thought and the probable economic value of a successful search for better alternatives Among the possibilities deserving attention is the prospect of washing the coal before conversion or combustion, a physical rather than chemical process to extract pure hydrocarbonaceous material free of mineral matter. Where production of methane from coal and water is the necessary objective, a catalytic process is indicated to take maximum advantage of the thermochemical near-neutrality of the reaction $2C + 2H_2O \rightarrow CO_2 + CH_4$ at or near ambient temperature. Where on-site combustion near a coal supply is required, means should be sought to burn the coal with minimum prior treatment. [4] No prior treatment would be needed if an effective and inexpensive flue gas clean-up process were available. Expensive chemical conversion of coal to a fuel for combustion should be avoided in favor of inexpensive direct combustion processes wherever possible.

Notes

① 对商用煤炭气化的障碍，实质上有技术方面的，也有经济和政治方面的。
② 公用设施，蒸气和水电系统一起共占总投资的约30%。
③ 到 2000 年，每年欠缺量将增至 20×10^{12} 立方英尺，比方说，从 1980 年开始每年要形成 10^{12} 立方英尺代用天然气的需用量。
④ 需要在煤源附近就地烧掉的地方，必须寻求具有最低预处理的燃烧煤的措施。

Reading Material B

High Btu Gasification

Low Btu gas production is limited to on-site power production applications almost exclusivelybecause of the relatively high cost of energy transportation. high Btu gas, on the other hand, has from 5 to 10 times the heating value, making energy transportation and distribution costs very substantially less. Since it is undesirable to pay the cost of transportation for inert materials or other substances of low heating value, high Btu gasification seeks to minimize the presence of such substances in favor of the production of, as nearly as possible, pure methane. It is thus clear why the presence of nitrogen is so deleterious to the quality of a pipeline gas, and why it is impractical to use a low Btu gasification process in connection with the production of a pipeline quality product. [1] One of the distinguishing features separating low Btu gasification processes from those producing pipeline quality gas is the need either to use pure oxygen to provide process heat by combustion, or to provide heat by a means that excludes nitrogen from the product. This subject has been reviewed thoroughly in earlier pages, and needs no further elaboration here.

Nearly all processes for the manufacture of pipeline quality gas can be fairly represented bythe overall process scheme, in which the nature of each of the process steps is not detailed. Thus the coal preparation step is peculiar in any given process to the nature of the gasification step, which may be carried out in a fixed bed gasifier requiring lump coal with minimum fines, a fluidized bed gasifier requiring crushed coal 100% through 8 mesh with only 10% passing through 200 mesh, or a transport reactor requiring ground coal so fine that 70% will pass through a 200 mesh screen. In any event, the raw gas leaving the gasification step will contain primarily carbon monoxide, carbon dioxide, hydrogen, excess steam, some methane, and an amount of hydrogen sulfide depending upon the nature of the coal being processed. Numerous other substances may also be present in the raw gas, depending strongly upon the nature of the gasifier. Generally, raw gases are cooled somewhat and sent through a shift reaction, in which CO and steam interact to produce additional CO_2 and hydrogen. This reaction normally occurs at about 550—750°F over a solid catalyst of various possible compositions, including cobalt-molybdenum and nickel-molybdenum on a solid support. The converted gas, now richer in CO_2 and hydrogen and leaner in CO is sent to gas purification, where CO_2 and H_2S are removed. ②Carbon dioxide is emitted to the atmosphere, and H_2S is processed. for recovery of elemental sulfur. The stream of gas leaving purification has been adjusted to approximately 3 mols hydrogen/mol Co and is fed to the methanation unit. The methanation reaction is highly exothermic, and since it occurs on a thermally sensitive supported nickel catalyst, heat removal from the methanator becomes an important design problem. Normally the heat is removed at a temperature level of about 800-900°F by generation of steam to be used elsewhere in the process. The water generated in the reaction is nearly pure (small amounts of methanol, acetone, etc.) and may be retained for recycle to steam generation for the process. The moist methane product leaving the methanator must subsequently be dried and, if necessary, compressed to pipeline pressure specification.

The majority of high Btu gasification processes depend upon the use of air or oxygen and steam; a few processes employ the separate production of hydrogen followed by hydrogasification. The latter procedure has the characteristic of eliminating the shift and methanation parts of the process scheme, and employs somewhat altered techniques for purification of the product methane. Since the majority of the processes employ shift, purification, and methanation stepswhich are sensibly independent of the nature of the gasification step, the nature of thegasifier becomes the major factor in distinguishing the various processes for the production ofpipeline quality gas.

Notes

①It is thus clear why⋯and why it is impracticalto⋯　and 并列连接两个由 why 引起的主语从句，用 it 作形式主语
②将含 CO_2 及 H_2S 较多和 CO 较少的转化煤气送到气体净化工段，去除 CO_2 和 H_2S.

UNIT THREE

Text   Fundamentals of Industrial Ventilation

[1]   The purpose of ventilation is to maintain in the building a prescribed condition and cleanliness of the air (in other words, the temperature, air velocity and concentrations). This task in the last analysis is resolved as follows. The vitiated air is removed from the building (extract ventilation), whilst in its place clean air is introduced, often specially treated (inflow ventilation)

[2]   In essence this boils down to heat transfer and mass transfer between the incoming air and the air already within the building. If owing to excessive internal heat production the temperature of the air in the building tends to exceed the specified norms, cooler air is introduced and mixed with the indoor air; the temperature of the air (owing to heat transfer) then remains at the norm. If harmful gases or vapours are released, their concentration is heldwithin specified limits by dilution with the clean incoming air.

[3]   More often than not mass and heat transfer take place simultaneously. For instance, the production of convective heat is very often accompanied by the releases of gases and highly dispersed dust.

[4]   Ventilation can be affected by fans (mechanical ventilation) or by the difference between the densities of the columns of internal and external air, and also by the action of wind (natural ventilation)

[5]   Ventilation can be general or local. Local extract ventilation is intended for removing polluted air at source, to prevent the dispersal of impurities throughout the building. As much of the impurity as possible is removed in this way so that a minimum has to be diluted by the incoming air. ① Local exhaust is not essentially ventilation proper. ②

[6]   Local ventilation thus limits the area of dispersal. This is assisted by the use of fixed screens or by air curtains. The impurity is removed by suction of the polluted air, and this can be combined with a jet of air which impels the impurity towards the suction opening.

[7]   If air is introduced into a building, some excess pressure is set up in it. In the steady state this pressure will be such that the total quantity of air leaving the building through specially provided vents, or through random cracks in the external surfaces, is equal to that which is introduced. ③ A similar phenomenon will occur with the extract of air from the building. Here a negative pressure (rarefaction) is set up in the building, and in consequence air will be sucked in through gaps from outside and from adjacent rooms to take the place of the extracted.

[8]   In certain cases this air has an unfavourable effect. For instance, if cold outdoor air enters a building in which much water vapour is produced it would create mist on mixing

with the internal hot and moist air. If the inflow from outside or from adjacent rooms satisfies the hygienic requirements, it can be used to replace general mechanical ventilation by natural ventilation.

[9]　　Ventilation is essentially the science of the control of air change in buildings.

[10]　　In solving the problems of ventilation, the following questions arise: (1)what quantity of air should be supplied to the building per unit of time, what quantity should be extracted and how? (2) What characteristics should the incoming air have, and is preliminary treatment of the air necessary(heating, cooling, dehumidifying, conditioning, dust removal, etc.)? (3) What should be the disposition of the inlets and outlets? (4) What should be the design of all the elements which determine the rate of air change?

[11]　　To resolve the issues of general ventilation it is necessary to know the quantity of impurity entering per unit time into the air of the building. It is also essential to know how the impurity is dispersed within the building, and how its distribution can be influenced by ventilation.

[12]　　By extracting the air from areas with high concentrations of impurity, one considerably reduces the quantity of air needed for ventilation. For instance, in iron foundries the concentration of carbon monoxide (CO) in upper levels can be $0.04\ g/m^3$, whereas in the work area it should not exceed the permissible norm $0.02\ g/m^3$.[④]This stratification of the concentration is maintained by a supply of fresh air near the floor, and by extracting the vitiated air from high level. If the fresh air were supplied near the ceiling, in descending it would disturb the stratification and mix with the vitiated air,[⑤] and with the same air change the concentration of CO in the work area would be $0.03\ g/m^3$. To obtain a concentration of $0.02\ g/m^3$ one would have to increase the quantity of ventilation air by a factor of about 1.5. Thus the question of the estimated quantity of ventilating air is directly related to the question of the arrangements for ventilation.

[13]　　To calculate and design local ventilation in the form of air douches, it is necessary to know the properties of the jet, the laws governing the variation of its velocity, temperature and concentration and the geometric dimensions of the jet. To obtain the hygienically prescribed parameters of the air at the workplace, one needs to know the initial parameters of the air and then find the forms of nozzles to produce a jet which would satisfy these requirements.

New Words and Expressions

ventilation * [ˌventiˈleiʃən]	n.	通风
prescribe [prisˈkraib]	vt.	规定、指令
concentration * [ˌkɔnsənˈtreiʃən]	n.	浓度
in the last analysis		总之，归根到底
vitiate * [ˈviʃieit]	vt.	使污浊，污染

extract * [iks'trækt]	vt., n.	抽出、排出
inflow * ['in-fləu]	n.	进气、吸风、流入
boil down to		归结为；简化为
norm [nɔːm]	n.	标准、定额
dilute * [dai'ljuːt]	vt.	稀释、搀入、冲淡
dilution [dai'ljuːʃən]	n.	稀释
more often than not		往往，时常，大半
convective * [kən'vektiv]	a.	对流的
disperse * [dis'pəːs]	vt.	扩散，散布
dispersal * [dis'pəːsəl]	n.	扩散
density * ['densiti]	n.	密度
at source		在源头，在始发地
exhaust [ig'zɔːst]	vt.; n.	排气
vent * [vent]	n.	排气孔，通风孔
random ['rændəm]	a.	偶然的，任意的
adjacent * [ə'dʒeisənt]	a.	相邻的
hygienic [hai'dʒiːnik]	a.	卫生的
disposition * [ˌdispə'ziʃən]	n.	处理
impurity [im'pjuəriti]	n.	杂质，夹杂物
iron foundry		铸铁厂
carbon monoxide		一氧化碳
stratification * [ˌstrætifikeiʃən]	n.	层次，分层现象
descend * [di'send]	vi.	下降，降落
by a factor of M		增加到 M 倍
douche * [duːʃ]	v.; n.	灌洗，喷淋
jet [dʒet]	n.	射流，喷嘴
variation [ˌvɛəri'eiʃən]	n.	变化
geometric [dʒiə'metrik]	a.	几何的，图形的
dimension [di'menʃən]	n.	维度；尺寸；因次
parameter [pə'ræmitə]	n.	系数，参数
nozzle ['nɔzl]	n.	喷嘴

Notes

①As much of the impurities as possible 作句子主语。

②局部排风实际上不是真正的通风。proper，形容词，用于名词后，意为：真的，严格意义上的。例如 the sphere of architecture proper 严格意义上的建筑学领域。

③Such that 如此……，以致……例如：

The situation was such that the experimenter found it difficult to predict.

情况如此，连实验员也觉得难以预料。

④whereas，conj 然而，引起表示相反情况的并列从句。

⑤in descending 当（新鲜空气）下沉时。

Exercises

Reading Comprehension

Ⅰ.Choose the best answer for each of the following.

1. It is possible to maintain in a building a prescribed condition and cleanliness of the air by _____ .

   A. extract ventilation

   B. inflow ventilation

   C. first extraction ventilation and then inflow ventilation

   D. extract ventilation and inflow ventilation at the same time.

2. The temperature of the air in a building remains at the norm because of _____ .

   A. heat transfer　　　　B. mass transfer

   C. dilution　　　　　　D. all of the above

3. Local exhaust is not essentially ventilation because it is used to _____ .

   A. prevent impurities　　　　B. introduce fresh air

   C. remove polluted air at source　　D. dilute the concentration of the air

4. If some excess pressure is set up in a building，the total quantity of air leaving the building is _____ that which is introduced.

   A. more than　　　　B. equal to

   C. less than　　　　D. defined by

5. The stratification of the concentration in iron factories is maintained by _____ .

   A. supplying fresh air near the floor

   B. extracting the vitiated air from high level

   C. keeping the air unchanged

   D. A and B

6. The difference between the densities of the Volumes of internal and external air can bring about _____ .

   A. ventilation　　　　B. natural ventilation

   C. mechanical ventilation　　D. air concentration

Ⅱ.Are the following statements true or false?

1. If a negative pressure is set up in the building，air will be drawn in through gaps from outside. （　）

2. The question that the design of all the elements which determine the rate of air change is not related with ventilation. （　）

3. The question of the estimated quantity of ventilating air is directly related to the question of the arrangements for ventilation. ( )

4. In designing local ventilation in the form of air douches, it is unnecessary to know the properties of the jet. ( )

Vocabulary

I . Fill in the blanks with some of the words listed below, changing the form where necessary.

> vitiate disperse exhaust source
> dilute ventilation concentration relate

1. Pollution from smoke and dust _____ the air.

2. A vacuum is created by _____ air from a container.

3. A solution _____ with water.

4. Some droplets of an immiscible（不能混和的）liquid can _____ in water to form a colloid（胶体）

5. The word _____ means literally the causing of air movement or wind, but has acquired the meaning of a system which gives a regulated supply of air to an enclosed space.

II . Complete each of the following statements with one of the four choices given below.

1. Control for heat exposures may be achieved by control _____, local exhaust, radiation shielding, general or dilution ventilation, or local relief ventilation.

   A. in the beginning　　B. at first　　C. at source　　D. in time

2. The investigation further shows that the increasing rate exceeds the medium value _____ about 5.

   A. by a factor of　　B. by factor　　C. with the factor of　　D. in a factor of

3. The acid solution is of weak _____.

   A. phenomena　　B. dense　　C. concentration　　D. liquid

4. The volume of a fixed mass of gas can _____ the pressure of the gas at a constant temperature.

   A. relate　　B. related to　　C. be referred as　　D. be known as

5. Thermal comfort ventilation _____ the provision of comfortable indoor thermal conditions, involving the prevention of discomfort due to feelings of warmth and skin wetness.

   A. prescribes　　B. disperses　　C. dilutes　　D. boils down to

Translation　　　　　　　　　　　　增词和减词

由于英汉两种语言的遣词造句的差异，因此翻译不可能是等量的逐词死译，应在词量上有所增减。增词法就是按意义和汉语表达上的需要增加汉字来再现原文内容。减词法是指原文中的某些词在译文中不译出来，因为译文中虽无其词，但已有其意，或者在译文中是不言而喻的。

增词法主要用于英语省略结构，短语结构，出现有指代关系或名词表示动作意义的句子结构。

例 1. A fluid is a substance which <u>when in static equilibrium</u> cannot sustain tangential or sheer forces. （省略结构）

液体是一种物质，当<u>它处</u>在静力平衡时，不能承受正切力，即剪力。

例 2. <u>Lifting heavy objects</u>, we always have to exert sufficient force to overcome the pull of gravity. （分词短语结构）

<u>当举重物时</u>，我们总是必须使出充分的力去克服地球的引力。

例 3. Structural members are divided into <u>those</u> in direct stress, <u>those</u> in bending and <u>those</u> with direct stress and bending. （指代关系）

结构构件分为受轴向应力的<u>构件</u>，受弯<u>构件</u>以及既受轴力又受弯的构件。

例 4. D-A is <u>vaporization</u> in the evaporator. （名词含动作意义）

D-A 是蒸发器内的蒸发<u>过程</u>。

减词法主要表现在英语冠词、代词、介词、引导词等结构词的省译。

例 1.1. To obtain satisfactory concentration, <u>one</u> would have to increase <u>the</u> quality <u>of</u> ventilation air.

为了获得满意的浓度，必须增加通风空气量。

例 2.2. <u>It</u> is because of this law <u>that</u> electricity can be changed into heat energy or mechanical energy.

正是由于这个定律，电可以变成热能或机械能。

Directions：

I. Translate the following into Chinese, adding Chinese characters or words where necessary.

1. Defects in the specimen, if any, can be detected by ultrasonic waves.

2. Single-span construction is usually adopted for the smaller factory building, while multiplespan, for the larger.

3. The design of this hotel adopts a combination of high-rise and low buildings.

4. In twenty four hours its strength is equal to that reached with ordinary Portland cement in thirty days.

5. This forging measures six inches by eight by two.

6. When current flowed across a junction in one direction, the junction was cooled; when the current flow was reversed, the same junction heated.

II. Translate the following into Chinese, leaving out English words of the original sentences where necessary.

1. This boiler is very effective provided that it be properly used.

2. It is said that you know a lot about computers.

3. The reactions which are exerted by the supports are in an upward direction.

4. These young people made it their business to take care of the old people in the neighbourhood.

5. It follows that not all substances are good conductors of electricity.

6. It is the introduction of air conditioning that greatly reduces the disadvantage of the interior corridor plan with its lack of through ventilation.

Reading Material A

Comfort Ventilation

Effective comfort ventilation is based on the principle that air must be delivered directly to the work zone with sufficient air motion and at a low enough temperature to cool the workerby convection and evaporation. In most cases, the objective is to provide tolerable workingconditions rather than complete comfort. In each case, the methods described for comfortventilation are based on the assumption that exhaust ventilation, radiation shielding, equipment insulation, and possible changes in process design have been fully used to minimizethe heat loads. In addition, supply air must not blow on or at hot equipment or hoods northrough the layers of hot ceiling air before reaching the work zone. In the former case, theventilation disturbs the capture velocity of the hood or thermal rise from the hot equipmentand distributes hot and/or contaminated air into the workroom. [1] In the latter case, hugevolumes of hot and possibly contaminated air are entrained and brought down to the work zone. [2] Because of the large volumes of ventilation required for industrial plants, heat conservationand recovery should be used, and will provide substantial savings.

In some cases, it is possible to provide unheated or partially heated makeup air to the building. Rotary, regenerative heat exchangers recover up to 80% of the heat represented by the difference between the exhaust and the outdoor air temperatures. [3] Reductions of 5 to 10℃ in the heating requirement for most industrial systems should be routine. While most of the heat conservation and recovery methods outlined in this section apply to heating, the saving possibility of air-conditioning systems is equally impressive. [4] Heat conservation and recoveryshould be incorporated in preliminary planning for an industrial plant. Some methods are:

1. In the original design of the building, process, and equipment, provide insulation and heat shields to minimize heat loads. Vaporproofing and reduction of glass area may be required. Changes in process design may be required to keep the building heat loads within reasonable bounds. Review the exhaust needs for hoods and process and keep

those to a practical, safe minimum.

2. Design the supply air systems for efficient distribution by delivering the air directly to the work zones; by mixing the supply with hot building air in the winter; by using recirculated air within the requirements of winter makeup; and by bringing unheated or partially heated air to hoods or process whenever possible.

3. Design the system to achieve highest efficiency and lowest residence time for contaminants. In the design, consider that it is psychologically sound and good practice to permit workers to adjust and modify the air patterns to which they are exposed;⑤ people desire direct personal control over their working environment.

4. Conserve exhaust air by using it; e. g. , office exhaust can be directed first to work areas, then to locker rooms or process areas, and finally, to the outside. Clean, heated air can be used from motor or generator rooms after it has been used for cooling the equipment. Similarly, the cooling systems for many large motors and generators have been arranged to discharge into the building in the winter to provide heat and to the outside in summer to avoid heat loads.

5. Supply air can be passed through air-to-air, liquid-to-air, or hot-gas-to-air heat exchangers to recover building or process heat.

6. Operate the system for economy. Shut the systems down at night or weekends whenever possible, and operate the makeup air in balance with the needs of operating process equipment and hoods. ⑥ Keep supply air temperatures at the minimum for heating and the maximum for cooling, consistent with the needs of process and employee comfort. Keep the building in balance so that uncomfortable drafts do not require excessive heating.

Notes

①在前一种情况下，通风干扰了排气罩的收吸速度或是从热设备出来的热量上升，且干扰了热的和/或被污染的空气进入工作室。

②在后一种情况下，大量的热和可能被污染的空气被卷吸并下降到工作区。

③回转型蓄热式热交换器可回收由排气温度与室外空气温度差所体现的热量的80％。

④当本节所概述的热量利用（守恒）和回收用于供暖时，空调系统的节能可能性同样给人以深刻的印象。

⑤在设计时要考虑到，允许工人们调节和改变他们所受到的气流型式，从心理上看这是合理的和好的作法。

⑥and operate the makeup…and hoods 起用补给空气，使与工艺设备和排气罩的需要相平衡。

Reading Material B

Roof Ventilators

Roof ventilators are basically heat escape ports located high in a building and properly enclosed for weathertightness. Stack effect plus some wind induction are the motive forces for gravity operation of continuous and round ventilators. [1] The latter can be equipped with fan barrel and motor, thus permitting gravity operation or motorized operation.

Many ventilator designs are available; two designs are the low ventilator that consists of a stack fan with a rainhood, and the ventilator with a split butterfly closure that floats open to discharge air and self-closes. Both use minimum enclosures and have little or no gravity capacity. Split butterfly dampers tend to make the fans noisy and are subject to damage because of slamming during strong wind conditions. [2] Because noise is frequently a problem in many powered roof ventilators, the manufacturer's sound rating should be reviewed.

Roof ventilators can be listed in diminishing order of heat removal capacity. The continuous ventilation monitor most effectively removes substantial concentrated heat loads. An efficient type is the streamlined continuous ventilator. It is designed to prevent backdraft, is weathertight, and usually has dampers that may be readily closed in winter to conserve building heat. Its capacity is limited only by the available roof area and the proper location and sizing of low level air inlets. Gravity ventilators have the advantage of low operating costs, do not generate noise, and are self-regulating (i. e. , a higher heat release results in higher air-flow through the ventilators) Care must be taken to ensure that a positive pressure exists at the ventilators, otherwise outside air will enter the ventilators. This is of particular importance during the heating season.

Next in capacity are: (1) round gravity or windband ventilator, (2) round gravity with fan and motor added, (3) low hood powered ventilator, and (4) vertical upblast powered ventilator. The shroud for the vertical upblast design has a peripheral baffle to deflect the air up instead of down. Vertical discharge is highly desirable to reduce roof damage caused by the hot air, if it contains condensable oil or solvent vapor. Ventilators with direct-connected motors are desirable, because of the locations of the units and the belt maintenance required for units having short shaft centerline distances. Round gravity ventilators have a low capacity and are applicable to warehouses with light heat loads and to manufacturing areas having high roofs and light loads.

Streamlined continuous ventilators must operate effectively without mechanical power. Efficient ventilator operation is generally obtained when the difference in elevation between the average air inlet level and the roof ventilation is at least 10 m and the exit temperature is 14℃ above the prevailing outdoor temperature.

To ensure this level of performance, sufficient low level openings must be provided for the incoming air. Manufacturers recommend 1.3 to 2.5 m/s inlet velocity. Insufficient inlet area and significant air currents are the most common reasons for gravity roof ventilators malfunction.③ A positive supply of air around the hot equipment may be necessary within large buildings where the external wall inlets are remote from the equipment.

The cost of electrical power for mechanical ventilation is offset by the advantage of constant airflow. Mechanical ventilation can also create the pressure differential necessary for good airflow, even with small inlets. Inlets should be sized correctly to avoidinfiltration and other problems caused by high negative pressure in the building. Often, amechanical system is justified to supply enough makeup air to maintain the work area underpositive pressure.

Careful study of airflow around buildings is necessary to avoid reintroducing contaminantsfrom the exhaust into the ventilation system. Even discharging the exhaust at the roof levelor from an area opposite the outside intake may still allow it to reenter the building evenwhen intakes are inside walls opposite the exhaust discharge point.

Notes

①抽气效应加上某种风的诱吸作用是连续式和圆形风机重力运行的推动力。
②对开式蝶阀会使风扇噪声增大，且因在大风时猛关而遭到损坏。
③进风口面积不足和气流量大，是重力式屋顶风机故障的最一般原因。

UNIT FOUR

Text　　Similarity and Experimental Methods

[1]　　Air in a building is in a state of motion due to natural and forced convection currents and their circulation. In this way vapours, gases, heat and fine dust are transferred and distributed.

[2]　　The fields of velocity and concentration are not independent of each other and so they have to be regarded as a complex of heterogeneous but interdependent processes, which are governed by the general laws of the conservation of matter and of energy. [1] The initial equations for solving these problems are the differential equations of (1) continuity; (2) motion; (3) heat conduction or mass transfer; (4) heat exchange at the boundary between solid bodies and fluids.

[3]　　These differential equations are applicable to a very wide range of phenomena—for instance, to the motion of air in the atmosphere, to the motion of water in a river and so on. To restrict the problem and determine the process uniquely, it is necessary, for steady state phenomena, to define the boundary conditions, i. e. such values of the required function which are known beforehand and are sufficient to define a unique solution of the differential equation.

[4]　　The application of mathematical analysis to the solution of complex technical problems in most cases is confined to the formulation of the problem, i. e. to forming the differential equations and establishing the boundary conditions, since the solving of the equations in most cases is still impracticable. In solving ventilation problems, owing to the great complexity ofthe phenomena and the impossibility of analytical solution, one often has to turn to experiments and testing.

[5]　　Sometimes the necessary experiments can be carried out in natural (actual) conditions; in other cases resort is had to the study of phenomena on a model (simulation) .[2] For studying ventilation problems by means of models one has to reproduce aerodynamic, thermal, and molecular processes often acting simultaneously, so as to determine what in reality will be the parameters which ensure the effectiveness of ventilation, viz the velocity of the air, temperature and the gas concentration.

[6]　　The laboratory-model method possesses a number of advantages over full-scale investigationsin actual conditions—namely, the possibility of studying installations in the development stage, the possibility of systematically studying the influence of some particular factor isolated from all other factors which condition the phenomenon as a whole, and the possibility of studying rapidly varying phenomena which elude actual observation. Furthermore, the cost of laboratory investigation is less than the cost of a field investigation. In setting up an experiment, on the full scale or on a model, one studies a particu-

lar phenomenon and then, by generalizing the results of the study, one tries to find a basis for calculating other related cases.

[7]　It is only legitimate to extend the results of a single test to analogous situations. How the results of an investigation of a single test carried out in actual conditions are extended to other conditions, and how the results of investigations on models can be converted to apply to actual conditions, is taught by the theory of similarity. ③One distinguishes geometric, mechanical and thermal similarity.

[8]　Geometric similarity, as is generally known, relates to equality of angles and the proportionality of similar sides in different geometric shapes. ④Mechanical similarity is understood to be kinematic or dynamical similarity of phenomena. Kinematic similarity presupposes proportionality between the velocities and accelerations of two streams ; dynamic similarity postulates the similarity of forces which cause similar motions.

[9]　In thermal similarity the temperatures and heat flows remain similar.

[10]　Similarity theory teaches that

　　1. mutually similar phenomena have identical similarity criteria (dimensionless groups);
　　2. any relationship between variable quantities characterizing some phenomenon can be represented as a relationship between similarity criteria,
　　3. those phenomena are similar for which the boundary conditions are similar and the similarity criteria are numerically identical. ⑤

[11]　The theory of similarity shows that in tests it is necessary to measure all those quantities which are contained in the similarity criteria, and the test results are to be handled by means of dimensionless quantities or groups.

[12]　The data of a single test can be extended to similar phenomena, i. e. to other phenomena with analogous boundary conditions provided the dimensionless groups (similarly criteria) formed from the quantities entering into the boundary conditions are numerically identical. By means of models one can study questions of mechanical, natural and combined ventilation, general and local, when air change is necessitated by the presence of sources of heat, moisture, noxious vapours, gases and dust.

[13]　Recourse is had to simulation when it becomes necessary to give a comparative evaluation of different systems of ventilation, to give an aerodynamic characterization of simple and wind-proofed roof-bay ventilation, and also in many other cases when an analytic solution is extremely difficult. ⑥Simulation is a reliable means of studying the very complex phenomena with which one is confronted in solving questions of ventilation. ⑦

[14]　The working medium in simulating ventilation phenomena may be air or water. Each has itsmerits and disadvantages. The technique of simulation with air is simpler.

New Words and Expressions

convection ＊　[kən'vekʃən]　　　　　　　　*n.*　　对流

circulation *	[ˈsəːkjuˈleiʃən]	n.	环流，循环
concentration *	[ˌkɔnsənˈtreiʃən]	n.	浓度
heterogeneous *	[ˌhetərəuˈdʒiːnjəs]	a.	非均质的，多相的，不均匀的
interdependent	[ˌintədiˈpendənt]	a.	相互关联的
conservation *	[ˌkɔnsə (:) ˈveiʃən]	n.	守恒
differential equation			微分方程
turn to…			向……求助，借助于……
resort	[riˈzɔːt]	n.	依赖，手段
aerodynamic *	[ˈɛərəudaiˈnæmik]	a.	空气动力的
viz	[viz]	ad.	（拉丁语）即，就是
full-scale			原型，足见比例
condition	[kənˈdiʃən]	vt.	决定，制约
elude *	[iˈluːd]	vt.	逃避，避免
generalize	[ˈdʒenərəlaiz]	vt.	归纳
legitimate	[liˈdʒitimit]	a.	正当的，合理的
analogous *	[əˈnæləgəs]	a.	类似的
proportionality *	[prəˌpɔʃənˈæləti]	n.	比例，平衡
kinematic *	[ˌkainiˈmætik]	a.	运动的
dynamical *	[daiˈnæmikəl]	a.	动力的
presuppose *	[ˌpriːsəˈpəuz]	vt.	以……为先决条件
postulate *	[ˈpɔstjulit]	vt.	以……为前提
variable *	[ˈvɛəiəbl]	n.	变量
characterize	[ˈkæriktəraiz]	vt.	表示特征
demensionless *	[diˈmenʃənlis]	a.	无量纲，无因次
necessitate	[niˈsesiteit]	v.	需要
noxious *	[ˈnɔkʃəs]	a.	有害的
have recourse to			求助于……
simulation	[ˌsimjuˈleiʃən]	n.	仿造，模型试验，模拟
wind-proofed			防风的
roof-bay			屋顶间隔
analytic solution			解析解
confront	[kənˈfrʌnt]	vt.	使面临
exposition	[ˌekspəuˈziʃən]	n.	解释，描述

Notes

①which 指代 heterogeneous but interdependent processes.
②in other cases resort is had to the study of phenomina on a model.
　　在其他情况下，就得求助于在模型上对现象进行研究。to have resort to… 向……求助。

resort is had to 为被动结构。

③and 并列连接两个由 how 引起的从句，作为一个整体概念作 is taught 的主语。

④as 引起非限定性定语从句，译为"正如所公认那样"。

⑤for which 引起限定性定语从句，修饰 phenomena。

⑥Recourse is had to simulation ，求助于模拟方法。Recourse is had 是 have recourse to（求助于…）的被动结构。

⑦With which one is confronted…

to confront sb with…使某人面临……；此限定性定语从句为被动结构。

Exercises

Reading Comprehension

Ⅰ. Choose the best answer for each of the following.

1. The fields of velocity and concentration are _____ .

    A. independent of each other

    B. heterogeneous but interdependent processes

    C. beyond the general laws of the conservation of matter and of energy

    D. steady state phenomena

2. "To define the boundary condition" means _____ .

    A. to restrict the problem and determine the process

    B. to define a unique solution of the differential equation

    C. to define a required function

    D. to define values of the required function known before-hand and sufficient to define a unique solution of the differential equation

3. People have to turn to experiments and testing in solving ventilation problems，because _____ .

    A. the application of mathematical analysis is confined to the formulation of the problem

    B. ventilation phenomena are complex technical problems

    C. ventilation phenomena are very complex and can't be solved with analytical solution

    D. people have to reproduce aerodynamic，thermal，and molecular processes.

4. The advantages of the laboratory-model method over full-scale investigations in actual conditions include _____ .

    A. the possibility of studying installations in the development stage and the influence of some particular factor conditioning the phenomenon as a whole

    B. the possibility of studying rapidly varying phenomena eluding actual observation

    C. a less investigation cost

D. all of the above

5. Which of the following is not taught in the theory of similarity?

　A. The identical similarity criteria of mutually similar phenomena

　B. The relations between similar phenomena, similar boundary conditions, and similarity criteria

　C. A relationship between similarity criteria

　D. Varying ventilation phenomena

II. Are the following statements true or false?

1. The theory of similarity does not include geometric similarity, mechanical similarity and thermal similarity.　　　　　　　　　　　　　　　　　　　　　( )

2. Geometric similarity relates to the velocity and acceleration　　　　　( )

3. Mechanical similarity refers to be the similarity of forces and similarity of motions.
　　　　　　　　　　　　　　　　　　　　　　　　　　　　　　　　( )

4. People have recourse to simulation because it can give a comparative evaluation of different systems of ventilation.　　　　　　　　　　　　　　　　　　　( )

5. When people are confronted with the very complex phenomena in solving questions of ventilation, they have to have recourse to simulation.　　　　　　　　( )

Vocabulary

I. Fill in the blanks with some of the words or expressions listed below, changing the form where necessary.

be applicable to	be confronted with	turn to	provided
be confined to	have resort to	simulation	on models

1. People have to _____ experiments and testing to solve ventilation problems when there is no analytical solution to them.

2. These equations _____ the motion of air in the atmosphere.

3. Since it is impracticable to solve the equations in most cases, the application of mathematical analysis to the solution of complex technical problems _____ forming the differential equations and establishing the boundary conditions.

4. When people can't carry out experiments in natural conditions they have to _____ the study of phenomena on a model.

5. In solving questions of ventilation people _____ various kinds of very complex phenomena.

II. Complete each of the following statements with one of the four choices given below.

1. When a mathematical analysis is extremely difficult to solve a problem, _____ is used as a reliable means of studying the very complex phenomena.

　A. simulator　　B. simulation　　C. similarity　　D. generalization

2. The next step is to isolate it from the workers who frequent the area _____ it is

not feasible to eliminate the contaminant from the workplace.

    A. providing   B. provided   C. which   D. as

3. One of the advantages of the laboratory-model method is that it is possible to study rapidly varying phenomena which _____ actual observation.

    A. elude   B. eliminate   C. elevate   D. equal

4. Vapours, gases, heat and fine dust are transferred and distributed because of natural and forced convection and their _____ .

    A. concentration   B. ventilation   C. circulation   D. conservation

5. The results of investigation _____ can be converted to apply to actual conditions.

    A. on site   B. on board   C. in model   D. on models

Translation   部分否定和否定转移

    英语表示否定概念形式多样，其中部分否定和否定转移，由于英汉两种表达差异甚大，常造成误解，值得特别重视。

    部分否定的结构有：

1. "Every…not+V. " = "not every…+V. " 并不是每……都……

    "Both…not+V. " = "not both" …+V. " 并不是两……都……

    "All…not+V. " = "not all…+V. " 并不是所有……都……

2. "Everybody+not+V. " = "not everybody+V. " 未必每个人

    "Everything not+V. " = "not everything+V. " 未必每件事

    "Everywhere not+V. " = "not everywhere+V. " 未必每个地方

例 1. Every machine here is not produced in our factory

    这里的机器不是每台都由我们厂生产的。

例 2. Both the bridges are not built of reinforced concrete.

    这两座桥不都是钢筋混凝土造的。

例 3. All the buildings in this area do not have to be heated.

    这地区的所有建筑物未必都需供热。

例 4. Everywhere is not good

    不是每个地方都好。

    否定转移指的是否定词 not 的否定对象和范围的转移，不是否定紧跟其后的动词，而是后面的从句或从句中的谓语。

例 1. I do not believe that percentage humidity and relative humidity are the same.

    我确信湿度率和相对湿度不是一回事。

例 2. He does not think that relative humidity is dependent of the temperature.

    他认为相对湿度与温度无关。

例 3. It is not supposed that the complete water supply system for the new paper mill is designed by the young water engineers.

据认为<u>这座新纸厂的全套给水系统不是那些年轻给水工程师设计的</u>。

Directions:

Translate the following into Chinese, paying attention to the negative forms.

1. All is not right.
2. The data are not altogether wrong.
3. Both the calculations are not correct.
4. Every conclusion made by Prof. Li in this book is not very scientific.
5. Everything can not be done well.
6. Designers do not always deal with materials.
7. I do not believe that heat transfer by convection can occur without conduction.
8. It is not supposed that most plastics conduct heat or electricity readily.
9. This version is not placed first because of simplicity. It is widely accepted.
10. He did not set out earlier than I did because he wanted to be the first to get there.

Reading Material A

Environmental Controls of Workplace

The means used to control exposures to harmful materials or conditions in the occupational environment can be categorized as engineering or administrative.

In nearly all cases, the most effective approach is the combination of controls into an integrated package. The elimination of an offending agent from the workplace, accompanied, if necessary, by its replacement with a safer material, should be considered first in any effortto control the environment. ① The substitution of less hazardous materials has become quite common in industry, as knowledge of dangers from certain materials becomes available. For example, hydrocarbon-solvent-based paints are being replaced by water-based paints. The use of asbestos is being severely curtailed. Purchasers of some organic solvents are specifying thatthese solvents contain only trace amounts of benzene contamination. The principle of elimination and substitution applies to equipment and processes as well as materials. Newer machinery is often designed to minimize dust generation and release, for example. Processescan be modified to incorporate contaminant-reduction techniques. The introduction of a rawmaterial in pellet form is less likely to generate dust than the same material presented as apowder.

If it is not feasible to eliminate the contaminant from the workplace, the next step is to isolate it from the workers who frequent the area. Distance and physical barriers, preferably around the process, but possibly around the workers, can provide protection. In either case, this method of control is usually accompanied by a ventilation system. When the process is isolated, the emphasis is on exhausting the contaminated air from the process. In contrast, when the worker is isolated, the emphasis should be on supplying clean air to the worker's station.

The use of ventilation is ubiquitous in the modern workplace. Virtually every industrial and commercial facility contains some form of ventilation system for environmental control. The intent may be comfort (temperature, humidity, odors), safety (flammable vapors), or health (toxic particles, gases and vapors, airborne contagious) The last resort for preventing exposures to toxic chemicals is personal protection, in the form of respirators and protective garments. [2] Respiratory protection is used when all other controls are inadequate or when the possible failure of those controls would produce a hazardous situation. Administrative controls such as worker rotation through hazardous areas can also be implemented. In the nuclear power industry, exposure to radiation is limited on a three-month as well as an annual basis. Any worker achieving the maximum permissible exposure before the end of the pertinent period is transferred to a low-radiation work area for the balance of time. [3] In hot environments, workers should be allowed to rest in a cold area on a frequent basis throughout the work shift to allow time for the body to recover from the thermal stress. Other administrative controls include biological monitoring, worker education. and equipment maintenance. In all cases, administrative controls should be combined with attempts to reduce the hazard through engineering controls.

Notes

①如有必要，从工作区消除引起不舒服的媒介物，代以安全材料，这是在任何想要控制环境的场合应首先考虑的。
②作为防止暴露于毒性化学物质的最后手段是个人防护，用防毒面具和防护衣服。
③任何一个工作人员，在一个适当的工作期结束以前就已经得到了最大允许辐照，这时，就要调换到低辐射区工作直到工作期满。

Reading Material B

Scale Model Measurement

Scale models can be used to quantify data on flow around buildings, to validate mathematical models for reentry, and to predict reentry for a given design configuration. The great advantage of scale models is that they can include such empirical factors as rough terrain, surrounding buildings, complex building shape, and other variables not fully accounted for by theoretical analysis. [1] Scale models can also be used to test reconstruction designs to evaluate, for example, the effect of a change in stack height on roof concentration contours when the wind is from the least favorable direction. Models are costly in both time and money and thus usually require strong justification before use.

The complex airflow around an existing or planned structure can be investigated with a geometrically scaled physical model where the flow field is simulated by air or water. Such models have been used extensively in civil engineering since being used by the French engineer, Eiffel.

General modeling criteria (Snyder, 1972, ASHRAE, 1985) are used to ensure that a group of parameters are chosen such that the model and the building are analogous. [2] One criterion is that there must be similarity of the natural wind. This requires modeling the flow characteristics of the atmospheric boundary layer where the flow is affected by the degree of surface roughness. The vertical thermal distribution is usually uniform in wind and water tunnels so that neutral stability conditions are modeled. Thermal stratification can be modeled in a specially designed facility. There must also be geometric similarity between the building and the surrounding topography and kinematic and dynamic similarity of the exhaust effluents. For modeling in the near field of a point source such as a stack, it is necessary to duplicate closely the local geometry in the area of the source (Plate, 1982). The interior of the model stack might require roughening, for example, to duplicate the exhaust flow properties. The exit and intake velocities must be equal in the model and protoype to ensure dynamic similarity.

The near field of a stack is determined not only by its configuration and exhaust rate but also by the turbulence of the atmospheric flow field. To best reproduce this turbulence, it is more important to model the buildings and topographic features in the stack vicinity than to have an exactly scaled profile of the approach wind.

Several tracer techniques have been used in wind tunnel studies. Early experiments depended on smoke patterns for mapping contours. Smoke can also be used for quantitative measurements with the use of a photometer. Another early method used ammonia as a tracer with sample analysis by titration. A variety of other tracers and detection systems have been used.

Notes

①缩尺模型的最大优点是它包括了一些经验因素诸如起伏地带，周围建筑物，复杂建筑外形和理论分析不能完全计及的其他变量。

②通用的模型准则是用来保证选择参数组要使模型和建筑物相似。

UNIT FIVE

Text   Natural Ventilation Fields of Application

[1]   Natural air change takes place in buildings as a result of wind and the difference in density between the indoor and outdoor air. Without control, such natural infiltration is haphazard, and the process can only legitimately be termed "ventilation" if the arrangements are designed[1] to maintain the desired state of the indoor air under a variety of outdoor conditions.

[2]   Temperature differences and wind speed can cause the transfer of enormous quantities of air. For instance, measurements show that the natural air change in an open-hearth plant or a rolling mill amounts to about 20 million kg/hr. In forges, ironworks and other hot shops the air transfer may also be millions of kilograms per hour.

[3]   A very large consumption of energy would be required to move such quantities by mechanical means. The great economic importance of natural ventilation is that it can bring about these air changes without expenditure of mechanical energy.

[4]   The time has long passed when it was necessary to demonstrate the benefits of natural ventilation and justify its application.[2] The proofs were simple and very convincing. They werebased on comparisons of mechanical ventilation and natural ventilation. In hot shops where all the emphasis was laid on mechanical ventilation, and natural air change, being regarded as unimportant, was not taken into account at all, it was found in all the tests that the volume of natural air change many times exceeded the volume of mechanical ventilation.[3] This revealed the negligible role of general mechanical ventilation despite its heavy installation and running costs. Mechanical ventilation in these cases was best used as a corrective to natural ventilation, in the form of air curtains and local air supply or extraction.

[5]   In the hot season of the year natural ventilation can be used in almost every branch of industry, except the comparatively few industrial undertakings which require pre-treatment of the air for technological reasons. In single-span workshops the outdoor air enters the premisesthrough vents at the foot of the walls, and vitiated air is removed from the shop through louvers in the roof. In multi-span shops, single vents in the walls of the building are not enough, and for the ventilation of working spaces far from the walls additional air has to be introduced from the roof via the spaces between the roof bays. In this arrangement it is necessary to have a good air supply through these spaces and to arrange hot and cold spans alternately. The outdoor air enters the building through the openings in the roof of the cold spans and is then distributed to the adjoining hot spans. The use of natural ventilation in winter assumes that the indoor excess of production of heat will be sufficient to heat the estimated volume of air, and that besides the openings in the roof bays,

there will be a seriesof vents (5-7 m above floor level) for the entry of cold air. The height of these vents is so calculated as to ensure that the incoming air is heated by mixing with the internal warm air while falling from this height to the work area.

[6]　　Natural air change is above all suitable in workshops in which a great deal of heat is liberated ("hot shops"), viz. blast furnaces, open-hearth furnaces, rolling mills, forges, foundries, and heat-treatment shops, boiler houses, engine rooms and so on. A combination of general natural and local mechanical ventilation, as already mentioned, is often specially useful in these cases.

[7]　　The effectiveness of natural ventilation depends on many factors which must be considered in using the building as well as in planning it.

[8]　　The main factors on which successful control of natural ventilation of industrial premises depends are the layout and siting of the sources of heat, the design of the building (number of spans, form and shape of the roof) and the arrangement of ventilation openings in walls and roof bays. The most satisfactory solutions are obtained when the architect and the engineer collaborate and take account of problems of natural ventilation as well as those numerous and complex requirements that industrial undertakings have to satisfy at the design stage.

[9]　　Many industrial buildings exist in which natural ventilation was provided for in the design stage and has since been satisfactory in use. On the other hand, there are numerous instances in which natural ventilation did not receive sufficient attention in the design of the premises. This lack of attention is now being paid for very dearly. ④

[10]　　To clarify the problems of natural ventilation we shall first of all discuss the effects of heat sources in a building in relation to the air currents they cause in single-bay and multibay buildings. The effect of wind on a building and the resulting pressure distribution will also be considered.

[11]　　In view of the great complexity of a theoretical study of these phenomena, they are best investigated experimentally with the aid of two-and three-dimensional models using air or wateras the working medium.

New Words and Expressions

infiltration * [inˈfiltreiʃən]	n.	渗入
haphazard [ˈhæpˌhæzəd]	a.	任意的，不规则的
legitimately [liˈdʒitimitli]	ad.	正规地，合理地
open-hearth		平炉
rolling mill		轧钢厂
expenditure [iksˈpenditʃə]	n.	消耗
negligible * [ˈneglidʒibl]	a.	微不足道的，可忽略不计的
corrective * [kəˈrektiv]	n.	补救

air curtain	n.	空气幕
undertaking [ʌndə'teikiŋ]	n.	企业
single-span		单跨
premises ['premisis]	n.	房屋，厂房
louver ['luːvə]	n.	气窗板，百叶
above all		首先，尤其
siting [saitiŋ]		所处地点
blast furnace		高（鼓风）炉
architect * ['ɑːkitekt]	n.	建筑师，设计师
collaborate * [kə'læbəreit]	v.	合作，共同研究
take account of…		注意到…，重视…
pay for		（为某过失）付出代价，吃亏
resulting * [ri'zʌltiŋ]	a.	所引起的
in view of		鉴于…，考虑到…
complexity * [kəm'pleksiti]	n.	繁杂性
working medium		工作介质

Notes

①be termed "ventilation" 被称作"通风"注意：term ＋宾 ＋宾补，把……称作……

②The time has long passed when it was necessary to demonstrate…

由 When 引起的定语从句修饰 the time，定语与被修饰词的分离，为了句子结构的平衡。

③natural air change，being regarded as unimportant，was not taken into account at all.

注意主语与谓语的分离现象，是由于状语 being regarded as unimportant 的插入而引起的。

④This lack of attention is now being paid for very dearly.

to pay for…为……付出代价，此处为被动结构。

Exercises

Reading Comprehension

Ⅰ. Choose the best answer for each of the following.

1. Ventilation is used for the purpose of _____ .

    A. natural infiltration

    B. the difference in density between indoor and outdoor air

    C. the desired state of the indoor air under various outdoor conditions

    D. natural air change in buildings

2. The air transfer in hot shops may be as large as millions of kilograms per hour, depending on _____ .

    A. natural infiltration

    B. temperature differences and wind speed

    C. a variety of outdoor conditions

    D. natural ventilation

3. The comparisons of mechanical ventilation and natural ventilation show that _____ .

    A. natural ventilation is more economic and more beneficial

    B. mechanical ventilation is more important and more efficient

    C. natural ventilation is a corrective to mechanical ventilation

    D. mechanical ventilation can replace natural ventilation

4. All the tests done in hot shops revealed that the volume of natural ventilation was _____ .

    A. as much as that of mechanical ventilation

    B. less than that of mechanical ventilation

    C. much more than that of mechanical ventilation

    D. too negligible to be taken into account

5. A combination of general natural and local mechanical ventilation is very useful in _____ .

    A. blast furnaces and open-hearth furnaces

    B. rolling mills, forges and foundries

    C. heat-treatment shops, boiler houses

    D. all of the above

Ⅱ. Are the following statements true or false?

1. Successful control of natural ventilation of industrial premises mainly depends on the air currents and pressure distribution. ( )

2. In order to obtain the most satisfactory solution to natural ventilation of buildings, both the problems of natural ventilation and the requirements to be satisfied must be taken into consideration at the design stage. ( )

3. In the design of industrial premises people have to pay for the insufficient attention to natural ventilation. ( )

4. It is necessary to discuss collaboration between architects and engineers for the problems of natural ventilation. ( )

5. The theoretical study of these phenomena is so complex that experiments should be done with the aid or two-and three-dimensional models. ( )

Vocabulary

Ⅰ. Fill in the blanks with some of the words or expressions listed below, changing the form where necessary.

layout	lack	alternately	justify	haphazard
take account		natural ventilation		in view of

1. Natural air change taking place in buildings is _____ but can be controlled.

2. _____ can bring about large quantity of air changes without any expenditure of mechanical energy.

3. The comparisons of mechanical ventilation and natural ventilation have demonstrated the benefits of natural ventilation and _____ its applications.

4. The problems of natural ventilation are so important that architects and engineers should _____ them in their designs.

5. It is necessary to introduce additional air for the ventilation of working spaces via the spaces between the roof bays and to arrange hot and cold spans _____ .

Ⅱ. Complete each of the following statements with one of the four choices given below.

1. Because of the negligible role of general mechanical ventilation, people think of mechanical ventilation as a _____ to natural ventilation.

   A. correlative   B. correction   C. corrector   D. corrective

2. _____ careful consideration about all the problems of natural ventilation in the design stage makes many industrial premises unsatisfactory in use.

   A. Short of   B. Because of   C. Lack of   D. Thanks to

3. Natural air change is above all suitable in blast furnaces where a great deal of heat _____ .

   A. is absorbed   B. is liberated   C. is transformed   D. is conserved

4. _____ the effectiveness of natural ventilation, natural air change should be taken into account in the design of buildings.

   A. In view of   B. In full view of   C. With the view   D. For the view of

5. The form of the roof and the _____ of the sources of heat are two of the main factors controlling natural ventilation of industrial premises.

   A. outlay   B. outline   C. layoff   D. layout

Translation   词类转换

英汉两种语言在结构和表达习惯上都有很大差别。因此,在英译汉中,不可能千篇一律地逐词对译。有时英语的名词可译成汉语动词,而英语的动词可译成汉语的名词,如此等等。这种词性改变的现象,称之为词类转换。

例1. Their perfect design of models underlined impressed the young engineers deeply.

42

完美的模型设计给青年工程师留下深刻的印象。（动词转译为名词，副词转译为形容词）

例 2. The application of mathematical analysis to the solution of complex technical problems is

almost impossible.

应用数学分析去解决复杂的技术问题是几乎不可能的。（名词转译为动词）

例 3. Concrete is as strong as stone.

混凝土的强度与石头一样。（形容词转译为名词）

例 4. The test should be made on washed samples.

应该用洗净剂的试样作试验。（介词转译为动词）

Directions：

Translate the following sentences into Chinese，paying attention to the underlined words.

1. A strange phenomenon similar to UFO was found that day.

2. Lightweight concrete is a development mainly of the last twenty years.

3. They experiment on animals.

4. Mercury weighs about thirteen times as much as water.

5. It is well known that heavy objects are more stable than light ones.

6. When there is time，holes should be properly designed.

7. We helped them out of a lot of difficulties.

8. Good，strong，long-lasting concrete didn't become generally possible until cheap coal was available and the cheap cement was available.

Reading Material A

Temperature Distribution in Hot Shops

In workshops with sources of heat，under certain conditions two zones are formed，one above the other，in each of which the circulation of air is independent.

As the thermal air current from any hot body rises，it entrains the surrounding air and so the total mass of moving air increases，whilst its velocity and temperature decrease. In a closed space with heat-conducting walls，the thermal stream rises to the ceiling，spreads out over it and then returns to its original source，replacing the air continuously rising above the heat source. Circulation of air is thus maintained. The presence of heat sources disturbs the equilibrium of the air throughout the closed space.

The temperature distribution is due mainly to the propagation，circulation and interaction of the convection currents and the incoming (natural and forced) flows of air and also， to a lesser extent, to the extract. [1] Thus the temperature distribution depends on the initial parameters and the momenta of all the air streams, on the layout of the heat sources and on the shape of the building in which the flows of air develop.

In shops with heat sources the temperature distribution is characterized by a higher tempera-ture at higher levels than at lower levels. Hot air tends to rise and in so doing interacts with other streams of air on the way and heat exchange takes place between them. A particle either continues its ascent, is stopped, or even starts to descend if, owing to a local stream of air, its temperature becomes less than that associated with the particular level. [2]

The temperature field produced by a single source of heat in an unventilated space with heat-conducting walls has been studied by Ye. V. Kudryavtsev, who carried out the following experiment. In a room with a thermally insulated window and door a 5-kW electric heater was suspended in the centre or in any corner of the room at different heights above the floor. The air temperature was measured at different levels in two positions, one near the heater, the other as far as possible away from it. Thermocouples at the same height above the floor showed the same temperature, i. e. isothermal conditions existed in any horizontal section. But at the height of the lower edge of the heater a considerable jump was discovered in the otherwise continuous vertical air-temperature profile. This temperature jump coincided with the level of the heater in no matter what position, or at what height, a heater of any capacity was set. [3]

When the heater was some distance above the floor and there was no air change in the room, there was practically no convectional motion below the heater, where the air temperature remained constant. On the other hand, above this level, a complex convective circulation was observed which led to a temperature rise throughout the space. [4] If the heater was placed on the floor, the circulation reached right up to the ceiling.

Experiment shows the air temperature gradient (from floor to ceiling) when the heater was 0.75 and 1.75 m from the floor. It will be seen from the diagram that the position of the temperature jump moves with the source of heat.

Notes

①温度分布主要起因于对流气及进入空气流（自然和强制）的扩散、循环及相互作用，在较小程度上还由于排风。
②质点或是继续上升，停止，或是由于局部气流而使质点温度低于某特定标高的温度时而开始下降。
③无论在什么位置或什么高度上设置任意容量的加热器，温度跃变线与加热器标高相吻合。
④另一方面，在此标高以上出现复杂的对流循环，这导致在整个空间的温度上升。

Reading Material B

Ventilation of Green Houses

Greenhouse ventilation primarily prevents excessive temperature rise because of insolation. Italso prevents CO_2 depletion and keeps relative humidity at a reasonable level. Ventilation (and cooling systems) should be designed to achieve uniform temperature distribution in the plant-growing zone. During cold weather, fresh air should normally be introduced through a variable-width slot inlet, keeping velocity between 3.5 and 5 m/s and to retard the tendency of coolair to settle directly to the floor and produce large, vertical temperature gradients. As notedearlier, perforated polyethylene tubing can effectively distribute ventilation air in thewinter. Perforations in the tubing at the 1000 and 1400 hour positions produce an upward airflow and prevent cold air from being directed onto the plants. Tubing of this kind can be usedin either positive or negative pressure ventilation systems.

In summer, the cooler air should be directed across the green-house at or near plant level. Typical maximum ventilation rates provide for up to 1 air change per minute, and distances between fans and inlets should be limited to 25 m to prevent excessive temperature rise. Such a system requires proper installation to ensure reasonably uniform airflow across all plants.

Most older greenhouses, and some newer ones, are ventilated by natural air exchange through ridge and side ventilators. Automatic vent controls are used in some cases. With natural ventilation systems, the degree of temperature control depends on the house configuration, external wind speed, and outside air temperature. If natural ventilation is to occur, wind or thermal buoyancy must create a pressure difference. Vent openings on both sides of the greenhouse and the ridge take the best advantage of pressure differences created by the wind.[1] Large vent openings supply sufficient ventilation when the wind is light or when thermal buoyancy forces are small. The total vent area should be from 15 to 25% of the floor area. For a single greenhouse, the combined sidewall vent area should equal the combined roof vent areafor best ventilation by thermal buoyancy. Both sidewall and ridge vent openings should becontinuous along the greenhouse. Sensors should be included in automatic control (or alarm) systems for times of rain and high wind, which could damage the crops.

Fans give a more positive control over ventilation than do naturally vented systems.[2] Generally, exhaust fans located in the side walls or ends of the greenhouse draw air through partially opened ridge vents, or end or side vents that may be equipped with evaporative pads. Inlet design is important, and inlets should be sized to maintain an airspeed between 3. 5 and 5 m/s at any ventilation stage. They should automatically adjust to maintain this speed asventilation capacity changes. A common inlet is a tophinged window vent located opposite the fans. Controls can be installed to vary the inlet opening automatically. Typically, the fans and inlets are controlled by (aspirated) thermostate located in the middle of the greenhouseat plant height.

The control over temperature rise achieved with fans relates directly to the air exchangerate. [3] As shown in Figure 11, air exchange rates between 0.75 and 1 change per minute are effective. At lower airflow rates, the temperature differential increases rapidly. At higher airflow rates, the reduction of temperature rise is relatively small, fan power requirements increase, and plant damage can occur from increased airspeed.

Notes

①暖房两侧的通风口和屋脊可充分利用由风产生的压差。
②风扇可对通风换气作出比自然排风系统更加可靠的控制。
③靠风扇达到温升的控制直接与换气量有关。

UNIT SIX

Text   **Dust Formation**

[1]   Immense quantities of dust are produced in crushing (ore dressing), milling, blasting, riddling, transfer of material from one conveyor to another, transportation and also in machining, viz. rough grinding, finish grinding or buffing, in scutching flax and cotton, knocking-out moulds in foundries, etc. Dust is also formed in paint spraying from the fine droplets of solvent and pigment. In etching, chromium-plating and electrolysis "gas bubbles" are formed, i. e. spherical liquid shells filled with hydrogen. Rising in a stream of air they burst, forming extremely fine particles which consist more often than not of the acid solution of the etching bath. [1]

[2]   The dust-content of the air is characterized either by the weight of dust per unit volume (mg/m^3), or by the number of particles per cm^3. To define the dust completely it is necessary to know both quantities.

[3]   According to the U. S. S. R. Hygiene Standard for the design of industrial premises the non-toxic dust-content of the air of a workplace should not exceed 2 mg/m^3 for dust containing morethan 10 per cent quartz, or for asbestos dust; for other types of non-toxic dust the maximum is 10 mg/m^3.

[4]   Dust can have an adverse effect on the health of workpeople. It is known, for instance, thatprolonged inhalation of large quantities of dust containing silica (SiO_2) or asbestos can causesilicosis or asbestosis respectively. Quartz sand and river sand, which consist of silica, are widely used in foundries as constituents of moulding and core sands, for sandblasting of castings, and as the main material for producing ceramics, glass, porcelain, etc.

[5]   Industrial dust, ejected from vents and ventilation systems, leads to atmospheric pollution around the factory site and in living quarters. In the atmosphere dust absorbs a great deal of sunlight, and in towns it also causes fogs since the dust particles act as nuclei for the condensation of water vapour. Furthermore, with some types of dust under certain conditions there may be great risk of fire or explosion.

[6]   Usually industrial dust is a mixture of particles of different substances, with sometimes one particular substance predominating. The various types of dust also differ in their physical properties, viz. particle size, density, shape, consistency, electric charge, adsorption capability, inflammability, explosiveness.

[7]   In industrial conditions, the particles in a cloud of dust may cover a wide range of size, from a fraction of 1 μ to 100 μ or more. The size distribution is determined by their origin, the type of machining, level of exposure and so on.

[8]   Three basic particle shapes are possible, namely laminar, fibrous and granu-

lar. Usually industrial dust is a mixture of these shapes with a large number of intermediate graduations. Of special importance are the size of the particles, and their shape, density, and electrical charge, i. e. those properties which determine the behaviour of the dust particles indoors. These properties are important technologically as well as regards hygiene. On the technical side, they affect the collection of the dust at its source and also its removal from the air. Large particles settle quickly. Heavy large particles several tens of microns in size do not enter into human respiratory organs. Light, fibrous, acicular dust, and also dust formed by condensation into loose, flocculent particles, hang in the air for very long periods and settle slowly.

[9]   It is considered that the size of the dust that can enter the lungs is mostly up to 5 μ with a maximum of 10 μ. The larger particles settle on the mucous membrane of the upper respiratory tracts (nose and throat) Particles less than 5 μ in size are the most dangerous in their effect on lung tissue. The view that particles 0. 5-0. 25 μ or less in size are relatively harmless is not shared by modern authorities in hygiene. There are grounds for the belief that if such particles are not retained in the nose, they may penetrate deep down into the lung tissue. [2]

[10]   Investigations show that particles up to 10 μin size predominate in the air of industrial premises, with 40-90 per cent being less than 2 μ. The percentage of particles less than 2 μ in inorganic mineral and metal dust is greater than that in organic vegetable and animal dust.

[11]   Particles less than 0. 1 μ in size are affected by the random Brownian motion. They either settle very slowly in zigzag fashion (particle radius 0. 1-0. 05 μ), or they do not settle at all, taking part in the molecular motion of the air (particle radius 0. 001 μ or less) and so diffusing in all directions. The size distribution of a dust cloud does not remain constant in time. Various factors may cause the particles to coagulate, and therefore to settle faster. The rate of coagulation depends on the homogeneity of size and shape of the particles and their electrical charge. Other things being equal, the coagulation is faster for greater size range. In poly-disperse systems the coagulation is quicker than in homogeneous systems, the larger particles acting as the nuclei for the coalescence of the finer particles. Highly disperse dust contains electrically charged particles, some positively charged and others, of the same substance, negatively. Particles with similar charges repel each other, but induction often converts the repulsion into attraction; particles with opposite charges coagulate more readily.

[12]   Each speck of dust is surrounded by a layer of adsorbed air, whose partial pressure is greater at the surface of the particle and then decreases rapidly to the pressure of the ambient air. It is for this reason that some fine powders do not cake after long periods of storage, but flow like liquids.

[13]   The volume of adsorbed air may be many times that of the dust on which it is adsorbed. Thus, for instance, 1 litre of soot may have 950 cm^3 of adsorbed air, which at nor-

mal temperature and pressure would occupy 2. 5 1. for only 50 cm^3 of soot. [3] It follows that the air is more compressed around the soot particles. Particles so mantled with air exhibit only a small tendency to coagulate.

[14]   The classification of dust by size is achieved by sieving it through a series of gauze sieves ranging from 42 μ upwards. The weight percentage of the various fractions is determined by weighing the residues on the sieves. Finer dust fractions smaller than 42 μ are treated in air elutriators，which enable the weight percentage of individual fractions to be determined and also allow these fractions to be classified according to their settling velocities.

New Words and Expressions

ore dressing		选矿
ridding ['ridiŋ]	n.	喷砂
conveyor [kən'veiə]	n.	传送带
buffing ['bʌfiŋ]	n.	抛光
scutch [skʌtf]	v.	打（麻）
flax [flæks]	n.	亚麻
knocking-out mould		铸模
solvent * ['sɔvənt]	n.	溶剂
pigment [pigmənt]	n.	颜料
etch * [etʃ]	v.	酸洗
chromium-plating		镀铬
adverse ['ædvəːs]	a.	相反的；不利的
inhalation [inhə'leiʃən]	n.	吸入
silica ['silikə]	n.	硅古，二氧化硅
asbestos [æs'bestəs]	n.	石棉
moulding [məudiŋ]		型砂
core sands		芯砂
ceramic [sir'ræmik]	n.	陶瓷，陶器
condensation * [kəndən'seiʃən]	n.	冷凝（作用）
electric charge		电荷
adsorption capability		吸附力
inflammability * [inflæm'biliti]	n.	可燃性
laminar ['læminə]	a.	薄层的
fibrous ['fibrəs]	a.	纤维状的
granular ['grænjulə]	a.	颗粒状的
graduation * [grædju'eiʃən]	n.	选分
flocculent ['flɔkjulənt]	a.	絮凝状的

mucous membrane			粘膜
coagulate * [kəu'ægiuleit]		v.	凝结
homogeneity * [hɔmədʒe'niːiti]		n.	均匀性
induction * [in'dʌkʃən]		n.	诱导（作用）
speck [spek]		n.	微粒
mantle * ['mæntl]		v.	覆盖
sieve * [siːv]		v.	筛选
gauze [gɔːz]		n.	网
residue * ['rezidju]		n.	剩余物
elutriator [i'ljutrieitə]		n.	淘选器

Notes

① ···more often than not···，······在大多数的情况下······。

② There are grounds for the belief that···。有理由相信······。

③ ···1 litre of soot may have 950 cm^3 of adsorbed air，which at normal temperature and pressure would occupy 2.5L. for only 50 cm^3 of soot.

"Which" 在此仅仅指代 "adsorbed air" 而不是 "950cm^3 of adsorbed air"。

Exercises

Reading Comprehension

I. Choose the best answer for each of the following.

1. In order to define the dust-content of the air completely we should know _____.

   A. the weight of dust per unit volume (mg/m^3)

   B. the number of particles per cm^3.

   C. both of the quantities above.

   D. none of the above.

2. Quarts sand and river sand are used as raw material in making _____.

   A. moulds and core sands

   B. gunpowder and glass

   C. kitchen ware and fuel

   D. some kinds of utensils

3. The shape of industrial dust is _____.

   A. a mixture of particles of various matters.

   B. laminar, fibrous or granular.

   C. a large number of intermediate graduations.

D. a predominating substance

4. Modern authorities in hygiene believe that particles 0.5-0.25 or less in size
   _____ .

   A. are not retained in the nose but penetrate deep down into the lung tissue.

   B. are relatively harmless.

   C. can be harmful for health.

   D. are not shared by people but fall onto the ground.

5. Particles less than 0.1 μ in size _____ .

   A. settle slowly or rapidly in zigzag fashion.

   B. do not settle at all but take part in the molecular motion of the air.

   C. diffuse in all directions.

   D. are affected by the random Brownian motion.

Ⅱ. Are the following statements true or false?

1. The hygiene standard set by the U.S.S.R for the design of industrial premises is that dust containing more than 10 per cent asbestos should be less than 10 mg/m^3. （　）

2. Industrial dusts not only differ in size and shape but also in other physical properties.
   （　）

3. Particles less than 5 μ in size settle on the mucous membrane and cause troubles with nose and throat.　（　）

4. Some fine powders surrounded by a layer of adsorbed air will turn to liquids.　（　）

5. The instruments to classify dust are gauze sieves and air elutriators.　（　）

Vocabulary

Ⅰ. Fill in the blanks with some of the words listed below, changing the form where necessary.

adverse	premises	condensation	graduation
conveyor	particle	respectively	speck

1. The shapes of industrial particles are laminar, fibrous, granular and a large number of intermediate _____ .

2. Special importance are the size, shape, density and electrical charge of the _____ .

3. Material transferred from one _____ to another can produce dust as well.

4. Inhalating dust which contain silica (SiO_2) or asbestos can cause silicosis or asbestosis _____ .

5. _____ effects on the health of people are caused by industrial pollution.

Ⅱ. Complete each of the following statements with one of the four choices given below.

1. Industrial dusts _____ their physical properties, viz. particle size, density, shape, consistency, electric charge, etc.

   A. differ at　　B. different from　　C. define as　　D. differ in

2. Every _____ of dust is surrounded by a layer of adsorbed air, whose partial pressure is bigger at the surface of this particle, then decreasing quickly to the pressure of the ambient air.

   A. speck　　B. drop　　C. piece　　D. bit

3. The random Brownian motion affects particles less than 0.1 _____ .

   A. in weight　　B. in volume　　C. in size　　D. in width

4. In designing industrial _____ there should be a hygiene standard limiting the dust-content of the air of workplace.

   A. pollution　　B. premises　　C. production　　D. material

5. In towns dust causes fogs because its particles act as nuclei to _____ water vapour.

   A. produce　　B. make　　C. absorb　　D. condensate

Translation　　　　　　　　　句子成分转换

　　英汉两种语言的句子结构和修辞不同，因此，通顺的汉语译文与英文原文在句法成分上并非一一对应。在英译汉时，根据汉语的表达习惯，有时英语句中的主语可译为汉语译文的谓语，而英语句中的谓语可译成汉语译文的主语，如此等等，被称之为句子成分转换。

1. A glance through his office window offers a panoramic view of the Washington Monument and the Lincoln Memorial.

   从他的办公室窗口可以一眼看到华盛顿纪念碑和林肯纪念堂。（主语转译为谓语）

2. The electronic computer is chiefly characterized by its accurate and rapid computation.

   电子计算机的主要特点是计算准确而又迅速。（谓语转译成主语）

3. There are three states of matter: solid, liquid and gas.

   物质有三态：固态、液态和气态。（定语转译成主语）

4. For almost all substances the density gets smaller as the temperature is raised.

   几乎所有物质的密度都会随温度增高而变小。（状语转译成定语）

5. People define the ability to conduct an electric current as conductivity.

   传导电流的能力定义为导电性。（宾语转译为主语）

6. The more carbon the steel contains, the harder and stronger it is.

   钢材的含碳量越高，强度和硬度就越大。（表语转译成主语）

Directions

Translate the following sentences into Chinese, paying attention to the underlined parts.

1. There is no water in the bottle.

2. The soils are tested throughout the building work.

3. Copper conducts electricity better than other materials.

4. We have the application of electronic computers to industrial designs.

5. Electronic computers <u>are</u> chiefly <u>characterized</u> by their accurate and rapid computation.

6. <u>The use of natural ventilation in winter</u> assumes that the indoor excess of production of heat

   will be sufficient to heat the estimated volume of air.

7. <u>The height of these vents is so calculated</u> as to ensure that the incoming air is heated by mixing with the internal warm air.

8. Convection takes place in a fluid because of a combination of conduction within the fluid and energy transport which is due to the fluid motion itself, <u>the fluid motion being produced either by artificial means or by density currents.</u>

Reading Material A

Propagation of Gases and Vapours in Indoor Air

Mass movements, i. e. air currents and circulation, are mainly responsible for the spread of gases and other contaminants throughout the room space. Diffusion (the exchange of molecules between adjacent layers originating in the difference between partial pressures orconcentrations) plays a negligible role.

Due to these mass movements the rate of spread is several hundred times greater than the rate of diffusion. In an environment with no perceptible air movement, there may yet be air currents of 0. 1-0. 2 m/sec, whereas the diffusion velocity is only of the order of 0. 01 cm/sec.

The behaviour of a gaseous impurity in air depends on the density of the gas, on its concentration in the mixture, and on the circulation of the air. Clearly, streams of any gas which is lighter than air move upwards, intermingle with the air and then, owing to circulation, return in diluted form to the lower area. Gases and vapours which are heavier than air have atendency to drop, though this is complicated by the convection currents at hot surfaces, and also by air currents due to other causes.

It should be borne in mind that a 1 degC rise in temperature reduces the density of air by 3 to 4 g/m^3, whereas the permissible concentrations of contaminants are most probably only milligrams per cubic metre of air. In especially unfavourable conditions the gas concentrations that occur in industrial conditions may, according to published data, reach 0. 4 g/m^3 for SO_2, 0. 127 g/m^3 for NH_3, 0. 43 g/m^3 for H_2S and 0. 1 g/m^3 for Cl; and even with such large concentrations, a temperature rise of only $1/4\,°C$, due to contact with a hot surface or mixing with a local current of warm air, is enough to cause the gas to rise. [1] Thus the spread of a gas is not determined by its specific gravity or its concentration but by its temperature.

Only a gas heavier than, and at the same temperature as, the surrounding air will tend to fall. For example, in unventilated shops without sources of heat, in which machine tools are sprayed with protective nitro-cellulose lacquers, the highest concentration of benzol vapour is found at floor level.

In workshops where gases are given off, there are usually hot surfaces that give rise to thermal currents; machines, drives, and workpeople also cause circulation of air. These air movements greatly disturb the natural tendency of heavy gas to fall, and they prevent the greatest concentration building up at floor level.

The erroneous notion that gas which is heavier than air must necessarily accumulate at floor level resulted from disregard of the industrial environment and it has led to some curious ventilation systems; the fallacies of some of these systems are exposed in published literature. For example, in a particular chlorine electrolysis shop special floor channels were providedalong which it was supposed that the chlorine would flow into the extraction apertures; inanother instance a floor grating was constructed. It is interesting that, in fact, the air showed no chlorine under the grating, but high concentrations under the ceiling.

Sometimes heavy vapours and gases do accumulate near floor level; this is only possible when there are no convection currents. Such substances as petrol or ether, which in evaporating absorb heat from the ambient air and cool it, have a tendency to drop to the floor, and then to spread in the form of currents throughout the entire space. [2]

The indoor distribution of concentration is often very complicated. In absolutely still air the gas spreads by diffusion, and its dispersion throughout the entire space then proceeds veryslowly. This sometimes occurs, for instance, in chemical stores and in non-ventilated premises. But in ventilated spaces, the concentration distribution is determined by the overall effect of the various air currents, and in a complex industrial environment it cannot be calculated in advance.

Notes

①a femperature rise···to cause the gas to rise. 因与热表面接触或与热空气流相混合，只要1/4℃的温升就足以引起气体上升。
②诸如汽油或乙醚这些物质，蒸发时从周围空气吸收热量并使其冷却，它们具有降至地面然后以气流的形式扩散到整个空间的倾向性。

Reading Material B

Special Laboratory Hoods

The laboratory hoods described above are valuable general-purpose control devices in the modern chemical laboratory. The laboratory hood provides a physical barrier to contain spills, splashes, and mild overpressure accidents. A modest face velocity will contain air contaminantsreleased from chemical operations. Although it has these impressive features, the laboratory hood should not be considered the only ventilation control available in chemistry laboratories. Standard procedures such as evaporation, distillation, and digestion are routinely conducted inlaboratories and a range of local exhaust hoods are available for these operations. Examples of these special-purpose hoods, which have the advantages of low initial cost, low airflow, and excellent capture efficiency, are described below.

Specimen digestion using strong oxidizers such as perchloric acid is frequently encountered in settings ranging from biological to metallurgical laboratories. This procedure requires excellent containment and air cleaning to ensure that violent reactions do not occur. Organic materials cannot be used in the hood or duct construction, and spray nozzles must be installed to wash down the duct work to prevent the buildup of unstable perchlorates. The hood used for perchloric acid digestion must be committed to this activity exclusively. Silverman and First (1962) have designed a scrubber for perchloric acid digestion which is placed directly in a standard laboratory hood. After cleaning, the scrubber exhaust stream is discharged to the laboratory hood exhaust stream. An integral scrubber effective against perchloric acid has beendescribed by Renton and Duffield (1986)

A second common procedure in chemical laboratories is paper chromatography. In this process a paper sheet onto which the liquid sample has been placed is put in a large jar in a solvent-saturated environment for the development of the chromatograph. [1] The changing of samples results in release of the solvent vapors to the air. Again, this work could be done in a conventional laboratory hood, but it can be controlled more efficiently by utilizing a mobile exterior hood which is placed directly behind the jar during transfers (Brief et al., 1963) This design provides excellent control using modest airflows of 250 to 300 cfm. The savings in installation and operating cost utilizing this special hood over the conventional laboratory hood are impressive. [2]

A common procedure in material control laboratories is the evaporation of a large number of samples. Rather than conducting this procedure in a chemical laboratory hood it can be controlled more efficiently by spot local exhaust (VS-206). A more difficult chemical laboratory procedure to control is distillation or reaction equipment mounted on a large rack with the potential for release of air contaminants at multiple locations. A "walk-in" hood can be provided for control, but the penalty of limited accessibility and large exhaust volumes must be accepted. An alternative approach is to mount the equipment in the open and provide oneor more flexible "drops" which can be positioned at critical release points. Normally a 3-in. -diameter flexible duct with an exhaust volume of 200 cfm is adequate to control all but major accidental releases.

Notes

①在此过程中，把涂有液体试样的纸片放入一个大瓶的溶液饱和环境中，使色层分离显影。

②使用这种特制的通风柜时，安装和运行费用的节约比起一般实验室通风柜来，是令人注目的。

UNIT SEVEN

Text   Air Douches

[1]   An air douche is a local current of air directed at a person. Unlike general ventilation, which has the task of maintaining a definite condition of the air throughout a building, the purpose of local currents (e. g. an air douche) is to produce particular air conditions in one or more parts of a building—for instance, at fixed workplace, or wherever workpeople congregate for long periods, or in rest areas. The intention is thus to maintain special conditions in limited space by the action of the air current. These conditions must satisfy prescribed hygienic and physiological requirements.

[2]   Air douches should be used.

1. if it is impossible to produce the required effect by means of general ventilation, e. g. at control posts in boiler and engine rooms, in power stations and combined heating and power stations;
2. when the required conditions can be obtained by general ventilation, but only with an immense volume of air at exorbitant cost, e. g. in very large drying rooms where only a few workers are employed. In such cases the use of air douches is also technically appropriate since any general reduction of the air temperature would greatly increase the heat loss of the drying equipment and so would increase the fuel consumption.

[3]   In the many cases when work is done in conditions of intense radiation, and general ventilation is inadequate to maintain the required air temperature and humidity and thereby preserve natural thermal regulation (normal heat transfer between the human body and the surrounding medium), an air douche can ameliorate the conditions. This applies in metallurgical and heavy engineering plants (where douches are needed near furnaces, rolling mills, hammers, presses and so on), and in glass works, dye works, bakeries, etc.

[4]   Air douches are also used in many plants with natural ventilation whenever the natural intake through casements, etc. , is insufficient to supply particular workplaces (in forges, foundries, heat-treatment shops, etc.)

[5]   Air douches are of special importance when no pre-treatment (heating, cooling, etc.)of the natural air supply is practicable; the air used for the douches can be pre-treated at low cost. The volume of air required for the douches is only a small fraction of the total natural air change.

[6]   Finally, in hot shops in regions with a high outdoor temperature, when general ventilation (natural or mechanical)holds the indoor air temperature 3-5 degC above the outdoor temperature, air douches can produce comfortable conditions at workplaces by using pre-cooled outdoor air.

[7]   It should be noted that with general mechanical ventilation too, the air supply must

be directed towards the workplace, i. e. the supply should conform to the requirements of any local air supply. Hence the siting and form of the inlets, the velocity and temperature of the air flow, etc. , must conform to the requirements which must be satisfied to achieve the necessary environment in the work area (i. e. specified air temperature and velocity distributions and contaminant concentrations).

[8]   By means of an air douche one can vary the velocity, temperature and humidity of the air and the concentration of impurity at a workplace.

[9]   The simplest is to alter the velocity while the other parameters remain constant. [1] This can be done by fans which set the air in the building in motion.

[10]   The temperature, humidity and concentration at the workplace are changed by supplying air from outside and, if necessary, by pre-treating it.

[11]   Air movement increases the heat loss from the body, which is very important when work is being done in conditions of radiant heat. Heat loss is also intensified by supplying air at a low temperature (compared with the ambient temperature indoors) and sometimes by sprinkling water. The droplets of water, falling onto exposed parts of objects and clothing and then evaporating, cause additional cooling.

[12]   In designing air douches for hot shops, one should above all try to lower the air temperature by natural ventilation.

[13]   For work in conditions of radiant heat, the following factors need to be taken into account:

(a) the intensity of the radiant heat at a fixed workplace, or if it is not fixed, wherever the worker is usually working;

(b) the duration of continuous exposure to radiation in the various sections of the work areaand also the duration of any breaks (the nature of radiation and work done);

(c) whether some particular part of the body is continuously subjected to radiation or whether by changes of position the entire surface of the body can be irradiated in turn.

[14]   As established by numerous investigations in production conditions, in cases where thermal radiation is present it is necessary to:

　1. arrange the air douches in the first instance in the zone where the worker is exposed to radiation for the longest periods of time, even if in this case the intensity of radiation is less than elsewhere (one needs to take into account both factors, i. e. the exposure and intensity of the thermal radiation) . [2]

　2. take into account that the thermal load on the body is least tolerable if the upper part of the trunk (chest, neck, head) is subjected to radiation. In the first instance, therefore, these parts of the body should be subjected to the jet.

[15]   The flow of air should be directed to that part of the body which is subjected to the more prolonged radiation, although the flow should as far as possible cover other parts of the body also.

[16]   In selecting the direction of the jet it is necessary to consider the possibility of

58

smoke, flames and sparks or even hot air becoming entrained in the jet if the inlet nozzle is positioned near such sources, e. g. furnace ports. Therefore the direction should be such that the jet of air is first incident on the workplace and only then should it encounter the sources of heat or contamination and so blow the impurities away from the workplace. It is also necessary to see that the impurities are not blown into adjacent work areas. ③

[17]   In summer, cooling of the air is very important for the effectiveness of the douches. The cheapest method of cooling is to humidify the air with water circulating in a closed circuit.

[18]   The width of the jet stream at the workplace should be about 1. 0 to 1. 2 m, except in cases when it is necessary to serve a much larger area.

New Words and Expressions

air douche		空气喷淋
congregate * ['kɔngrigeit]	v.	聚集
hygienic [hai'dʒiːnik]	a.	卫生的
physiological [fiziə'lɔdʒikəl]	a.	生理的
exorbitant [igzɔːbitənt]	a.	过渡的
thermal regulation		热量调整
ameliorate * [ə'miːljəreit]	v.	改善
metallurgical [metə'ləːdʒikəl]	a.	冶炼的
rolling mill		滚轧机
press [pres]	n.	压力锻机
casement ['keismənt]	n.	窗扉
inlet ['inlet]	n.	进气孔
contaminant [kən'tæminənt]	n.	污物
radiat heat		辐射热
ambient * ['æmbiənt]	a.	周围的
sprinkle ['spriŋkl]	v.	喷水
subject to		暴露
in the first instance		首先
thermal load		热负荷
tolerable * ['tɔlərəbl]	a.	能忍受
entrain * [in'trein]	v.	吸入
adjacent * [ə'dʒeisənt]	a.	邻近的
humidify * [hju'miditi]	v.	弄潮湿

Notes

①The simplest is to alter the velocity···.

本句中，在 "The simplest" 后面省去了 "thing to do"。

②even if in this case 即使在这种情况下······。也就是说当 "the intensity of radiation is less than elsewhere" 的时候。

③It is also necessary to see that···.

在本句中 "to see" 是 "to make sure" 的意思。

Exercises

Reading Comprehension

I. Choose the best answer for each of the following.

1. An air douche is a local current of air _____ .

 A. which has the task to maintain a definite condition of the air throughout a building.

 B. producing particular air conditions in one or more parts of a building.

 C. directed at fixed workplace where only one person works.

 D. which satisfies prescribed hygienic and physiological requirements.

2. Which of the following statements is not mentioned in the text?

 A. Air douches are needed when it is impossible to use general ventilation for the required air conditions.

 B. Air douches are used when there needs to be great volume of air at high expenses by general ventilation.

 C. Air douches should be used when fuel becomes expensive.

 D. When air douches are used, there is no need for the general reduction of the air temperature in the whole building.

3. For work in conditions of radiant heat, which of the following factors should be considered?

 A. The volume of air needed for air douches.

 B. How many breaks are there in the duration of exposure to radiation for the body of the worker?

 C. The intensity of the radiation heat at a fixed workplace where no one works.

 D. Which parts of the human body are subjected to radiation?

4. If thermal radiation is present, in the first instance, it is necessary to _____ .

 A. arrange the air douches in place where the worker stays for the longest periods of time.

B. arrange the air douches in the zone where the intensity of radiation is less than elsewhere.

C. measure the intensity of radiation in order to reduce it to the least degree.

D. pay equal attention to the duration and intensity of radiation

5. When installing the air douches _____ .

A. cold water is needed to prevent possible smoke, flame and sparks.

B. the width of the jet stream at the workplace should be considered.

C. the ambient air must be clarified and the impurities need to be blown away from the workplace.

D. seasons are of great importance, so it is better to do the work in summer.

Ⅱ. Are the following statements true or false?

1. Air douches will take the place of general ventilation because they can serve the functions which are impossible for general ventilation to do.   ( )

2. An air douche can ameliorate the air conditions in certain workplace without changing the temperature of the entire building.   ( )

3. The air used for the air douches can be pretreated at a much lower cost because the volume of air required for the douches is smaller.   ( )

4. If there is a air douche, we do not need natural ventilation, for air douches can lower the air temperature by itself.   ( )

5. The thermal load on the body is least tolerable when the chest, neck and head are subjected to radiation.   ( )

Vocabulary

Ⅰ. Fill in the following blanks with some of the words listed below, changing the form where necessary.

congregate	hygienic	ameliorate	contaminant
tolerable	adjacent	air current	parameter

1. One can change the velocity of the air and keep the other _____ constant.

2. Hence the intention is to maintain some special conditions in a limited space by the action of the _____ .

3. Sometime, work should be done in intense radiation, yet general ventilation is inadequate to maintain the required air temperature and humidity, air douches can _____ the conditions.

4. The purpose of local currents is to produce particular air conditions at fixed workplaces where workers _____ for long periods of time.

5. The air conditions in a workplace need to satisfy prescribed _____ and physiological requirements.

Ⅱ. Complete each of the following statements with one of the four choices given below.

1. While working in conditions of radiant heat, some particular parts of the human body will be continuously _____ to radiation.

   A. adapted to   B. subjected to   C. composed of   D. stuck to

2. When thermal radiation is present it is necessary to arrange the air douches _____ in the workplace where the worker is exposed to radiation for the longest periods of time.

   A. as a result   B. in terms of   C. as well as   D. in the first instance

3. In selecting the direction of the jet it is necessary to make sure that the impurities are not blown into _____ workplaces.

   A. adjacent   B. adjoin   C. adjunct   D. adjustable

4. One must take into account that the thermal load on the body is least _____ when the upper part of the trunk is exposed to radiation.

   A. insufficient   B. inadequate   C. tolerable   D. impossible

5. We are satisfied with the environment in the workplace, i. e. specified air temperature, velocity distributions and _____ concentrations.

   A. radiation   B. douche   C. temperature   D. contaminant

Translation

Review Exercises

I. Translate the following sentences into Chinese.

1. This experiment introduces a fact of an importance that cannot be overstressed.

2. The temperature of the air has then to be increased, to give a more agreeable relative humidity, which can be done by warming or by mixing with air which has not been cooled.

3. Industrial ventilation may be considered as comprising industrial environment control, industrial exhaust installations and drying systems.

4. The science of air-conditioning may be defined as that of providing and maintaining a desirable internal atmospheric environment irrespective of external conditions.

5. The question of the estimated quantity of ventilating air is directly related to the question of the arrangements for ventilation.

II. Point out the mistakes in the following translations and then put your correct ones.

1. All the oxygen supplied to the flame is not generally used.

2. A good specification will expand or clarify drawing notes, define quality of materials and workmanship, establish the scope of work, and spell out the responsibility of the prime contractor.

3. If the cost of equipment per hour of operation is considered, a heat pump is more economical to own than a cooling system with a separate heating unit.

4. The liquid flows from the pump by the force of gravity and is lifted only by atmo-

spheric pressure, which is not capable of lifting water more than about 30 feet.

5. We find buildings of the present day incorporating to a greater or lesser extent, almost as a common rule, some form of air-conditioning.

Reading Material A

Air Curtains

Even workshops which have considerable surplus heat release become chilled in the cold seasonof the year by the opening of gates and doors. Great masses of cold air burst in through themdue to gravity and wind. Being heavier than the air already in the building, this air movesover the floor in the lower part of the building.

Tests have shown that the heat loss associated with this influx, depending on the size of the doorway and the rate of inflow, amounts to many thousand kcal/hr. It would be uneconomic to meet this loss by extra heating even if it were practicable to do so. To reduce the entry of cold air, or even to stop it entirely, use can be made of an air curtain to deflect the cold air away from the door, or to let only some part of it pass through. This is done by a current of air acting upon natural flow. Essentially the phenomenon under consideration is due to the interaction of two streams of air, for without this interaction there would be no air curtain, only a simple plane jet of air.

Air curtains were first suggested by the author to replace "thermal curtains", which were intended to heat all the air as it enters a workshop. Since the warm air in these cases is blown from individual apertures at the side of and parallel to the plane of the gate, a thermal curtain cannot in any appreciable way stop the entry of cold air.

The air curtain is a comparatively thin plane jet projected from underneath or from one side of a rectangular opening to the other, or from top to bottom. In this form the curtain is to some extent an obstacle to the entry of cold outdoor air. It reduces the amount which enters and thereby makes it feasible to heat it. [1] Sometimes the need for heating can be obviated entirely if air form the warmer upper layers of the premises can be used for the air curtain; the air blowing into the shop can be deflected upwards. The calculation of air curtains was first published by the author jointly with I. A. Shepelev.

The problem was solved by the method of flow superposition known in aerodynamics by vector addition of the velocities of the jet with the velocities of the incoming air.

The problem was regarded as planar, assuming that in each cross-section of the jetperpendicular to the aperture one and the same geometric pattern is repeated. It was also supposed that the velocity of the incoming air depends only on the vertical coordinate, and distortion of the flow by the doorway was not taken into account. On the basis of these calculations a fairly large number of air curtains were set up in Soviet factories and these have since operated quite effectively.

Despite the imperfection of this theory, the right conclusion was obtained that the air-curtain effect is decided by the ratio of the momenta of the curtain jet and of the outdoor stream. This conclusion has been confirmed by tests. The effectiveness of the curtain remains unchanged if $(u2b)/v20 = $const.

The circulation was improved by Shepelev, who took account of the inherent velocity distribution in the jet, whereas previously only the axis of the jet had been considered. Later the calculation was refined by generalization of tests carried out with a model. During the tests a definite velocity was established in the doorway, and the air-flow rate through the door was measured with the curtain out of action and the pressure reduction in the model was also measured. On starting the air curtain, the pressure in the model increased owing to the "damping" action of the curtain. It was restored to its previous reading by throttling the fan discharge and then the quantity of the air passing through the model was measured again. The difference in flow rate was taken as the quantity of air which was held back by the action of the air curtain. [2] The assumption that the variation of pressure under the action of the air curtain can be ignored was not justified. This was shown by V. M. El'terman. who solved the problem of the air curtain by means of the theorem of momentum.

The calculation proposed by El'terman is expounded later, but for historical purposes a brief account is first given of Shepelev's analysis by means of stream functions, since it is amethod which can be used in solving other problems in ventilation.

Notes

①空气幕降低了进入的空气量，并使之有可能加热进入的空气。
②流量之差取作由空气幕挡住的空气量。

Reading Material B

Ventilated Chambers

In this system of local extraction, the impurity is confined to an enclosed space from which it is removed by mechanical or natural extraction. The process operators are outside the chamber, hence far greater concentrations can be discharged than would normally be permissible. The various kinds of enclosure in which such processes as drying, sandblasting and paint-spraying are carried on can be regarded as ventilated chambers.

Owing to the small number of openings in ventilated chambers, the impurities can be trapped effectively with the minimum consumption of air. However, contaminated air may escape into the air of the building through these openings or leaks, or it can be transferred on materials or workpieces when removed directly from the chamber into the building. For instance, cloth cancome straight from a drier emitting heat and vapours of dyes; a workpiece may be washed in petrol in a degreasing chamber and then the petrol remaining on the workpiece may afterwards evaporate in the building; after paint-spraying in a cabinet the workpiece may be a source of solvent vapours; and so on.

To avoid such residual effects, either the workpiece must be retained in the chamber or, if the technological process does not allow this, additional extraction may have to be provided.

The quantity of air that has to be extracted from a chamber is determined by the condition that no impurity should escape into the surrounding air through openings or leaks in the walls. In spite of the extraction of air from the chamber, leakage can take place for variousreasons, mainly due to local excess pressures inside the chamber and badly designed arrangements for the admission of the air to replace the quantity extracted.

Excess pressures can arise inside the chamber because of (1) rotation of machine parts under cover; (2) differences of air density inside and outside the chamber; and (3) pouring-pulverized materials.

When there are such local pressures within the chamber, only some of the admission openings may take in air, whilst the remainder (sometimes even a part of the same opening) eject air into the indoor atmosphere and thereby contaminate it. The following examples illustrate this.

In dye-finishing works, cloth is dried in drying chambers in which the temperature is maintained at 60-80℃. Conventional drying chambers are 1.5×10.0 m in area and about 4-4.5 m high. The cloth passes into the drier through openings, usually in the upper parts of the chamber. There are also several doors and other openings in the lower parts of the chamber for inspection of the operation and rectification of breakdowns (e.g. tearing of the cloth). The forced extraction from the chamber is from 3000 to 5000 m^3/hr, i.e. about 74 air changes per hr. [1] If the extraction is from a cold drier, indoor air will be sucked into the chamber through all the openings in accordance with their hydraulic resistances.

With the heated drier, owing to the static pressure difference between inside and out, air will enter through any leaks in the lower parts of the chamber and at the same time contaminated air from the drier will escape into the building through the upper openings. This is because the outward movement due to the static pressure differences is greater than the inward velocities due to the mechanical extraction.

Ventilated chambers may have natural or mechanical extraction. Consider first chambers with natural extraction. Here it is necessary for the temperature of the air in the chamber to be higher than the temperature in the building, i.e. the presence of a buoyancy force is necessary.

For satisfactory operation of the chamber it is also necessary to satisfy other conditions; the spent air should have sufficient reserve of energy to overcome the total resistance to the flow through the chamber from entry to exit; and to prevent contaminated air from entering the building, the neutral level in the chamber should not be below the upper edge of the opening. ②

Notes

① 小室的强制排风量从 3000 至 5000m³/hr，即每小时约 74 次换气。

② the spent air should have…of the opening 消耗的空气应有足够的能量储备，用来克服气流从入口到出口通过小室的总阻力；防止污染空气进入建筑物，小室中的中性面应低于开口的上边缘。

UNIT EIGHT

Text   Comfort and Discomfort

[1]   One of the goals of the environmental engineer and architect is to ensure comfortable conditions in a building. Thermal pleasure can only be achieved locally over part of the body or temporarily in the context of a situation which is in itself uncomfortable. Continuous thermal pleasure extending over a period of hours is not possible We are left simply with the idea of comfort as a lack of discomfort; this may seem an uninspiring definition, but nevertheless it presents a real practical challenge.

[2]   General thermal discomfort will be felt if a person is either too hot or too cold. In addition there are several potential sources of local discomfort, such as cold feet or draughts.

[3]   Any guide to comfort must relate these forms of discomfort to the physical variables of the environment, so that a permissible range of the variables may be recommended. It is conventional to treat overall thermal discomfort in terms of thermal sensation.

[4]   For other forms of discomfort it is not possible to base the definition of discomfort simply on a scale of overall thermal sensation. It is possible to be thermally neutral and so want the temperature neither raised nor lowered, yet still be uncomfortable because of some non-uniformity in the environment, such as a draught or radiant asymmetry. The most direct way of finding if someone is uncomfortable is simply to ask him. Usually the subject is asked to make a decision as to whether he is comfortable or uncomfortable, or whether he finds the thermal conditions acceptable or uncomfortable, Different people may be expected to become uncomfortable at different levels of external stress, so if the proportion of people voting uncomfortable is plotted against the level of stimulus, we should expect to get a curve of the shape. This is an ideal presentation, since the end user of the information is now able to trade off the proportion of people made uncomfortable against the cost of controlling the uncomfortable stimulus.

[5]   How well can we achieve such a presentation in practice? In laboratory studies the control and measurement of the potentially comfortable stimulus can be done to any required degree of accuracy. The stimulus might be, for instance, radiant asymmetry. A subject is then exposed to several levels of radiant asymmetry, with the other environmental variables held constant; the subject is asked to say if he is uncomfortable or not. After sufficient subjects have been exposed to various levels of radiant energy, a curve of the form may be plotted.

[6]   This experimental paradigm has formed the basis for much of the work on comfort, but has some weaknesses. The subject is asked to make a decision about whether he is uncomfortable or not; he has to make this decision in the unfamiliar surroundings of a labora-

tory after a limited exposure time. The results may then be applied to a population at its normal place of work. This ignores the fact that a person's judgement may be very dependent on context. ① For instance, the radiant asymmetry provided by direct sunshine is far higher than the level which is regarded as satisfactory from a radiant heating system, yet people seek out and welcome sunshine. While complaints of draughts are common in modern offices, a gentle walking pace produces an air speed over the body of greater than 1 m/s, which would normally be regarded as very draughty, yet no one complains of draught discomfort while walking. The response to a stimulus depends on the general surroundings and expectation of the person.

[7]   A particular example is the range effect. When an observer experiences a range of stimuli and is asked to rate them on a category scale, he tends to rate them by putting the stimuli from the middle of the range into the central categories of the rating scale. This has been clearly demonstrated in experiments on the acceptability of noise. Subjects exposed to a range of sound levels tend to place the boundary between acceptable and unacceptable noise at the centre of the range of noise which they have been exposed. Thus people who are exposed to high noise levels will apparently tolerate more noise than people who have only been exposed to low noise levels. The range effects do not apply only to the range of stimuli provided by the experimenter. People carry their own standards with them, based on their general experience, with which they compare a new stimulus. Thus, the meaning of the words comfortable or uncomfort able will not have an absolute value, but will be relative to his experience and expectation. ②When Gagge et al. (1967)put young men in an environmental chamber at 48 ℃ , the subjects rated the environment as slightly uncomfortable. There is little doubt that the equivalent environment in an office would be regarded as intolerable. However, the subjects knew they were in a physiological laboratory, were expecting to sweat, and did not object strongly to the experience.

[8]   It is clear, however, that their comfort rating cannot be transferred to a different situation. The standards of acceptability are set by the range of stimuli that people are used to. Poulton (1977) points out that this implies that the goal of providing a universally acceptable environment may be ever receding. If people do make judgements of acceptability on the basis of their own experience, then the maximum acceptable level will fall as the general level falls. If the noise level in a district is reduced, the level at which a noise becomes unacceptable will also be reduced and so the loudest noise will always be too loud. Air conditioning engineers are often heard to complain that standards of expectation rise as fast as the standard of air conditioning, so that the level of complaints stays constant.

New Words and Expressions

uninspiring [ʌnin'spaiəri]   a. 平凡的

challenge ['tʃæləndʒ]	n.	异议
draught [drɑ:ft]	n.	吹风
thermally neutral		热中性状态
non-uniformity		不均匀性
radiant asymmetry	n.	辐射不对称
subject ['sʌbdʒikt]	v.	受验者
trade off		交替使用
plot * [plɔt]	v.	测绘
presentation * [prezən'teiʃən]	n.	表达
paradigm ['pærədaim]	n.	范例
range effect		量级分布效果
category ['kætigəri]	n.	类别
environmental chamber		环境实验室
recede * [ri'si:d]	v.	失去重要性
stay constant		不变的

Notes

①…dependent on context

　……依赖于先后环境变化。

②but will be relative to his experience and expectation.

　是相对他的经验与期望而言的。

Exercises

Reading Comprehension

Ⅰ. Choose the best answer for each of the following

1. The general thermal discomfort is usually judged by _____ .

　A. the context of a situation

　B. how people feel

　C. cold feet or draughts

　D. some parts of body

2. When the environment is thermally neutral, _____ .

　A. there may be still other factors which make people uncomfortable

　B. people feel completely comfortable

　C. people want the temperature raised or lowered

　D. people feel uncomfortable because of some non-uniformity in the environment.

3. The "curve" mentioned in the text shows _____ .

A. the different levels of external stress of the subjects.

B. the levels of radiant asymmetry.

C. how the subjects are traded off.

D. the proportion of people voting uncomfortable against the level of stimulus.

4. According to the author, people's judgement on discomfort _____ .

A. may be very dependent on the environment.

B. is absolutely subjective.

C. is decided by their temporary mood.

D. may be more or less dependent on their expectation.

5. The level of complaints will never reduce because _____ .

A. the improvement can not catch up people's expectation.

B. the environment is getting worse and worse.

C. people's acceptability reduces while the environment improves.

D. people are becoming more and more intolerable.

II. Are the following statements true or false?

1. Thermal pleasure can never remain continuously, because environment keeps changing all the time. ( )

2. The simplest way to find if a person is uncomfortable is to ask him ( )

3. The result of laboratory studies can not be applied to a population at its normal place of work. ( )

4. Subjects exposed to a range of sound level tend to draw the same line between acceptable and unacceptable noise at the centre of the range of noise. ( )

5. The last paragraph indicates that the only way to quiet complaints is to make people used to their environment. ( )

Vocabulary

I. Fill in the blanks with some of the words listed below, changing the forms where necessary.

draught	paradigm	recede	trade
lack	category	stimulus	context

1. We have to accept the idea of comfort as _____ of discomfort, which seems to be uninspiring.

2. With ideal presentation of the curve, the end user is able to _____ off the proportion of people made uncomfortable against the cost of controlling the uncomfortable stimulus.

3. _____ is a non-uniformity in the environment that makes people feel uncomfortable.

4. When the observer had experienced a range of stimuli, he was asked to rate them on

a _____ scale.

5. The idea of providing comfortable environment for the people may be ever _____ .

Ⅱ. Complete each of the following statements with one of the four choices given below.

1. By carrying out experiments, this _____ has formed the basis for many people to work on comfort.

    A. paradigm   B. environment   C. expectation   D. curve

2. When air conditioning improves, the expectation of user rises, too, so the level of complaints _____ .

    A. reduces   B. upgrades   C. stays constant   D. lowers down

3. When the _____ were put in an environmental chamber, They rated the environment as uncomfortable.

    A. engineers   B. observers   C. judges   D. subjects

4. People tend to compare their general experience with a new _____ .

    A. expectation   B. stimulus   C. environment   D. condition

5. Comfort can be felt by people only in the _____ of uncomfortable situation.

    A. context   B. content   C. asymmetry   D. category

Translation   被动句的翻译

Ⅰ. 译成汉语被动句

被动句强调的主语，汉语时以原文主语作译文主语来构成被动句，以体现这种强调。

1. 有 by 引出动作发出者时，常在动作发出者前加"通过"、"由"、"用"等字构成汉语被动句。

举例：The direction of force can be shown by an arrow.

力的方向可用箭头表示。

2. 没有 by 引出动作发出者时，表明动作发出者没有必要，汉译时也如此。常在谓语动词前加"被"、"受到"、"得到"、"遭到"等译成被动句。

举例：Several methods are used for developing concrete quality.

若干种方法被用来改进水泥质量。

Ⅱ. 译成汉语主动句

不是所有的英语被动句都得译成汉语被动句，有些译成汉语主动句更便于表达原意，符合汉语的表达习惯。

例 1. The complete water supply system for the new paper mill was designed by three young water engineers.

三个年轻给水工程师设计了这座新纸厂的全套给水系统。

例 2. Within the last 40 years new methods of concrete construction have been introduced.

近 40 年来，采用了几种制作混凝土的新方法。（无主语）

Directions:

Translate the following into Chinese, paying attention to the underlined parts.

1. The metric system is now used by almost all the countries in the world.
2. Iron is extracted from the ore by smelting in the blast furnace.
3. The word "work" and "power" are often confused or interchanged in colloquial use.
4. Electricity itself has been known to man for thousands of years.
5. Gases are frequently regarded as compressible, liquids as incompressible.
6. Attention has been paid to the new measures to prevent corrosion.
7. Large quantities of steam are used by modern industry in the generation of power.
8. The available energy contained in a fuel is converted to heat energy by a process known as combustion.

Reading Material A

Ceiling Heating

A heated ceiling emits heat into the room largely by radiation. A layer of warm air forms immediately under the ceiling and is held there by its own buoyancy. The convective transfer from the ceiling into the room is therefore very low; a convection transfer coefficient of about 1 W/m^2K is found, compared with the radiation transfer coefficient of 6 W/m^2K. The air in the room is therefore not heated directly by the ceiling. The radiation leaving the ceiling warms up the floor, walls and furniture, which subsequently warms up the air. The result is that ceiling heating produces a fairly uniform air temperature in the heated room, with the room surfaces, and particularly the floor, tuning at a temperature slightly higher than the air temperature.

Although the air temperature is fairly uniform, there is a possibility that the asymmetric nature of the radiation may cause discomfort. The degree of radiant asymmetry at a point is measured by the vector radiant temperature, which was defined previously. The radiant environment produced by the heated ceiling may then be described by the mean radiant temperature and the vector radiant temperature, conventionally measured at a height 1 m above the floor in the occupied position. This cannot be a complete description; both the mean radiant temperature and the vector radiant temperature will normally vary with height, as will the air temperature. [1] The head and feet of a person may therefore experience different heat losses, with the risk of local discomfort. However, for design purposes it will normally be adequate to describe the asymmetry in terms of a single number, the vector radiant temperature at a height of 1 m. In order to set a maximum design value, we must refer to the results of experiments.

Several experiments have been carried out on the comfort conditions produced by heated ceilings. To make a meaningful comparison between them, it was necessary to recalculate the radiant temperature. Only by expressing the results in a common unit is it possible to compare different experiments. One of the earlier experiments, and one which had a great influence in setting comfort recommendations in Europe, was carried out by Chrenko (1953) In this experiment a person sat under a heated ceiling for half an hour, and then gave ratings of his thermal comfort, feelings of pleasantness and discomfort. The walls and floor were held at a constant temperature of 19℃ and the temperature of the ceiling panel was varied up to a maximum of 50℃. It was found that the incidence of feelings of unpleasantness rose steadily as the ceiling temperature increased. Chrenko expressed his recommendation in terms of elevation of the mean radiant temperature at head level above the unheated mean radiant temperature and stated that this should not exceed 2.2K; the limit was associated with an expected frequency of 20% of unpleasant sensations. Estimating the vector radiant temperature from the original paper shows that the recommended upper limit corresponds to a vector radiant temperature of about 6 K.

Interpretation of Chrenko's results is made difficult by the fact that the warmth conditions were not held constant; as the ceiling temperature was increased, overall warmth increased and so there was a risk that discomfort from overheating might be confused with discomfort from the asymmetric radiation. [2]

Notes

①这并非完整的描述方法，平均辐射温度和定向辐射温度二者通常随高度而变化，如同空气温度随高度而变化那样。

②温暖条件未能保持恒定，当天花板温度上升时，总温暖度增大，从而会形成因过热的不舒适性可能与因不对称辐射的不舒适性相混淆的危险性，这使得Chronko的试验结果的整理分析遇到了困难。

Reading Material B

Underfloor Heating

Heating a space by means of a warm floor started with the Roman hypocaust, and survives in modern times, using either water pipes or electric heating cables buried in a concrete slab. [1] It is universal practice to heat the whole of the floor area to a uniform temperature. One advantage is that the relatively low temperatures required make the system suitable for heat sources such as heat pumps or solar systems. which work most efficiently with low-temperature output.

Short term discomfort from walking on a warm floor while wearing shoes is most unlikely. However, warm floors can produce discomfort over a long period of time. The skin temperature of the feet varies greatly with general vasomotor tone and there is not really a unique temperature for foot comfort. A person who is alert, i. e. slightly aroused, will have a foot temperature which is lower than the average skin temperature. Relaxation, as when falling asleep, causes the foot temperature to rise sharply. Heating the feet may combat the general vascular tone and produce local vasodilatation. [2] This may be unpleasant, producing the feeling of hot swollen feet, and in extreme cases may upset the general thermoregulatory system. During the war there were many attempts to produce heated clothing for air crew, and it was found that if the feet were overheated compared with the rest of the body the unpleasant situation of simultaneous sweating and shivering could be produced—Burton (1963). Herrington and Lorenzi (1949) measured comfort and skin temperatures with both floor and ceiling heating. They also observed an undesirable rise of foot temperature with a heated floor. They considered that a floor temperature of over 24℃ was undesirable, but gave 27 ℃ as the temperature at which the effects were clearly demonstrable.

The Kansas State University carried out a series of experiments on floor temperature and comfort. Both seated and standing postures were used, and the exposure time was three hours. The percentage of standing people reporting discomfort rose from 2% to 15% when the floor temperature increased from 24 to 26. 7℃—Nevins et al. (1967). However, the authors concluded that temperatures of 29. 5℃ could be used without causing serious discomfort. This emphasizes the different criteria of acceptability which have been used by different been found to be too high in British experience. Chrenko (1956) mentions floor-heated hospitals, where the nurses complained him to recommend that for long-term occupation floor temperatures should not exceed 25℃ for walking, or 27℃ for sedentary occupants. These figures have been used successfully in the design of electric underfloor heating, and agree with the other evidence quoted above.

Notes

①the Roman hypocaust，罗马式火坑供暖。
②local vasodilation，局部血管舒张。

UNIT NINE

Text   Heating by Steam and High-pressure Hot Water

[1]   Generation of Steam: It will be as well to recapitulate here that steam is produced when heat is applied to water in a partially filled closed vessel; and that, when boiling point isreached, the addition of further heat causes a change of state to occur from water to steam. The quantity of heat involved in the process is considerable. 2258kJ/kg at atmospheric pressure, compared with 420 to raise it to boiling point from $0\,^{\circ}\mathrm{C}$.

[2]   In a closed vessel, the steam has no means of escape and the addition of further heatcauses the pressure to rise. Means for preventing the rise from being above the strength of the vessel are provided by safety valves. As the pressure rises so does the temperature, Thus, this further heat entering the water is in the form of sensible heat in the liquid and steam, the latent heat falling as the pressure rises.

[3]   The utilization of steam for heating involves the process of condensation, in which the latent heat is removed by the heat-emitting surfaces of the heating system and reverts to water at the same temperature as the steam. This hot water or condense must be removed as soon as it is formed, or the heating apparatus will become water-logged and useless. The condense is, however, under pressure and, as it is released to atmospheric pressure, it suffers a reduction in temperature. In effect, part of the heat in the condense above atmospheric boiling point goes to re-evaporate a proportion of the liquid into steam at the lower pressure, this being termed flash-steam. [1] Use can be made of this in a variety of ways, but if it is not usefully employed it constitutes a loss, as also does the remaining heat in the condense if this is run to waste. [2] Thus, in practice, condense is collected and returned to the boiler for re-use, which at the same time affords a supply of distilled water and saves on water consumption.

[4]   Unfortunately, condense also may carry with it uncondensible gases such as chlorine, CO_2 and O_2 which are liable to cause severe corrosion of condense lines.

[5]   Condense Return: Having been condensed in the heating equipment it is grossly wasteful todischarge condense to drain. It may represent as much as 20 per cent on the fuel bill. Thus itis normally returned for re-use in the boiler, as explained already.

[6]   At the drain point of the heat emitting apparatus or calorifier, some means is required to allow water to pass but not steam. This device is termed a steam trap. Various types exist, and these fall into three broad classes, identified by the means adopted to distinguish and separate condensate from steam, as follows: 1. Mechanical, incorporating (a) Open top bucket (b) Inverted bucket (c) Ball float; 2. Thermostatic, with various elements (a) Balanced pressure (b) liquid expansion (c) Bi-metallic; 3. Miscellaneous, including (a) Labyrinth (b) Thermodynamic (c) Impulse.

[7]　　Choice of trap type depends upon a number of factors: load characteristics (constant orfluctuating); inlet and outlet pressures; associated thermostatic or other controls on the steam equipment; and the relative levels of trap and condense main piping to name but a few. Heating by High-pressure Hot Water

[8]　　The father of all high-pressure hot-water systems was Perkins, whose patent was filed in 1831. In his system, the piping was extremely strong, about 22 mm bore, and formed one continuous coil, part of it passing through the boiler and the remainder formed the heating surface in the rooms to be heated. Expansion of the water was allowed for in a closed vessel at the top. Two or more coils could be used where one was insufficient. As the water was heated, its expansion compressed the air in the expansion vessel and considerable pressures were reached. The principle was that the formation of steam was prevented by the pressure to which the water in the system was subjected. The system is now obsolete, though examples may still be found at work chiefly in churches and chapels.

[9]　　Temperature Ranges: The higher the initial temperature, obviously the greater the temperature drop which can be allowed between flow and return, and, correspondingly, the larger the heat content per unit mass flow of water, requiring smaller pipe sizes for a given load. On the other hand, the higher the pressure the more costly the boilers and other equipment.

[10]　　The lower pressure system requires more heating surface for a given output. For smaller installations, however, there are many compensating advantages.

[11]　　For this and for other reasons, it has come to be accepted that there is no point in designing for high pressures for systems under say 2000 to 3000 kW, below which ratings medium-pressures are most suitable.[3] The high-pressure system comes into its own with increasing size and extensive runs of mains.

[12]　　Comparison with Steam: Hot water in a closed system under pressure may be run at any temperature up to its design maximum. Where serving space-heating apparatus, the temperature of the water can be varied according to the weather, so saving on mains heat losses and by better control generally. Variability of temperature is not possible with steam, which must be either on or off and any attempt at throttling is liable to cause water logging at the remote ends.

(This assumes that the vacuum steam system with its further complications is ruled out anyway.)

[13]　　Hot water requires no steam traps. The potential loss of heat through flash steam and condense return may amount to ten per cent or more of the fuel bill. Traps also require maintenance, as do other steam accessories.

[14]　　Hot-water mains may be run with complete freedom as to levels, whereas steam mains require careful grading and draining. Also corrosion of condense lines is avoided.

[15]　　In terms of pipe sizes and cost it can be shown that, taken overall, there is little difference in the two systems.

New Words and Expressions

recapitulate * [ˌriːkəˈpitʃuleit]	v.	概括，摘要（说明）
vessel [ˈvesl]	n.	容器，器皿
utilization [juːtilaiˈzeiʃein]	n.	应用
revert * [riˈvəːt]	v.	恢复原状
condense * [kənˈdens]	n.	冷凝液，冷凝结水
re-evaporate * [iˈvæpəreit]	vt.	自蒸发，再蒸发
uncondensible [ˌʌnkənˈdensəbl]	a.	不凝性的
chlorine [ˈklɔːriːn]	n.	氯
corrosion [kəˈrəuʒən]	n.	腐蚀
grossly [grəusli]	a.	极度地，十分地
calorifier	n.	散热器
term * [təːm]	vt.	把…称作
trap [træp]	n.	疏水器，凝汽阀
condensate [kənˈdenseit]	n.	凝结水，冷凝液
thermostatic [ˌθəːməˈstætik]	a.	恒温式（的）
bi-metallic	a.	双金属的
miscellaneous [misˈleiniəs]	a.	各式各样的，其它类型的
labyrinth [ˈlæbərinθ]	n.	迷宫
thermodynamic [θəːmədaiˈnæmik]	a.	热力式，热力学的
impulse [ˈimpʌls]	n.	脉冲
fluctuating [ˈflʌktʃueit]	a.	波动的
to name but a few		（插入语）不过举几个（例子）
patent * [ˈpeitnt]	n.	专利
absolete	a.	过时的，已废弃的，废弃
chapel [ˈtʃæpl]	n.	小教堂
compensate [kɔmpenseit]	v.	补偿
mains [meinz]	n.	总管，总线，主管道
variability [vɛəriəˈbiliti]	n.	变化性，易变，变化的倾向
throttle [ˈθrɔtl]	vt.；n.	节流，节流阀
water logging	n.	积水，浸透水
be ruled out		不考虑，不接受
grading [greidiŋ]	n.	定坡度
taken over all		总之，整个说来
accessory [əkˈsesəri]	a.	辅助的；n.（pl）辅助设备

Notes

①this being termed flash-steam，分词独立结构，作状语表示补充说明。

②as also does the remaining heat in the condense if this is run to waste.

　as 引出方式状语从句，并倒装。

③there is no point in designing for high pressures for systems under say2000 to 3000kW.

　there is no point in …意为"没有必要做……"systems under say 2000 to

　3000 kW 中，say，意为"比如说。"

Exercises

Reading Comprehension

Ⅰ. Choose the best answer for each of the following.

1. Steam is generated by _____ .

　A. applying heat to water in a partially filled closed vessel

　B. further heating of the boiling water in a partially closed vessel

　C. additional heat to water in a closed vessel

　D. heating a completely filled closed container

2. In the process of condensation _____ .

　A. it is not necessary to remove hot condense when it is formed

　B. flash-steam constitutes a loss

　C. the latent heat is removed and reverts to water at the same temperature as the
　　steam

　D. heating apparatus becomes useless

3. A steam trap is a device which _____ .

　A. provides some means to allow water to pass but not steam

　B. can discharge condense to drain

　C. can distinguish and separate water from steam

　D. can make condense return for re-use

4. Choice of trap type is determined by many factors except _____ .

　A. inlet and outlet pressures

　B. associated thermostatic or other controls on the steam equipment

　C. open top bucket

　D. the relative levels of trap

5. The comparison between hot water and steam shows that _____ .

　A. the temperature of hot water can be controlled whereas the temperature of steam
　　can not.

B. they both have different temperatures according to weather

C. hot water mains and steam mains may be run freely

D. they both need steam traps

II. Are the following statements true or false?

1. The re-use of condense collected and returned to the boiler supplies distilled water and saves water consumption. ( )

2. Condense also may carry with it chlorine, CO_2 and O_2 without causing too much corrosion of condense lines. ( )

3. High-pressure Hot Water system invented by Perkins is now widely used all over the world. ( )

4. For smaller installations, the lower pressure system has many compensating advantages. ( )

5. It is not supposed that the higher the presssure, the more costly the boilers and other equipment. ( )

Vocabulary

I. Fill in blanks with some of the words listed below, changing the form where necessary.

| recapitulate | latent | revert | discharge |
| remainder | obsolete | variability | corrosion |

1. It's possible for some uncondensible gases in the condense to cause _____ of condense lines.

2. The main part of the apparatus was kept in the large workshop, while the _____ of it was kept in the small one.

3. The _____ heat in the water can still warm the whole set of equipment in such cold weather.

4. Ten years ago, such machines were found at work in many factories, however they are _____ now.

5. The latent in the process of condensation is removed as soon as it's formed and _____ to water, otherwise the heating apparatus will become water-logged.

II. Complete each of the following statements with one of the four choices given below.

1. The well-known professor only _____ that the addition of further heat may cause some changes of the working process.

A. illustrate   B. recapitulate   C. elucidate   D. explain

2. It will be difficult to complete the new experiment because of _____ of temperature.

A. variability   B. unstability   C. mobility   D. mutation

3. They have tried the new method since the last failure in working out the problem and

the _____ of the method has brought them a great success.

A. operation   B. exploitation   C. utilization   D. conduction

4. Although there are many similarities between the two machines, it's _____ to discover some differences.

A. liable   B. accountable   C. amenable   D. answerable

5. It's obvious that after having been condensed in the heating equipment it is greatly wasteful to _____ condense to drain.

A. emit   B. disburden

C. exclude   D. discharge

Translation   静态结构句的翻译

静态结构句与被动句结构相同，但表意却有区别。被动句强调动作，而静态结构句强调状态或性质。静态结构句不可能出现由 by 引出的动作发出者，汉语时，都译成汉语主动句，表示状态或性质。

静态结构的惯用句型：

It is said that…据说   It is told that…据说

It is found that…据发现   It is reported that…据报导

It is believed that…人们确信   It is considered that…普遍认为

It is estimated that…据估计   It is suggested that…普遍认为

It is understood that…据了解   It is well known that…众所周知

It is claimed that…据声称   It is supposed that…据推测

It is acknowledged that…普遍承认   It has been established that…现已公认

It is presumed that…据假定

Directions：

Translate the following sentences into Chinese, paying attention to the underlined parts.

1. It has been established that there is no work unless there is motion.

2. It is estimated that the switching time of the new type transistor is shortened 3 times.

3. It is supposed that sun is 330.000 times as large as the earth.

4. It is well known that the greater the height, the less air there is and the lower the pressure.

5. The outside of the convector is made of steel plates. The inside is lined with bricks. The converter is tipped on to its side.

6. The picture presented in the preceding paragraph is still very much oversimplified. The formation and eventual combustion of carbon particles clearly are not concentrated very near the stoichiometric surface. The reactions governing carbon parti-

cle formation <u>are</u>, for some reason, <u>delayed.</u>

7. Those aggregates which <u>are dug</u> nearby must <u>be sized</u>, <u>washed</u>, free of clay or silt, and <u>recombined</u> in the correct proportions.

8. When all the exploration functions <u>are completed</u>, the actual drilling of the well is accomplished. The gas, or rude oil, <u>is brought</u> to the earth's surface and is blocked at this point, The well remains in this state until the gas or oil <u>is needed.</u>

Reading Material A

Reduce Transmission Heat Losses through Walls

Heat loss through a wall is a function of its resistance to heat flow modified by the effect of solar radiation (reduces heat loss) and wind (increases heat loss) on the outside surface. The effect of solar radiation is modified by the absorption coefficient of the outside surfaces; dark colors (high absorption coefficient) will reduce the heat loss more than light colors (low absorption coefficient)

The mass of the wall and its attendant thermal inertia have an overall modifying effect onheat loss by delaying the impact of outdoor temperature changes on the heated space. This timedelay allows the wall to act dynamically as a thermal storage system, smoothing out peaks in heat flow and reducing yearly heat loss. [1] Low mass walls of 10-20 1bs. /square foot willhave approximately 2% greater yearly heat loss than high mass walls of 80-90 1bs. /square foot, assuming both walls have the same overall "U" value conductance and absorption coefficient.

A computer program was developed to study the reaction of walls to varying climatic conditions and runs were made for 12 cities chosen to provide a typical cross section of climates.

Heat loss through walls is greatest in locations having high degree days but for any one location varies with the wall orientation; heat loss is highest through north walls and least through south walls due to the beneficial effect of the sun. The difference is more marked in walls having a high absorption coefficient.

The overall "U" value of walls may be decreased by the addition of insulating material to the inside surface, to the outside surface, or to fill cavities within the wall structure.

Addition of insulation to the outside of walls can be accomplished with relative ease inone or two story buildings, but becomes increasingly difficult for the higher stories because of the requirement for access staging. Insulation added to the outside of walls must be weatherproof and vapor-sealed to prevent deterioration of its insulating properties due to the ingress of moisture. External insulation could be added in the form of prefabricated insulating panels finished to give the most advantageous absorption coefficient. A design problem likely to occur when adding insulation to the outside surface of walls is treatment of window openings and door openings; it must be resolved architecturally for each individual case. ② The appearance of the building will be changed and may be subject to approval to meet local fine arts standards or covenant requirements.

Addition of insulation to the inside surface of walls can be accomplished with the same ease for single and multi-story buildings (as access is from the floor of each story treated)

It may, however, entail moving furniture and fittings away from the wall and could interrupt normal operation of the building. Internal insulation must be protected from moisture by a vapor barrier and from degradation by wear and tear either by having an integral finished surface or by being covered by a protective finish such as wood paneling or gypsum plasterboard. Design problems likely to occur when adding insulation to the internal surfaces of walls are treatment of window and door openings, architraves and reveals, the junction between the insulation and the floor and ceiling; and repositioning equipment such as heaters, electric receptacles, etc., that are recessed in the existing wall.

Notes

①时间延迟能使墙可充当动态蓄热系统，消除热流峰值，并降低年热损失量。
②在墙壁外表面加绝热层时，可能会出现的设计问题是窗孔和门孔的处理，对于每一种个别情况必须从建筑角度加以解决。

Reading Material B

Non-metallic Hot Water Distribution Piping

Fibre glass reinforced plastic (FRP) "Bondstrand" piping was developed in the United Statesin 1955 mainly for the purpose of conveying all types of liquids for which metal piping was not suited and its origin was associated with requirements by major chemical industries for piping such substances as acids, alkali, oxidizing agents, chlorine compounds, salt water, dyes, condensate, food industry liquids, oil and petroleum products, etc. There are different varieties of Bondstrand piping in production, featuring either epoxy or polyester resin liners, fibre glass reinforced by a mechanical process of continuous filament winding under tension at an exact helix angle. ①

All FRP materials are chemically and biologically inert; the pipe exterior does not require painting, protective coating or cathodic protection when buried. Structurally it is nearly equal to steel but its weight is one fifth to one eighth that of steel.

Heating water development of FRP, within classification of pipe-in-pipe mains, factory prefabricated and insulated for direct installation in the ground, features the chemically inert epoxy resin bonded fibre glass spirally wound reinforced construction. The material of high insulation value has great strength and is corrosion free. The piping is rated for water temperature of 120℃ and pressure of 10 bar.

Insulation is conventional using rigid polyurethane foam encased in a heavy low density polyethylene jacket. End seals are fitted to each end of pipe or fitment unit to provide external water barrier as insulation protection.

In addition to such an inherent advantage as being inert to internal and external corrosion the other positive characteristic is light weight, greatly facilitating handling and transport. As an example, a standard prefabricated and insulated 6 metre long unit containing service pipe 80 mm internal diameter × 3. 6 mm thick weighs 23 kg whereas the equivalent steel pipe/plastic casing unit is 58 kg.

Furthermore, with a coefficient of thermal linear expansion at 0. 0153 mm/m℃ axial expansion forces, due to the very low modulus of elasticity of ca 16×106 kN/m² and nature of construction, are moderate and tend to reduce with increased temperature. The piping therefore does not require compensation devices; in the course of installation axial forces are contained and absorbed within the pipe held between specially calculated and designed concrete anchor blocks which are provided at changes in direction, at reducers, bends, elbows and branches. [2]

Thermal transmission coefficient of the pipe is 0. 30 W/m · ℃ and its inert reaction to soil and other surroundings makes insulation of joints unnecessary especially as such connections are usually embedded in the concrete anchors.

All fitments are manufactured in the same glass fibre reinforced epoxy resin as the pipework. All connections are made by specialized techniques using proprietary 2-part resin adhesive. Correct attachment of pipe units and fitments ensures connections of a strength at least equal to that of the piping material.

Trenching for the FRP piping should be of similar nature to that for any pipe-in-pipe system, with installation on a sand base and sand covering prior to final backfill. The bearing capacity of solid soil base must be ascertained to ensure effective constructi on of concrete anchor blocks.

This FRP system is finding an increasing market in the low temperature (100 ℃) district heating field where aggressive soils rule out the use of steel systems. Also, it is particularly suited to condensate lines where corrosion causes a constant need for replacement of conventional steel pipework. Tests carried out at the Department of the Environment research rig at Cardington showed very favourable results especially with regard to heat loss.

Notes

①现生产各式各样的粘结原丝玻璃钢管，其特点是环氧树脂或聚酯树脂衬里，在张力下以

准确螺旋角用连续缠绕机械工艺的玻璃纤维增强。

②因而管道无需补偿装置，在安装过程中轴向力被固定在经专门计算和设计的混凝土支座之间的管子遏制和吸收，支座设在管道的变向处、变径处、转弯、肘弯及分支处。

UNIT TEN

Text　　　　Efficiency Is Fashionable Again

[1]　　The word synallagmatic is a legal term defined as "imposing reciprocal obligations and characterized by mutual rights and duties. " The word does not define cogeneration, but it is aiming in the right direction. "Partnership" does a better job. "Achieving reciprocal benefits " comes closest to what results in an effective cogeneration arrangement. Synergism is also clearly involved.

[2]　　The practice of cogeneration occurred in many forms long before the name was attached. According to a U. S. Department of Energy technical report on the subject, "In broadest terms, cogeneration denotes any form of the simultaneous production of electrical or mechanical energy and useful thermal energy (usually in the form of hot liquids or gases) . Cogeneration systems include dual-purpose power plants, waste-heat utilization systems, certain types of district-heating systems, and total energy systems. "

[3]　　District heating systems are examples of cogeneration when an electric utility or industry with its own power plant supplies thermal energy in the form of steam or hot water to customers. When a district heating system does not involve electrical generation but simply the burning of fuel to supply heat, cogeneration does not occur.

[4]　　Total energy systems, such as the system operated by the Regency Square Shopping Center, Jacksonville, Florida, produces electricity, heating, and cooling, typically for a compact development such as a shopping center, medical complex, university campus, or comparable institutions.

[5]　　Traditional energy systems in the United States have ordinarily delivered only one product, either electricity or heat. When cogeneration is introduced, one system is designed to deliverboth electricity and thermal energy, with a substantial improvement in fuel and operational efficiency as a result. In a cogeneration operation, thermal energy that would otherwise be discharged as waste is put to use.[①] This can make a system significantly more efficient than before in terms of energy savings and reduced fuel requirements.

[6]　　Cogeneration offers the following benefits:

●Flexibility in the use of fuels: Various alternative fuels in plentiful supply can be used rather than oil and natural gas.

●Efficiency: National energy self-sufficiency is promoted, because energy waste is eliminated or reduced.

●Cost advantage: By using less fuel to achieve objectives, cogeneration saves both energy and capital.

●Environmental Improvements: Cogeneration systems need less fuel to produce a stipulated amount of energy, which means a corresponding reduction in the pollutants released as a consequence of burning fuel.

●Resource Conservation: By achieving more with less fuel, cogeneration saves depletable fuel resources as well as the energy that would be required to extract and deliver those resources. ②

●Dependability: Reliable power is more likely to be available during periods of emergency such as natural disaster, adverse weather, or a local blackout.

[7]　For several decades cogeneration was known about as a means of conserving energy, and all the above advantages were recognized, but little was done to introduce cogeneration. Deliberately wasting energy was a predictable result of cheap energy supplies.

[8]　In the 1980s conventional energy supplies are less easy to acquire, less certain, and their prices are much higher. In the United States, cogeneration as a result is beginning to be noticed rather than ignored. Saving fuel, reducing expense, protecting the environment, and assuring reliable power have become important goals only cogeneration can effectively reach. ③ The technology of cogeneration is not new, since various forms of it date back to the 19th century. This familiarity is itself an advantage, because delays for research and development are not necessary before implementation.

[9]　"Cogeneration is a viable technological alternative that offers the United States one more strategy for working toward its goal of energy self-sufficiency both now and over the long term," stated the Department of Energy report on Cogeneration.

[10]　Two basic types of cogeneration systems are available: (1) topping system, which produces electricity and exhausts thermal energy which is used for district heating or comparable functions. (2) bottoming system, which produces thermal energy for an industrial process or district heating and part of the thermal energy is withdrawn to generate electricity. Each system has particular equipment requirements. Which system is used depends on the special needsand situation of the user.

[11]　Utilities commonly supply district heating steam or hot water through a topping system. Institutions, shopping centers, and similar complexes as well as industries may first need steam for heating/cooling or process operations, and find it expedient to drive a turbine with a fraction of the steam to supply electricity in a bottoming operation.

New Words and Expressions

reciprocal [ri'siprəkl]	a.	相互起作用的
synergism ['sinədʒizəm]	n.	协合作用
dual-purpose ['djuːəl]	n.	两种目的
complex ['kɔmpleks]	n.	综合设施
discharge [dis'tʃɑːd]	vt.	排出，流放
depletable [di'pliːtəbl]	a.	非再生的
implementation [ˌimplimen'teiʃən]	n.	实施

expedient [ik'spi:diənt]	a.	适宜的
turbine ['tə:bain]	n.	汽轮机
impose [im'pauz]	vt.	把…强加
obligation [ˌɔbli'geiʃən]	n.	义务，责任
simultaneous [ˌsiml'teiniəs]	a.	同时发生的
utility [ju:'tiləti]	n.	公共事业设备
comparable ['kɔmpərəbl]	a.	可比较的
operational [ˌpə'reiʃənl]	a.	用于操作的
flexibility [ˌfleksə'biləti]	n.	机动性，灵活性
stipulate ['stipjuleit]	vt.	订立协议，允诺
corresponding [ˌkɔri'spɔndiŋ]	a.	符合的，一致的
emergency [i'mə:dʒənsi]	n.	紧急情况
blackout ['blækaut]	n.	灯光管制，中断
predictable [pri'diktəbl]	a.	可预测的
in the form of		以…的形式
be likely to		有可能
date back		始于
in terms of		从…方面来说
be defined as		被定义为

Notes

①be put to use：使用，利用。

②as well as：在此相当于 and。

③Saving fuel，reducing…protecting…assuring reliable power…

并列动名词短词作主语。

Exercises

Reading Comprehension

Ⅰ.Choose the best answer for each of the following.

1. It's known that cogeneration of which the practice occurred long before denotes any of the following forms except the simultaneous production of _____ .

   A. electrical energy   B. thermal energy

   C. mechanical energy   D. liquids or gases

2. Traditional energy systems in the United States have ordinarily delivered only one product such as _____ .

   A. electricity   B. steam   C. cooling   D. hot water

3. Through cogeneration, national energy self-sufficiency is promoted because of
_____ .

　　A. the adequate production of electricity.

　　B. the sufficient production of heat.

　　C. the plentiful supply of fuels.

　　D. the elimination of energy waste.

4. Owing to cogeneration, reliable power is more possible to be available during periods
of _____ .

　　A. natural calamity 　　　B. harmful weather

　　C. shortage of water 　　　D. Both A and B.

5. It's said that cogeneration can effectively reach some important goals, for example,

_____ .

　　A. making full use of fuel.

　　B. reducing unjust expense.

　　C. changing the environment.

　　D. offering reliable power.

Ⅱ. Are the following statements true or false?

1. Although it's not easy to define cogeneration explicitly, the word synallagmatic is
aiming in the right direction. 　　　　　　　　　　　　　　　　　　　　( )

2. The naming of cogeneration had existed actually long before the practice of cogeneration which occurred in varied forms. 　　　　　　　　　　　　　　　　　( )

3. Cogeneration systems merely include certain types of district-heating systems and to-
tal-energy systems which offer the simultaneous production of electrical or mechanical energy. 　　　　　　　　　　　　　　　　　　　　　　　　　　　( )

4. Only when an electric utility or industry with its own power plant supplies thermal
energy in the form of steam or hot water to customers are district heating systems
the examples of cogeneration. 　　　　　　　　　　　　　　　　　　　( )

5. Cogeneration also occurs when a district heating system involves electrical generation,
not simply the burning of fuel to supply heat. 　　　　　　　　　　　　　( )

Vocabulary

Ⅰ. Fill in the blanks with some of the words listed below, changing the form where necessary.

discharge	viable	denote	depletable
implementation	effective	elimination	predictable

1. Cogeneration which _____ any form of the simultaneous production of mechanical energy and so on includes dual-purpose power plants.

2. Some substance which originally should be _____ was put to use again by utiliz-

ing the new instrument.

3. Cogeneration by using less fuel saves _____ fuel resources which can not be easily regained.

4. The familiarity of the technology of cogeneration is an advantage especially before the _____ of the technology.

5. The United States can enjoy one more strategy for working toward its goal of energy self-sufficiency because cogeneration offers a _____ technological alternative.

Ⅱ. Complete each of the following statements with one of the four choices given below.

1. Most workers in the plant are working hard in order to make an _____ cogeneration arrangement.

   A. efficient   B. effective   C. effectual   D. efficacious

2. This newly-established system was excellent in terms of energy conservation and _____ fuel requirements.

   A. reduced   B. diminished   C. lessened   D. dwindled

3. The _____ supply of water made it possible to carry out this experiment involving the need of a great deal of water.

   A. bountiful   B. generous   C. plentiful   D. plenteous

4. The _____ of energy waste will take a long time for lack of advanced technology.

   A. deletion   B. liquidation   C. removal   D. elimination

5. None of them is sure of the _____ result brought by making use of the new measure aiming at preventing air pollution.

   A. prescient   B. predictable   C. prophetic   D. portentous

Translation   倍数增加的翻译

    表示倍数增加有两个概念：净增加倍数和增加后的倍数（含基数）。英语表示这两个概念时，常用下述是四种表达法，在汉译时要特别注意"增加了…倍"和"增加到…倍"的区别。

例1. The output value of this factory has been raised by three times. （V. ＋by＋倍数）

    该厂的产值提高了三倍。

例2. The quantity of such products has multiplied four times since 1992. （V. ＋倍数）

    这类产品自 1992 年以来已增加到四倍。

例3. In case of electronic scanning the beam width has increased by a factor of two. （V. ＋by a factor of ＋整数）

    用电子扫描时，波束宽度增加到两倍。

例4. The power has increased threefold. （V. ＋-fold）

    功率增加到三倍。

Directions:

Translate the following into Chinese, paying attention to the underlined parts.

1. The sun is <u>330,000 times as large as</u> the earth.
2. The oxygen atom is <u>16 times heavier than</u> the hydrogen atom.
3. Mercury weighs <u>more than</u> water <u>by about 14 times.</u>
4. The beam width is <u>broader by a factor of two.</u>
5. The amount of coal left was estimated to be <u>again as much as</u> all the coal that had been mined.
6. The output of coal <u>has been increased three times</u> as against 1990.
7. A temperature rise of 100℃ increases the conductivity of a semiconductor <u>by 50 times.</u>
8. The annual total of telephone calls between the two cities <u>has increased sevenfold.</u>
9. Halving the repeater spacing made it possible <u>to quadruple</u> the bandwidth.
10. The molecules of nitrogen and oxygen respectively are <u>14 times and 16 times more massive</u> than the hydrogen molecules.

Reading Material A

Past Experience and Design Criterion of District Heating

District heating is not a new concept, although in Britain its serious initiation did not materialise until after the Second World War. Prior to 1939 coal was cheap and plentiful, the cost and wellbeing of labour was not as critical a consideration as today and little attention was paid to environmental and air pollution. Individual open coal fires formed the staple means of providing residential and a large proportion of commercial accommodation with a certain degree of warmth at a thermal efficiency of 10-12 per cent, albeit with much smoke and loss of heat, although individual coal and coke fired boilers were also used for comparatively minor central heating of schools, office blocks and other functional buildings by means of hot water or steam radiators. Of course industrial complexes frequently offered better standards because of the availability of surplus steam as used for industrial heat, generated in indestructible Lancashire boilers and other similar smoky heat producers. In the past it has often been a "tongue-in-cheek" contention that the Gulf Stream climate and inherent hardiness of the population combined to make life on the British Isles bearable; any unexpected excesses in low winter temperatures (which seemed to occur very frequently) became useful for maintaining full employment of meteorological statisticians, provided a traditionally excellent subject for small talk and in any case could always be counteracted by means of 750 watt electric fires.[1] It may possibly not be surprising that numerous varieties of rheumatic ailments were much in evidence. In the past years the fuel and labour syndrome also applied to other countries enjoying climatic conditions not dissimilar to those in Britain, (excluding the Gulf Stream, of course) also environmental pollution was not given much thought; it was however realised by the inhabitants that under certain winter ambient conditions, man's own natural source of heat generation was not adequate to allow him to perform his everyday toils and chores in reasonable comfort and without consequent reduction in productive effort and absenteeism caused by sickness.

Recent Interpretations and Design Criteria

Some property developers, in order to economise on first cost investments in rentable new buildings, installed so-called "central heating" in the form of off-peak electricity, a verycostly type of heating which cannot possibly constitute anything more than "background warming".

It is not intended to enlarge upon details and analyses of past and present day environmental influences, nor upon modern realistic appreciation as to what constitutes a condition of comfort and well-being; detailed information related to such criteria and associated design data as well as statistical assessments are nowadays available within the context of numerous excellent transactions and publications, such as the IHVE Guide.[2] Sufficient to say, the Continent of Europe and the United States, be it within our own range of degree days or in areas having colder climates, took cognizance of the facts related to man's comfort rather earlier than we did and laid down mandatory design criteria to safeguard indoor conditions of comfort in winter. As an example, dictated by altitude above sea level and geographical location.

Germany uses base ambient design temperature criteria of-12℃ to-18℃ in conjunction with indoor living space temperature of +18℃. Even the south of France refers heating design to-3℃ winter ambient. In the past the British recommended outdoor standard was quoted at 0℃ (32°F) for +18℃ indoors. This ambient base temperature has been amended to a more realistic and flexible range of-2℃ to-3℃, as a result of recommendations by professional bodies.

Notes

①In the past…on the British Isles bearable 过去常常有一种"言不由衷"的说法，即海湾洋流气候和居民的耐劳共同使得不列颠群岛上的生活可以忍受。

②It is not intended…and well－being 不打算评述过去和当今环境影响的详情及分析，也不想详述关于什么是构成舒适和幸福的现代实际评价。

Reading Material B

Load Diversity Factor

Large district heating systems are planned on basis of calculated heat loss for accommodation in question, related to base design temperatures applicable for particular locations. In addition provision of domestic hot water and mains losses have to be catered for. Such calculations of heat loss comprise the sum of individual hourly peak demands for consumers within the area. In practice these peak demands are not constant and do not coincide; variations are created by such factors as time of day, weather, ventilation, personal habits and solar and other incidental heat gains. Both, heating and domestic water loads peak at different times of day, depending upon nature of the accommodation (residential, commercial, etc.) and upon consumer's individual requirements. Design allowances to suit every individual case cannot possibly be calculated but it has been definitely established that it is quite unlikely for all design loads to be applied simultaneously and that the actual thermal load on boiler plant and network is invariably considerably less than the calculated sum of all separate design demands. The ratio, actual peak load at boiler house (actual peak demand of all consumers plus losses) to the calculated design summation of individual peak thermal loads, isdefined as the load diversity factor. This factor has to be taken into account in the course of design calculations, both for space heating and for domestic hot water. Long-term monitoring observations also at-1℃ ambient, at a large variety of operational installations, proved that peak space heating demands average around 60% of total connected load, with mains losses allowed for. Corresponding daily space heating demand also averages at 60% of design prediction.

The same tests also show that individual domestic hot water consumptions which never coincide, are much less that the designed overall figures, with consequent diversities as low as 30%being observed. It appears that at design stage the total domestic hot water load is defined as boiler power required to simultaneously heat all the water stored in calorifiers to the requisite temperature in a prescribed recovery time. It is impossible to generalise but it is considered essential that attention be paid to the nature of consumers as well as to recovery times at design stage,applying a reasonably realistic diversity factor of, say 50%. [1]

To quote an example, if a total calculated system peak demand, including summation of peak heat losses and of domestic hot water loads, is reduced by 40% as per realistic diversity factor and a 15-20% boiler reserve is added, the total would still be some 30% less than a plant rating obtained from summary of all calculated peak demands, without reserve.

It is evident that the application of realistic diversity factors to a particular scheme has a direct bearing upon the matching of load to boiler installed capacity and to the sizing of distribution mains, thus offering realistic plant load factors with consequent savings in investment and operational costs.

It may be of interest to note that in the past, lack of appreciation of realistic diversity factors for large west European heating systems has been encountered, usually in districts with design bases in the region of-12℃ and lower. Such low outdoor temperatures are experienced only during very limited periods in winter; relatively large district heating systems built some two decades ago were much over boilered and the distribution mains were over sized.[2] Such plants were known to operate continuously at around one half of installed boiler capacity in winter even during periods of lowest ambient temperatures.

Notes

①在设计阶段对用户的性质,以及复原时间要加以注意,采用合理的实际负荷不同时系数 例如,50%。这虽不能归纳成理论但可认为是必要的。

②relatively large distriet heating systems…were over aiged 20多年前建造的较大区域供热 系统,其锅炉设置过量,输热主干管也尺寸过大。

UNIT ELEVEN

Text   Network Planning

[1]   Distribution layouts. Shape, design and cost of network layout for distribution are very much functions of fluid characteristics, shape and location of area and siting and concentrations of consumer loads. A ringmain ex boiler house has some advantages insofar as it would allow peripheral location of distribution points and a good flexibility for isolation of sub-networks. For certain layouts a single main, starting and finishing at boiler house, may bepossible. Disadvantages are associated with necessity for high circulation pump duties, large bore main pipe-work and problems with the balancing of temperatures and heat loads. Conventional design of networks, especially if existing housing is involved, seldom justifies aring main unless for small systems.

[2]   The common practice, more easily adaptable for most conurbation planning and to the widest area spreads, features the "tree branch" network layout, possibly comprising multiple sets of flow and return branches from generation source, with each pair of mains providing for its associated zone within a sub-district. Depending upon extent of its network, each separate circuit may be served by its own circulation pump. It is usual practice then to provide for reserve pump or pumps to be connected into flow lines in such a manner as to ensure standby capacity. The reserve pumps are suitably sized for summer primary hot water circulation for domestic use.

[3]   Distribution mains. Current practice still occasionally refers to a choice between such alternatives as single, twin, triple or quadruple pipe systems. The single pipeline, apart from a rare ringmain layout, is used for steam as primary fluid over such vast networks as to make condensate return lines prohibitive in first cost and maintenance expenditures and where it becomes more economical to run treated water to waste. Another alternative for a single pipe system is for the primary flow water to eventually become used up for various direct domestic or municipal services or for processes. Such practice is apparently represented in the Soviet Union. The single pipeline apart from introducing the obvious economy of omitting a return main, must be considered economically and technically unsuitable within context of West European practices.

[4]   A twin pipe system is the most common and widely used form of distribution; it comprises aflow and a separate return line. The system is also quite usual for steam distribution where the return condensate line has to be smaller in bore than the steam main. Nowadays all types of hot water distribution systems are based upon the two-pipe layout which offers optimum design and economical advantages, thus greatly facilitating most aspects of operation. For district distribution and sub-distribution networks sealed systems only come into consideration and internal condition of pipework has to be main-

94

tained clean and corrosion free by suitable water preparation.

[5]   Triple pipeline systems found limited use for high pressure hot water in Western Europe around the mid-sixties; since the lower water temperatures and pressures became prevalent and increased use was made of efficient direct-in-the-ground mains, the third pipe whose duty was to act as conveyor of primary heating water for domestic use during off-heat periods, went out of fashion. ① Although this third pipe may offer certain advantages related to a comparatively smaller bulk of water having to be moved during the summer months with consequently slightly lower distribution losses, some of these contentions proved rather illusory. Reasons for this were connected with provision and maintenance costs for the third pipe and the fact that in the summer isolation of the winter heating flow main, with its large water content, created problems of preservative treatment to obviate stagnancy. ② Experience with twin pipes proved that with modern effectively insulated mains the extra heat loss from the larger combined flow main, in use also during the summer, is virtually negligible. ③ A typical technical problem encountered with a three-pipe system involved failure of effective heating water modulation with consequent overheating of accommodation during spring and autumn periods. This was caused by excessive rise in combined return water temperatures due to low take-off from large domestic hot water calorifiers.

[6]   A four pipe system intended to cater for separated primary heating and domestic service water networks with central calorifiers installed remote from users, possibly in a boiler house, is now in a state of virtual obsolescence. Its muted advantages have been off-set by extra cost and the fact that the two domestic service pipes have to carry untreated town water, a possible source of trouble.

New Words and Expressions

ringmain ['riŋmein]	n.	循环管道
insofar as		到这样的程度，就…而论
peripheral [pə'rifərəl]	a.	周围的
bore [bɔː]	n.	孔型
conurbation [kənə'beiʃən]	n.	（具有许多收星城的）大城区
standby ['stændbai]	a.	备用的
primary ['praiməri]	a.	原生（水）的
condensate [kən'denseit]	n.	冷凝水
prohibitive [prəhibitiv]	a.	禁止的
optimum ['ɔptiməm]	a.	最佳的
corrosion [kə'rəuʒən]	n.	腐蚀
prevalent ['prevələnt]	a.	普及的
out of fashion		过时的

bulk [bʌlk]	n.	容积
contention [kən'tenʃən]	n.	论点
illusory [i'ljuːsəri]	a.	错觉的
provision [prə'viʒən]	n.	安装
isolation [aisə'leiʃən]	n.	隔绝
obviate ['ɔbvieit]	v.	预先防止
stagnancy ['stægnənsi]	n.	滞流
negligible [neg'lidʒibl]	a.	可以忽视的
modulation [mɔdju'leiʃən]	n.	调协
accommodation [əkɔmə'deiʃən]	n.	设备
calorifier [kə'lɔrifai]	n.	加热器

Notes

①Triple pipeline system···went out of fashion.

在本句中，"since" 引导了一个原因状语从句。

②Reasons for this···. stagnancy.

在本句中，"the fact" 后面的 "that" 引导一个长的同位语从句。

③Experience with twin pipe proved···. negligible.

在本句中，"that" 引导一个宾语从句．在这一从句中，"the extra heat loss" 是主语。

Exercises

Reading Comprehension

Ⅰ. Choose the best answer for each of the following.

1. The disadvantage of the ringmain system is that _____ .

   A. it has only a single main starting and finishing at boiler house.

   B. it needs a high circulation pump and a large bore main pipe work.

   C. it only suits small systems.

   D. it has difficulties in installation.

2. The "tree branch" network is a common practice _____ .

   A. which needs to have reserve pumps.

   B. for conurbation planning only

   C. which is a widely used layout for the city and country alike.

   D. suitable for sub-district.

3. The "single pipe system" used in the Soviet Union is _____ .

   A. not a good practice in the west European countries.

   B. the best system.

C. not economically and technically suitable for use.

D. a good system in west Europe.

4. The "triple pipeline system" requires _____ .

A. costs for provision and maintenance and preservative treatment to obviate stagnancy.

B. smaller bulk of water and high cost for maintenance of the third pipe.

C. ineffective insulation and extra heat loss.

D. None of the above.

5. According to the Text which system seems to be the best for hot water distribution?

A. Single   B. Twin   C. Triple   D. Quadruple

Ⅱ. Are the following statements true or false?

1. In current practice the four network systems (single, twine, triple, and quadruple) are equally in wide use.   ( )

2. In the single pipeline system in the Soviet Union, there may be no returning condensate.   ( )

3. In using the twin pipeline system people do not need to worry about the corrosion problem.   ( )

4. The triple pipeline system is going out of fashion.   ( )

5. The quadruple pipe system is proved to be the most promising one in the future.
                                                                                 ( )

Vocabulary

Ⅰ. Fill in the blanks with some of the words listed below, changing forms where necessary.

condensate	standby	optimum	modulation
accommodation	isolation	practice	bulk

1. A reserve pump is provided in this system for _____ capacity.

2. Because of high cost for provision and difficulties for maintenance, this network layout is proved to be a poor _____ .

3. Large _____ of water needs to be pre-treated before the usage so the larger bore pipework is introduced.

4. All of the hot water distribution systems are now based on the two-pipe layout, because it offers _____ design and economical advantages.

5. This radio has a frequency _____ system.

Ⅱ. Complete each of the following statements with one of the four choices given below.

1. The disadvantages of this arrangement are the frequent technical failures and the high cost by overheating the _____ .

A. pipe   B. system   C. network   D. accommodation

97

2. The suit is smart and of good quality but is _____ , so people don't like it.

    A. out of fashion   B. out of order   C. out of question   D. out of use

3. In such a vast network, the _____ return line can be omitted by using up the treated water for domestic and municipal services.

    A. waste   B. maintenance   C. condensate   D. pipework

4. This material needs to have heat _____ .

    A. forging   B. processing   C. control   D. production

5. In the summer the third pipe should be _____ from the winter heating flow main.

    A. connected   B. used   C. applied   D. isolated

Translation   **数量或倍数减少的译法**

表示数量（或倍数）减少有两个概念：净减少值和减少后的数值。译为"减少了…"和"减少到…"。

英语常用表达法和译法例举如下：

例 1. The cost was reduced to 30%. （V. ＋to＋整数或分数，百分数）

    成本减少到 30%。

例 2. The cost is cut down by one third. （V. ＋ by ＋整数或分数，百分数）

    成本减少了 1/3。

例 3. Switching time of the new type transistor is shortened 3 times. （V. ＋倍数）

    新型晶体管的开关时间缩短到 1/3。

例 4. The newly-designed calculator will reduce the error probability by a factor of 15. （V. ＋ by a factor of…）

    这台新设计的计算器将使误差率降到 1/15。

例 5. The weight of the computer-aided machine is decreased by a six-fold. （V. ＋by a x-fold）

    这台由计算机辅助的新机器的重量减少到 1/6。

Directions：

Translate the following into Chinese, paying attention to the underlined parts.

1. By the year 2000 the world's annual oil output is expected to fall to 35 percent.

2. An increase in the oxygen content of coal by 1% reduces the calorific value by about 1.7%.

3. The pressure will be reduced to one-fourth of its original value.

4. The line AB is half as long as the line CD.

5. The power output of the machine is twice less than its input.

6. The voltage has dropped five times.

7. The new equipment will <u>reduce</u> the error probability <u>by seven times</u>.

8. Tests indicate this might <u>reduce</u> activity <u>by a factor between 10 and 100</u>.

9. The principal advantage over the old fashioned typewriter <u>is a four-fold reduction</u> in weight.

10. Magnetic fields of the metal contaminants within the human body are generally about <u>a million times weaker than</u> the earth's field.

Reading Material A

The Industrial Cogeneration

Industrial cogeneration often involves an arrangement to deliver excess electricity generated in the system to the electric grid. Using a grid in this manner to make unneeded electricity from an industrial plant available to other private electricity users is called "wheeling". With such provisions, the cogeneration operation need not maintain extensive standby equipment. Mechanisms and regulations are in effect in the United States to encourage such developments, thus further reducing energy waste. Providing for the redistribution of excess power through the grid helps assure that power generating potential is not neglected simply because there is nothing to do with the power once the needs of the cogeneration system are met. [1]

When an effective energy partnership of this sort is set up between a utility and an industry with cogeneration capability, substantial cost and fuel saving benefits result. Utilities provide a valuable service to industry and achieve efficient energy utilization through this approach, and the utilities themselves may also be well served. By purchasing excess industrial power, the utility could thereby fill peak load demands without falling back on less efficient equipment to generate additional power.

The ability of an industrial cogenerator to sell or buy electricity through the grid frees industry from concerns about outages and makes cogeneration more attractive as a reliable and profitable company operation.

One aspect of industrial conservation stands out, for American industry has within its grasp an Alaskan oil strike, a major new source of energy waiting to be developed. This type of conservation energy deserves special attention because of its potential scale and because itsavailability largely depends upon requisite decisions being made in the political process. The source is sometimes called combined heat and power, a term awkward enough to be designated CHP, and perhaps for that reason better known in the United States as cogeneration, but the meaning is simple enough-the combined production of electricity and heat (the latter for either processor space-heating purposes).

During the 1970s as the so-called "oil crunch" developed, recognition of the benefits available through industrial and utility cogeneration spread widely. A 1974 Ford Foundation report argued the merits of cogeneration which seeks to improve efficiency by producing both steam and electricity together. When electricity is produced alone, only about 30 to 40 percent of the fuel is converted to electricity; but in combined systems, about 80 percent of the fuel energy can be used to produce both steam and electricity. Large savings result when the electricity is generated near the industrial plant so that the waste heat that would posea thermal pollution problem at a central power station can be put to use for industrial process steam. The net savings in total energy requirements for steam and electricity can be about 30 percent. There are good reasons why most industries should consider self-generation asa byproduct of steam production at industrial installations appears to be practical and economical on a wide scale. [2]

The logic of self-reliance has an increasingly broad appeal among industrialists. Some American industries such as Dow Chemical Company were taking this advice many years before it become fashionable enough for attention from prestigious foundations.

Notes

①考虑到多余电力通过电网的再分配，辅助作用应使其确信电力生产潜力不能简单地被忽视，因为一旦联产系统的需要能够满足就与电力无关了。

②有更好的理由认为，很多工业部门为什么应当考虑自己发电，作为工业装置上生产水蒸气的副产品在广泛程度上看来似乎是现实和经济的。

Reading Material B

The Diaphragm Tank

Principles. The idea of utilising compressed air as a pressure medium has also led to developments of diaphragm tank, in which air or inert gas such as nitrogen, under pressure in the expansion tank, is kept physically separated from the water surface in the tank during operation. Some 15-18 years ago the diaphragm pressure/expansion tank was introduced in the U. S. and on the Continent of Europe for small and medium sized sealed systems in order to abolish the high level open expansion containers with their inherent installation, corrosion and frost problems. This sealed tank comprises a closed cylindrical or circular steel vessel sited on or about the floor level of the boilerhouse and it can be sited either horizontally or vertically. The vessel usually consists of two valves flanged together in the middle and containing a pressure cushion of air or nitrogen on one side of an internal flexible membrane made of elastomer (special synthetic rubber) which, it is claimed, is age- and (within limits) temperature resistant. [1] The vessel is connected to system water on the opposite side from the pressure cushion. In smaller pressure units, i. e. rated up to 0. 12 MW at maximum pressure of 3 bar, the membrane is usually permanently flanged-in at the circumferential centre inside the vessel. Alternatively, some makes provide exchangeable diaphragms in form of a balloon with single entry fixing and filled with the pressurising gas. The water side of the tank is connected into system return main at the suction side of a circulation pump (if installed) and the gas filled half has a spring-loaded filler valve for topping up with the gas as required. When the system is heated, water expands and its pressure in the closed system rises above that of the tank medium. This allows water to enter the tank, compressing the gaseous medium separated from it by the membrane, until expansion of the water corresponds to the operational temperature. A balance is then achieved and system water remains under pressure by the gas in accordance with Boyles Law, but separated from it by the membrane.

Domestic ratings. The above described expansion tank is the elementary operational principle of the pressurising method and in its simple form has application within certain technical limits, for small and medium sized installations. Tanks of this type are used for systems having rapid reaction heating controls, i. e. with oil or gas firing. To preserve the rubber diaphragm, tank temperature must not be allowed to exceed 50℃ and therefore the vessel must be connected into the system return as near as possible to boiler; alternatively, with larger sizes and higher return temperatures, an intermediate break-vessel must be connected between system connection and pressure tank.

The simple "domestic size" pressure tank is limited to a maximum system temperature of 100 ℃ and volume of up to 80 1, hence, being suitable for average sized heating plants of up to 120000 W installed rating. It is particularly suitable for modernisation of obsolescent lowtemperature systems where it may replace high level expansion tanks. Although the static level of system above the membrane vessel of this type usually does not exceed 15 m water column (1. 5bar) with corresponding maximum working pressure limited to 3. 0 bar, special modern designs cater for pressures up to 6-7 bar. As with all sealed systems, protection must be provided against overpressure by means of a safety valve. Makers recommend provision of an overriding high-limit control thermostat to fail-safe the boiler in the event of failure of the control thermostat, as fitted. In a heating system where isolation from water supply is possible, a low-water cut-out switch is recommended to ensure that should water pressure drop, the switch would shut off the boiler. [2]

Notes

①and containing a pressure cushion…femperature resistent. 在由弹性体（特制合成橡胶）制成的内部柔性膜的一侧装有一空气或氮气压力缓冲垫，据称该弹性膜是抗老化和耐温的（在一定极限内）。

②在可能与供水隔开的供暖系统中，推荐用一个低水压切断开关，以确保：倘若水压降低，开关就关断锅炉。

UNIT TWELVE

Text   Thermal Expansion of Piping and Its Compensation

[1]   A very relevant consideration requiring careful attention is the fact that with temperature of a length of pipe raised or lowered, there is a corresponding increase or decrease in its length and cross-sectional area because of the inherent coefficient of thermal expansion for the particular pipe material. The coefficient of expansion for carbon steel is 0.012 mm/m℃ and for copper 0.0168mm/m℃. Respective module of elasticity are for steel $E = 207 \times 1.06$ kN/m² and for copper $E = 103 \times 106$ kN/m². As an example, assuming a base temperature for water conducting piping at 0℃, a steel pipe of any diameter if heated to 120 ℃ would experience a linear extension of 1.4 mm and a similarly if heated to copper pipe would extend by 2.016 mm for each metre of their respective lengths. The unit axial force in the steel pipe however would be 39% greater than for copper. The change in pipe diameter is of no practical consequence to linear extension but the axial forces created by expansion or contraction are considerable and capable of fracturing any fitments which may tend to impose a restraint; the magnitude of such forces is related to pipe size. As an example, in straight pipes of same length but different diameters, rigidly held at both ends and with temperature raised by say 100℃, total magnitude of linear forces against fixed points would be near enough proportionate to the respective diameters.

[2]   It is therefore essential that design of any piping layout makes adequate compensatory provision for such thermal influence by relieving the system of linear stresses which would be directly related to length of pipework between fixed points and the range of operational temperatures.

[3]   Compensation for forces due to thermal expansion. The ideal pipework as far as expansion is concerned, is one where maximum free movement with the minimum of restraint is possible. [1]Hence the simplest and most economical way to ensure compensation and relief of forces is to take advantage of changes in direction, or where this is not part of the layout and long straight runs are involved it may be feasible to introduce deliberate dog-leg offset changes in direction at suitable intervals.

[4]   As an alternative, at calculated intervals in a straight pipe run specially designed expansion loops or "U" bends should be inserted. Depending upon design and space availability, expansion bends within a straight pipe run can feature the so called double offset "U" band or the horseshoe type or "lyre" loop. [2] The last named are seldom used for large heating networks; they can be supplied in manufacturers' standard units but require elaborate constructional works for underground installation.

[5]   Anchored thermal movement in underground piping would normally be absorbed by three basic types of expansion bends and these include the "U" bend, the "L" bend and the

"Z" bend. In cases of 90 changes in direction the "L" and "Z" bends are used. Principles involved in the design of provision for expansion between anchor points are virtually the same for all three types of compensator. The offset "U" bend is usually made up from four 90° elbows and straight pipes; it permits good thermal displacement and imposes smaller anchor loads than the other types of loop. This shape of expansion bend is the standardised pattern for prefabricated pipe-in-pipe systems.

[6]   All thermal compensators are installed to accommodate an equal amount of expansion or contraction; therefore to obtain full advantage of the length of thermal movement it is necessary to extend the unit during installation thus opening up the loop by an extent roughly equal the half the overall calculated thermal movement. This is done by "cold-pull" or other mechanical means. The total amount of extension between two fixed points has to be calculated on basis of ambient temperature prevailing and operational design temperatures so that distribution of stresses and reactions at lower and higher temperatures are controlled within permissible limits. Pre-stressing does not affect the fatigue life of piping therefore it does not feature in calculation of pipework stresses.

[7]   There are numerous specialist publications dealing with design and stressing calculations for piping and especially for proprietary piping and expansion units; comprehensive experience backed design data as well as charts and graphs may be obtained in manufacturers' publications, offering solutions for every kind of pipe stressing problem. ③

[8]   As an alternative to above mentioned methods of compensation for thermal expansion and usable in places where space is restricted, is the more expensive bellows or telescopic type mechanical compensator. There are many proprietary types and models on the market and the following types of compensators are generally used:

[9]   The bellows type expansion unit in form of an axial compensator provides for expansion movement in a pipe along its axis; motion in this bellows is due to tension or compression only There are also articulated bellows units which combine angular and lateral movements; they consist of double compensator units restrained by straps pinned over the centre of each bellowsor double tied thus being restrained over its length. Such compensators are suitable for accommodating very pipeline expansion and also for combinations of angular and lateral movements.

New Words and Expressions

thermal expansion		热膨胀
inherent [in'hiərənt]	*a.*	具有的
coefficient [kaui'fiʃəut]	*n.*	模数
elasticity * [elis'tisiti]	*n.*	弹性
linear ['liniə]	*a.*	线性的

axial force			轴向力
contraction *	[kən'trækʃən]	*n.*	收缩
magnitude *	[mæghitjud]	*n.*	大小
rigidly	['rigidli]	*ad.*	固定地
compensatory provision			补偿措施
restraint *	[ristreint]	*n.*	限制
take advantage of			利用
deliberate	[di'libəreit]	*a.*	故意的
dog-leg	['dɔg'leg]		折线形的
offset *	['ɔfset]	*n.*	补偿
lyre	[laiə]	*n.*	竖琴
elbow	[elbəu]	*n.*	弯头
proprietary	[prə'praiətəri]	*a.*	有专利权的
bellows	['beləuz]	*n.*	波纹管
angular	['æŋgjul]	*a.*	角的
lateral *	['lætərəl]	*a.*	水平的
strap	[stræp]	*n.*	环，板条

Notes

①…maximum free movement with the minimum of restraint…
　具最小约束力的最大自由移动量……。
②depending upon design and space availability……
　根据设计和可利用的空间……。
③expansion unit 膨胀节。

Exercises

Reading Comprehension

Ⅰ. Choose the best answer for each of the following.

1. The factor capable to fracture a pipe is mainly _____ .

   A. the axial forces caused by expansion or contraction.

   B. the linear extension of the pipe.

   C. the change of the temperature.

   D. the size of the pipe.

2. It is easy and economical to make compensation for force due to thermal expansion by _____ .

   A. putting dog-leg offset changes in direction at intervals.

B. inserting expansion loops or "U" bands

C. putting the horseshoe type or "lyre" loop.

D. making use of changes in direction.

3. Which of the following bends is the standardised pattern for prefabricated pipe-in-pipe system?

   A. The "S" bend.

   B. The "V" bend.

   C. The "Z" bend.

   D. The "L" bend.

4. Pre-stressing does not feature in calculating stresses of pipework, because _____ .

   A. it is not important in "cold-pull" .

   B. it does not reduce the time of using the compensator.

   C. the installation is done by mechanical means.

   D. none of the above.

5. Which of the following compensators is mentioned in the text?

   A. Articulated bellows which combine angular and lateral movements.

   B. Bellows type expansion unit in form of an axial compensator.

   C. Double off set "V" bend.

   D. All of the above.

Ⅱ. Are the following statements true or false.

1. The length and cross-sectional area of a pipe increases or decreases correspondingly with its inherent coefficient of thermal expansion. ( )

2. In designing a pipework, people try to let it have as much free movement as possible. ( )

3. All thermal compensators should be installed to accommodate an equal amount of expansion or contraction of a pipe work. ( )

4. There are many specialist publications which warn people of the pipe stressing problem. ( )

5. The best compensator is the articulated bellows, because it is suitable for accommodating very large pipeline expansion. ( )

Vocabulary

Ⅰ. Fill in the following blanks with some of the words listed below, changing forms where necessary.

linear	compensation	deliberate	advantage
coefficient	elasticity	contraction	insert

1. Expansion loops can be _____ in a straight pipe run.

2. This material has _____ so it can be bent and then becomes straight again.

3. To ensure compensation and relief of forces of a pipework，the designer takes full _____ of changes in direction.

4. When the pipe is heated，its total magnitude of _____ forces against fixed points would be almost proportionate to its diameter.

5. The convective transfer is very low，compared with the radiation transfer _____ .

Ⅱ. Complete each of the following statements with one of the four choices given below.

1. _____ offset changes in direction are introduced at suitable intervals to guarantee compensation and relief of forces.

    A. Elbow   B. Dogleg   C. Bellows   D. Strap

2. To make compensatory _____ for thermal influence is very important in designing a pipework.

    A. expansion   B. impose   C. contraction   D. provision

3. A pipe expends or _____ as the ambient temperature is raised or lowered.

    A. breaks   B. shortens   C. contracts   D. disappears

4. It is essential to ensure _____ for forces caused by thermal expansion.

    A. quality   B. compensation   C. length   D. temperature

5. It is _____ to apply the theory of thermal expansion and compensation in designing a pipework.

    A. feasible   B. flexible   C. impossible   D. efficient

Translation   定语从句的合译法

合译法就是把定语从句译成汉语的"的"字结构，放在被修饰的词语前面。合译法主要用于结构短，内容负载小的限定性（也可能非限性）从句的翻译。

例 1. In the English-speaking countries，a professional engineer who wishes to be fully qualified must join at least one engineering institution.

在说英语的国家里，凡是希望成为完全合格的职业工程师必须至少加入一个工程学会。

例 2. The apparatus by means of which protons can be separated from neutrons in a nucleus is called a cyclotron.

用于使原子核中的质子与中子分离的装置叫做回旋加速器。

例 3. Around the home submersible or jet pumps supply domestic well water in areas where municipal water supplies are unavailable.

在住宅周围，潜水泵或射流泵为没有市政供水的区域供应家庭用井水。

例 4. Some apartment buildings，where maximum economy was sought，have as many as 16 apartments per floor.（非限定性定语从句）

某些旨在谋求最高利润的公寓大楼，每层设计有多至 16 套客房。

Directions:

Translate the following sentences into Chinese, paying attention to the attributive clauses.

1. The energy which coal provides is the solar energy which was stored by plants millions of years ago.
2. The sun from which we get all our heat is a very good power provider.
3. Air moves from places where the pressure is high to places where the pressure is low.
4. The amount of solar energy which is lost on the way in the atmosphere is about equal to the amount which is received at the surface of the earth.
5. The carbon, of which coal is largely composed, has combined with oxygen from the air and formed carbon dioxide.
6. If the carbon content of the steel is below 0. 2 percent, the product is mild steel which is quite ductile.
7. The rate at which the molecules move depends upon the energy they have.
8. There must be no dust at all in the room where the electronic computer is kept.
9. It must be said that pollution is a pressing problem which we must deal with.
10. The time (when) nuclear fission takes place vast energy is released.

Reading Material A

Comeback of an Energy Oldtimer

District heating lost favor among utilities because they could earn greater profits concentrating on the production of electricity. District heating lost favor with the public because oil and gas were plentiful and low-priced, and individuals were sold on the challengeable idea that oil or gas heating are private and convenient like the family automobile. Each home should be self-reliant and independent with a furnace of its own. Of course, if it happened to be a gas furnace, the gas arrived by pipeline the same as hot wateror steam in a district heating operation. If the furnace burned number 1 or number 2 home heating oil, the oil was discharged into the basement tank by means of a long hose from an oildelivery truck. Independence has been an illusion in home heating since chopping wood ceased to be an American practice except for the rustic privileged few. [1]

District heating is regaining favor slowly because the illusion of independence counts for little when the oil in your house costs nearly as much as the gasoline in your car, which costs more today than it cost yesterday, and it cost too much yesterday.

District heating couldn't be worse and might be better. This is the assumption fostered by the new realities of energy in the 1970s and the 1980s. But despite the fact that district heating and cogeneration to eliminate traditional utility waste have been around a long time, are becoming standard practice in other parts of the world, and are available to American communities for the taking, the number of takers remains small.

It is worthwhile to consider various district heating activities in communities, institutions, and industries that are making progress in the United States, frequently with thanks to the foresight and farsightedness of a few individuals who have studied the history of district heating, or who learned about its potential in Europe, or who just pay attention to the fuel combusted annually in America and the amount of real energy benefit that is gained. The facts that U. S. energy consumption is overwhelmingly greater than that of any other country on earth and that U. S. energy waste equals the energy consumption of most countries on earth have been well-publicized. Doing something about the consumption and the waste has been labeled with the 12-letter dirty word "conservation". [2]

District heating is basically an energy conservation technology. If and when district heating begins achieving its full potential in the United States, conservation may cease to be a dirty word to those Americans who consider it vaguely unconstitutional and decidedly unreasonable, uncomfortable, and unnecessary to turn down the thermostat. This old-technology that time has rendered new again seems ideal as a way to make the pains and fangs of conservation considerably less difficult.

Following are representative district heating projects briefly discussed. Cataloguing all the district heating/cogeneration activities and projects current in the U. S., either off the drawing board or on it, would be encyclopedic in scope and is beyond the needs of this survey. The examples cited are intended to suggest the range of options involved in this technology and the versatility it allows.

District heating can be and probably in time will be used with virtually every conceivable energy source. The same is true of the cogeneration principle. If an energy source is capable of generating electricity, there is probably also the capacity to some degree of delivering thermal energy as well for district heating applications.

Notes

①在家庭取暖中独立性已成为一种假象，因为劈柴不再是美国的习惯，除了对乡间的特许的少数以外。

②对于消费和浪费所采取的举措则被称之为由 12 个英文字母组成的一个不吉利的字眼 "conservation"

Reading Material B

Prefabricated Rigid Pipe-in-pipe System

Encased factory prefabricated and preinsulated piping for laying direct in the ground to convey liquids at high or low temperatures originated with varying success in the United States some 50 years ago. Systems with steel outer protection jackets designed for pressure tight operation were experiencing extensive development during the early post-war years. The original designs were not much cheaper than ducted mains but often less reliable because of difficulties associated with the then available insulation materials and their introduction to pipework. Other major problems included protection of outer steel jackets against corrosion and making reliable watertight external joints between jackets of respective prefabricated sections especially in the region of expansion compensation at anchor points and at branches. Some early pipe-in-pipe systems introduced in Europe experienced major failures for reasons of inadequate field testing and use of untried external casing materials in place of steel. There was also a lack of appreciation of problems involved in the direct burying of piping, be it due to baddrainage characteristics of the soil or its chemical influences. As an example, an early continental design featured chemically unstable rock wool insulation. After some 4-5 years' use external signs such as steaming of rainfall and melting of snow, led to localised site excavations where it was discovered that hot water was virtually flowing through formed insulation, the steel piping having disintegrated due to corrosive action of sulphur content inthe rock wool insulation. [1]

Recent developments in insulation materials such as calcium silicate and polyurethane compounds, much improved manufacturing and assembly techniques, efficient field testing and other research related to pressure tight systems ensured improved reliability of co-axial pipe distribution.

Manufacturers of modern factory prefabricated piping offer 5-10 years' guarantees for their products. Test excavations of piping laid 6-8 years ago, often confirm that long term trouble free and maintenance free operation may be expected although there is insufficient practical experience as yet to confirm that spans of life in the region of 20 or more years can be assured.

It must be emphasised that reliability and efficiency of any continuous finished network of this nature is only as good as the assembly work force employed, be it welders, insulators, testers or site supervision. [2] A comparatively minor error in fitting or welding can result in major warranty claims and financial loss.

Much credit is due to development and research associated with thermal efficiency and safety of different proprietary systems carried out by the Department of the Environment and H & V Research Association as well as to the issue of relevant British Standards.

Pressure tight pipe-in-pipe systems are nowadays delivered to site in complete tested units of 7 to 14 metres in length together with appropriate prefabricated fittings, elbows, bends, tees, anchors, branch pieces, complete manhole valve pits, etc., for site assembly and installation into specially prepared but comparatively simple trenching in order to constitute complete piping networks. Needless to say such installation and backfilling is much more rapidly executed and at much lower cost than can be ascribed to ducted pipework and thus introduces major economies in builders' work.

There are two defined basic principles applicable to rigid steel carrier pipe prefabricated co-axial systems.

Notes

①使用4～5年之后，诸如雨水蒸发和雪融化的外表痕迹导致局部穿孔，在该处发现热水实际上通过型块绝热上流出，由于岩棉绝热层中硫含量的腐蚀作用而钢管剥裂。

②必须加以强调的是：这种性质的任何连续完工的管网的可靠性与经济性实际上体现了所雇安装人员的实力，如焊接工，密封工，检验员或工地监督。

UNIT THIRTEEN

Text　　　　　　　Smoke Tube Economic Boiler

3-Pass Smoke Tube Economic Boiler

[1]　Experience to date has shown that if centralised heat generation by boiler plant is required optimum cost-effectiveness, with but few exceptions, is achieved using the modern version of the well known, time honoured principle of the 3-pass "Economic" all welded steel boiler. Latest models of this type have been developed to offer value for money commensurate with efficiency, economy, reliability and compactness. Design and construction can vary in detail depending upon manufacturer and the limits to which the boiler is built to comply with mandatory standards, dimensions and materials' specifications in relation to its cost. Many years type development culminated in certain criteria associated with modern good manufacturing and operational practices and characteristics offering high average generating efficiencies and anticipated life span around 25-30 years assuming reasonably efficient standards of operation and maintenance. ① As related to any product, high quality is seldom associated with low first cost and the client must always think twice before accepting the cheapest tender. In considering 3-pass smoke tube boiler plant for a particular service it is most advisableto ensure provision of boilers specifically designed for the duty within scope of media to begenerated and of requisite operational parameters.

[2]　A steam boiler adapted for hot water may well have excessive capacity for water in the upper portion of the shell giving rise to inferior circulation because of incorrect heat distribution effecting water flow. ② In a hot water boiler it is important for return water circulation to follow a natural flow pattern for rapid mixing to compensate for possible stratification and cold pockets and also to avoid thermal shock due to difference between flow and return temperatures.

[3]　Conversely if a hot water boiler is adapted for a steam space within a larger shell it also experiences consequent change in volume and displacement of heating zones around furnace and tubes originally meant for water. ③ This results in imbalance effecting combustion, circulation and thermal capacity especially at part loads.

[4]　Adaptation of high pressure boilers for low pressure operation, be it for steam or from steam to hot water can cause low back-end temperatures and inferior circulation because of considerable difference in mean operational temperatures of media at different pressures and an out-of-balance of water volumes involved. ④ Such adaptation may also entail a higher first cost.

[5]　Efficiency of the Economic boiler. The average modern 3-pass. Economic boiler should be capable of generating with equally high efficiency when burning light or heavy oils, natural and other gases or coal. It has then to be equipped with an appropriately

matched burner or solid fuel grate. It has also been developed to offer high performance if fitted with matched multi-fuel burners or special grates for certain types of refuse or wood.

[6]　　Modern 3-pass smoke tube boilers and combustion systems can be expected to achieve generating efficiencies around 85—87% at 75% to 100% load and not less than 85% at one-third toone-half load under ideal conditions.

[7]　　The 3-pass smoke tube boiler can be looked upon as an ultimate development of the 3-pass Lancashire type with the second and third passes comprising nests of tubes instead of masonry ducts thus ensuring the better efficiency because of higher specific rating commensurate with higher flue gas velocities. By present day standards the economic may be considered to have a comparatively large water capacity, contributing to heat storage and adaptability to variable and intermittent heat loads without forfeiting functional reaction and flexibility.

[8]　　Furnace tube. The first pass of the smoke tube boiler is the furnace tube designed for combustion flame propagation and radiant heat transfer; it comprises 10-15% of the total boiler heating surface but accounts for ca 45-55% of boiler heat output. The load on this part of heating surface and the consequent stressing of the material are therefore high obviously because the magnitude of heat transfer by radiation is primarily a function of flame temperature which would be in the region of 1000℃. Modern furnace volumes are usually so designed as to maintain combustion intensity not in excess of 2. 0 to 2. 2 MW/m³ to ensure that burner settings are effectively controllable and heat dissipation through furnace walls does not approach the upper critical temperature range of steel plate.

[9]　　The furnace tube can be either corrugated or smooth. Of the two, the more traditional corrugated furnace offers a greater heat transfer contact surface but this is counteracted by the fact that it is more difficult to keep clean and maintain. [5]In the course of the last decade or so the smooth-bore flame tube has found many adherents because of its greater rigidity and ease of removal of soot and other combustion products. Furthermore,[6] first cost is reduced and replacement is simpler and cheaper.

[10]　　Smoke tubes. After the first pass, combustion gases enter the rear reversing chamber which is usually surrounded by water (wetback) to improve balance of heat transfer. Gases are then led through appropriate nests of smoke tubes comprising the second pass into the reversing chamber at the boiler front and then into the third pass of smoke tubes which convey the gases into the rear flue outlet.

[11]　　Heat transfer rate over the convection heating surfaces of the smoke tubes is much lower than radiant transfer of the furnace tube; it is not only related to temperature but is also a function of gas velocity and the character of gas stream. Thus the heat transfer can be increased by raising the velocity of a constant volume of gas by reducing the area of tubes. This is only possible within certain practical limits; resistance to gas through-put can introduce excessive load on burner fan with consequent increase in power costs. At the

same time excessive thermal stressing can shorten the life of a boiler.

New Words and Expressions

optimum * ['ɔptiməm]	a.	最佳的，最有利的
cost-effectiveness		成本效益
compactness [kɔm'pæktnis]	n.	紧凑
commensurate * [kə'menʃərit]	a.	相称的
comply (with) [kəm'plai]	v.	遵照，符合
mandatory ['mændətəri]	a.	指令性的，强制性的
culminate * ['kʌlmineit]	v.	达到极点，到顶峰
client ['klaiənt]	n.	顾客
tender ['tendə]	n.	提供物
requisite ['rekwizit]	a.	必不可少的
compensate * ['kɔmpenseit]	v.	补偿，弥补
combustion * [kəm'bʌstʃən]	n.	燃烧
entail [in'teil]	vt.	需要
burner * ['bəːnə]	n.	燃烧器
grate * [greit]	n.	炉排，炉篦
refuse * ['refjuːs]	n.	废料，残渣
Lancashire ['læŋkəˌʃiə]	n.	兰开夏锅炉
masonry ['meisnri]	n.	炉墙，砌筑
duct * [dʌkt]	n.	管道
rating * ['reitiŋ]	n.	额定功率，额定性能
intermittent [ˌintə'mitənt]	a.	断续的，周期性的
forfeit * ['fɔːfit]	v.	丧失
propagation * [ˌprɔpə'geiʃən]	n.	传播，扩散，分布
magnitude * ['mægnitjuːd]	n.	数值，量值
ca (=circa 拉丁语) ['səːkə]	prep.	大约
dissipation * [ˌdisi'peiʃən]	n.	消散·散失
corrugated ['kɔrugeitid]	a.	波纹形的
counteract * [ˌkauntə'rækt]	vt.	抵消
smooth-bore	a.	光腔
adherent [əd'hiərənt]	n.	拥护者
soot [sut]	n.	煤烟灰
chamber * ['tʃeimbə]	n.	燃烧室，腔
flue [fluː]	n.	烟筒，烟道
throughout * ['θruːaut]	n.	通过量
first cost		造价，主要成本

Notes

①associated with modern good manufacturing and operational practices and characteristics offering,……and maintenance. Associated with 后跟 practices 和 characteristics 两个宾语；

offering 有 efficiencies 和 life span 两个宾语，以及 assuming 引起的状语，构成现在分词短语作定语，修饰 characteristics。

②may well 完全有可能，理所当然地。

③originally meant for water 过去分词短语作定语修饰 furnace and tubes。

④be it for steam or from steam to hot water. it 指代 adaptation. 是 should it be for steam or from steam to hot water 的省略而引起的倒装现象，表示虚拟假定。

Exercises

Reading Comprehension

Ⅰ. Choose the best answer for each of the following.

1. The latest models of 3-pass smoke tube economic boiler are _____ .

    A. well known and time honoured

    B. efficient but not economic

    C. both reliable and compact

    D. efficient，economic，reliable and compact

2. A steam boiler adapted for hot water is likely to give rise to inferior circulation because _____ .

    A. heat distribution affecting water flow is incorrect

    B. stratification and cold pockets are possible

    C. thermal shock is avoided

    D. there is a difference between flow and return temperature

3. Adaptation of a hot water boiler for a steam space within a larger shell can cause _____ .

    A. combustion

    B. circulation

    C. thermal capacity

    D. imbalance effecting combustion，circulation thermal capacity

4. If high pressure boilers are adapted for low pressure operation and used for steam or from steam to hot water，it can result in low back-end temperatures and inferior circulation because _____ .

    A. it follows a natural flow pattern

B. there is considerable difference in mean operational temperatures of media at different pressures and an out-of-balance of water volumes involved

C. it experiences changes in volume of heating zones

D. it causes changes in displacement of heating zones

5. As an ultimate development of the 3-pass Lancashire type with the second and the third _____ passes comprising nests of tubes instead of masonry ducts, the 3-pass smoke tube boiler can

A. generate 87% at one-half load under ideal conditions

B. forfeit functional reaction and flexibility

C. ensure the better efficiency because of higher specific rating

D. contribute to heat storage and adaptability to variable and intermittent heat loads.

II. Are the following statements true or false?

1. The furnace tube is designed for combustion flame propagation and radiant heat transfer   ( )

2. The corrugated furnace tube can be well maintained and kept clean without difficulties.   ( )

3. The smooth-bore flame tube is popular because it is of greater rigidity and easy to remove soot and other combustion products   ( )

4. The rear reversing chamber is usually surrounded by water in order to convey the gases into the rear flue outlet.   ( )

5. While resistance to gas through-out introduces excessive load on burner fan with consequent increase in power costs, excessive thermal stressing can shorten the life of a boiler.   ( )

Vocabulary

I . Fill in the blanks with some of the words or expressions listed below, changing the form where necessary.

replacement	dissipation	forfeit	excessive	counteract
commensurate with		cost-effectiveness		compensate for

1. The more traditional corrugated furnace offers a greater heat transfer contact, which _____ by the fact that it is more difficult to keep clean and maintain.

2. Higher specific rating _____ higher flue gas velocities can ensure a better efficiency.

3. The modern version of the well-known, time honoured principle of the 3-pass smoke tube economic boiler can bring about optimum _____ .

4. _____ load can be introduced on burner fan with consequent increase in power costs.

5. Because of its reduced first cost, its simple and cheap _____ , the smooth-bore

flame tube is very popular.

Ⅱ. Complete each of the following statements with one of the four choices give below.

1. If a steam boiler _____ for hot water, it may well have excessive capacity for water in the upper portion of the shell and give rise to inferior circulation.

A. is adopted   B. is installed   C. is adapted   D. is designed

2. A furnace tube is designed for combustion flame propagation and radiant _____ .

A. heat transfer   B. ion transfer   C. transfer check   D. transfer valve

3. Modern furnace volumes are so designed as to keep heat _____ through furnace walls below the upper critical temperature range of steel plate.

A. disaggregation   B. dissipation   C. disassimilation   D. discharge

4. The economic boiler can contribute to heat storage and adaptability to variable and intermittent heat loads, and no functional reaction and flexibility can _____ .

A. be delivered   B. be discharged   C. be formed   D. be forfeited

5. In order to _____ possible stratification and cold pockets, it is essential for return water circulation to follow a natural flow pattern for rapid mixing.

A. compensate for   B. search for   C. take over   D. keep away

Translation　　　　　　　　　　　**英语从句的分译法**

分译法就是把定语从句抽出来单独译成一个分句，与前分句在语法关系和逻辑意义上衔接起来，保持全句的完整与连贯。分译法主要用于非限定性定语从句，但偶尔也用于结构复杂、内容负载大且与被修饰词语关系较松弛的限定性定语从句。

Ⅰ. 译成并列分句或独立句

例1. There are different kinds of liquid solvents, the most important of which is water.
　　　有许多不同种类的液体溶剂，其中最重要的是水。（并列分句）

例2. The central processing unit (CPU) controls and carries out all the calculations, and the memory or store, where the information as well as the programs are stored.
　　　计算机主机对全部计算进行控制、操作和储存。所有的信息和程序均储藏在主机里。（独立句）

Ⅱ. 译成状语从句

当定语从句表示含有原因、目的、结果、条件、方式、时间、让步等意义时，可根据具体行文需要，译成原因、目的、结果、条件、方式、让步等状语从句。

例1. Some pozzolanas have been known to prevent the action between cement and certain aggregates which causes the aggregate to expand and weaken or burst the concrete.
　　　人们已经知道有些火山灰能防止水泥和某些骨料之间的反应，因为这种反应使骨料膨胀，造成混凝土强度削弱或爆裂。（原因状语）

例2. The cantilever has only one support, which restrains it from rotating or moving horizontally or vertically at that end.
　　　悬臂梁仅有一个支点，它使悬臂梁不在此端产生水平或垂直旋转或移动。（目的状

116

语）

例 3. The insulation value of the lightweight aggregate is only important in the roof insulation, which is greatly improved.

轻骨料的隔热值只对屋面的隔热重要，（所以）它可使屋面的隔热性能大为改善。（结果状语）

Directions:

Translate the following sentences, paying attention to the attributive clauses.

1. A fuel is a material which will burn at a reasonable temperature and produce heat.
2. Radio telescopes are giant dish-shaped antennas by means of which we can collect radio waves coming from outer space.
3. Fine grains of dust can reflect blue light, which coarse grains of dust cannot.
4. The process of combining with oxygen is oxidation, of which burning is one type.
5. Solid carbon dioxide has a low temperature, which makes it suitable for refrigeration.
6. The motion of ions is the motion of such atoms as have gained or lost electrons, which in most cases takes place in chemical solution.
7. A solid fuel, like coal or wood, can only burn at the surface, where it comes into contact with the air.
8. In an electric lamp there should not be any oxygen in which the wires may burn away.
9. Copper, which is used so widely for carrying electricity, offers very little resistance.
10. Electronic computers, which have many advantages, cannot carry out creative work and replace man.

Reading Material A

Stoichiometric Combustion of Oil Fuels[①]

It is intended to give an overall picture of the utilisation of liquid and gases fuels without delving in any detail into the various proprietary burner types and designs.[②] The burner must be matched to boiler design and characteristics and this means primarily that the burner rating and flame shape must at all loads be compatible with boiler load ratings, combustion chamber shape and boiler internal resistance to passage of flue gases thus maintaining prescribed heat transfer per unit heating surface at optimum furnace heat. This concerns burner flame intensity related to above conditions and its function at best possible efficiency, i. e. , ensuring combustion with a near stoichiometric fuel/air ratio.

Stoichiometric combustion represents ideally complete conversion by oxidisation of all combustible particles in the fuel; this can be achieved by introduction of a stoichiometric air/fuel ratio which contains the exact oxygen requirement for complete combustion, i. e. , the absence of any unburnt or part burnt particles of CO, H_2, carbonhydrates and carbon in the shape of coke or soot. Furthermore, ideally, absence of excess oxygen would ensure that sulphurcontent oxidises to SO_2 and not to SO_3.

Combustion technology however cannot fully realise this ideal and the complicated chemical/physical process of this nature can only be executed within certain practical limits; ideal near stoichiometric combustion therefore accepts approximately 0—1.0% excess air as a criterion. [3] Exact determination of stoichiometric air/fuel ratio for combustion of a particularoil can only be calculated from the knowledge of elementary analysis of the fuel, its specific gravity and sulphur content; such details also relate to determination of flue gas volumes related to stoichiometric combustion.

Full advantages of near stoichiometric combustion are associated with an assumption of ideal matching and operation of burners. Overall thermal efficiency of a particular boiler installation is related to the flue gas loss which in turn depends upon excess air and exhaust temperatures encountered in course of combustion. Stoichiometric firing limits this influence to that of flue gas temperature only. If excess air falls short of near stoichiometric figure of 1.0%, flue gas loss becomes a function of exhaust temperature and unburnt constituents such as CO, H_2, etc. , with the inert combustion product CO_2 in the flue gas, decreasing because of incomplete oxydisation. [4] A limit to flue gas temperature is set by necessity for an adequate temperature gradient between flue gas and heating surfaces but the decisive lower limit is imposed by possible danger of low temperature dewpoint corrosion created by the sulphur content of the fuel.

Near stoichiometric combustion would ensure that the influence of acid dewpoint of sulphur upon low temperature corrosion is considerably lessened by reducing oxydisation of sulphur to SO_3. Reduction of excess air to near stoichiometric limit also causes a decrease in flue gas loss; at the same time the theoretical flame temperature rises. Increased combustion temperature and reduced proportion of inert gas volume are associated with acceleration of combustion reaction. Fuel oil does not burn in its liquid state but only after atomisation and vapourisation, whereby gases thus formed in intimate combination with the oxydising medium air or oxygen, create a combustible mixture. High surrounding temperatures enable the combustion temperature of the mixture, which can be considered of constant magnitude, to be achieved more rapidly thus accelerating complete burn out of the oil fuel. [5] To approach this ideal and so maintain efficiency of combustion, it is important that the burner is capable of constantly creating sufficiently fine vapourisation of fuel to offer as large a combustion contact surfaceas possible but offering sufficient tolerance to allow for minor variations in fuel characteristics.

The ability to approach stoichiometric combustion enables more efficient utilisation of the cheaper grades of fuel oils and exercises a decisive influence in counteracting low temporature corrosion in boilers and flues liable to be caused by sulphur.

Notes

①燃料油化学计量比燃烧。

②想要得出液体和气体燃料应用的总概念，不必详细研究各种获专利的燃烧器型式及设计。

③ideal near stoichiometric combustion…as a criterion 理想的近化学计量比燃烧允许大约 $0\sim10\%$ 的过量空气作为判据。

④If excess air…becomes a function of… 如果过量空气未能达到近化学计量比数的 10%，则排烟损失是…的函数。

⑤高环境温度能使可视为常数的燃烧温度很快就达到，从而加速燃料油的完全燃尽。

Reading Material B

Furnace and Boiler

The configuration of the furnace part of the combustion system must be matched to the grate rating offering optimum space and time for complete burning of all solid and gaseous matter comprising the refuse culminating with consistently blended inert flue gases. This is a veryimportant part of the plant design because faulty combustion caused by incorrect oxygen admixture is liable to give rise to serious fireside deposits and corrosion.

Boiler types used for recovery of thermal energy from refuse can be designed to generate hot water or high pressure (also superheated) steam and in overall concept are of conventional water tube type as used in power station practice but requiring adaptation of heat transfer surfaces to suit the low calorific value of refuse as fuel. The corner tube water wall boiler has found favour with modern plants because of its heating surface layout and compactness.[①]

Experience has shown that water tube boilers designed integral with incinerator furnace become smaller and more compact than separate waste heat boilers and allow a furnace configuration more suited to efficient combustion.

Early incinerator plants featured waste heat boilers as separate conventional units connected to the furnace instead of being an integral part of it.[②] This often gave rise to operating problems due to tube fouling and corrosion; there was a tendency therefore of restricting such plant to moderate operational parameters. For the same reasons fire tube boilers also proved unsuitable for the duty.

It is practice for boilers integral with incinerator plant to have natural circulation and gasvelocities are maintained at around 6 m/s to minimise deposits on heating surfaces and reduce erosion and corrosion of tubes. Primary flue gas temperatures should preferably not exceed 750℃ to obviate slag deposits. In older plants with uncooled firebrick lined side walls corrosion troubles may well have been accentuated by the fact that the heat value of refuse has been increasing with its chemical composition tending to vary and the additional heat release resulted in softening of ash and much increased slagging on the uncooled walls. [3]

Any incinerator plant usually has to be individually designed to suit various specified requirements and operational criteria. The overall matching of grate, furnace and boiler is therefore very much a "one off" problem. [4] Specialist environmental engineering firms such as the major incineration grate manufacturers are best qualified to offer advice and design the plant as a whole and this would include boilers. It is therefore impossible to generalise about the various technical details involved.

Boiler fireside surfaces must be cleaned regularly by means of soot blowers using steam or compressed air. Possibilities of corrosive attacks show a relationship to operational pressures and temperatures with damage to boiler tubes appearing to stem mainly from high temperatures whereas low temperature corrosion can result from gases at less than 200 ℃. Incorrect combustion control with after burning of combustible gases due to incorrect oxygen balance possibly caused by particular furnace configuration contributing to wrong distribution of primary air for a complete burn out, can be considered a major cause of corrosion damage. [5] In modern plants automatic combustion control systems ensure more uniform incineration and therefore heat release by automatic synchronisation of fuel feed on grate, combustion air quantity and distribution and boiler output.

Trends from past and present experience indicate that because of increasing calorific values of modern waste the magnitude of preheating of combustion air has to be reduced and in certain cases fully eliminated. Modern systems do not by pass returning flue gases to the underneath of grates; combustion air is drawn by forced draught fan suction from the garbage store bunker thus creating negative pressure necessary to exhaust foul fumes from the refuse silo area.

Notes

①由于角管式水壁锅炉加热面布局及紧凑性而深受现代厂站的欢迎。
②早期焚烧装置的特点是废热锅炉连至炉膛的通常的分设单元，而不是它的组成部分。
③在具有未冷却耐火砖衬砌的侧墙的老式装置上，腐蚀问题由下列事实加以强调，即…
④锅、炉与炉篦的总体匹配确实是一个"同时一次解的"问题。
⑤炉室形状促使完全燃烧所需一次空气的不良分布，由此可能产生氧的不平衡，进而造成可燃气体二次燃烧的不恰当控制，这可视为腐蚀损坏的主要原因。

UNIT FOURTEEN

Text   Water Treatment

[1]   Internal Treatment of Water. There are numerous chemicals, some called boiler compounds, onthe market and recommended for "internal" water softening and other treatment. Their duty is to stabilise hardness agents, prevent scaling or make deposits easily removable. Such chemicals are also used for neutralisation of residual hardness in systems after external treatment. Chemicals of this nature are introduced at a more or less constant rate in dissolved state into feed tanks or systems. The most frequently used chemicals are phosphates; trisodium phosphate ($Na_3 Po_4$) is the best known compound. Its reaction with calcium and magnesium salts results in consolable calcium and magnesium phosphates. Other internal treatment agents are calcium hydroxide, sodium carbonate, sodium hydroxide, tannins and amines.

[2]   The most effective method of introducing internal treatment compounds to ensure a reasonable degree of quantity control is by means of dosage apparatus consisting of one or more containers having manual or motor driven agitators and a dosage pump.

[3]   As a general rule internal treatment alone, for waters of much more than 5° (UK) (70 p. p. m.) hardness is not recommended because system and make-up quantities and water composition may become critical and precipitated sludge and salts are liable to increase density of water and solidification of sludge with consequent propensity to foaming and priming in steam plant and circulation complications.

[4]   Internal treatment is generally used within limits for smallish systems, say up to 2-3 MW or as residual treatment and to raise pH value to a requisite amount.

[5]   External Treatment of Water. External softening of system and make-up water is the more effective and comprehensive method of water treatment for any size of plant and network and it can suit most water characteristics. Nowadays external treatment involves the principle of ion-exchange, which ensures water of virtually zero hardness. [1]

[6]   The ion-exchange process can be described as follows. Molecules of dissolved salts are dissociated in form of free electrically charged ions in liquid solution. In the force field they tend to be attracted to opposite charges: positive cations to the negative cathodes and negative anions to the positive anode. Ion-exchange materials are insoluble artificial resins to which activated chemical groups with tied dissociable ions, are attached. Ion exchangers are classified in accordance with dissociation characteristics of the activating groups, strongly, medium or weakly active. [2]

[7]   Base exchange water treatment. In the base exchange process, raw water containing calcium and magnesium salts passes through a bed of cation synthetic resin activated by sodium base. Calcium and magnesium salts are exchanged for quantitatively equivalent

salts of sodium (sodiumbicarbonate) and soft water.

[8]　　This neutral ion exchange does not change the salt content of water, also pH value and therefore content of free and tied carbonic acid remain constant. Water softened by the base exchange process is free of calcium and magnesium hardness agents. Sodium bicarbonate is dissolved in water and deposits are prevented. There is a tendency for dissociation of sodium bicarbonate at temperatures above 110℃ resulting in some part-tied and tied carbon dioxide being released as aggressive agent.

[9]　　When the active exchange material ceases to be effective due to saturation by calcium and magnesium, its softening power is regenerated by flushing with solution of brine. The high concentration of sodium ions in the brine replaces calcium and magnesium chlorides in the exchange material and reactivates it. Calcium and magnesium chlorides are flushed out with brine to sewage.

[10]　　There is no practical limit to regeneration and exchange material does not become exhausted. In the case of such mechanical impurities as iron content above 0.3 mg/1 or manganese over 0.2 mg/1 being introduced by raw water,[3] the exchange material can become contaminated thus experiencing reduced capacity. If such impure waters are involved, introduction of a special pre-filter is good practice; foreign bodies cannot be dislodged from the exchanger bed in the course of regeneration and frequent renewal of the material would be necessary.

[11]　　The base exchange softener consists of a specially lined steel cylinder, half filled exchange material and provided with suitable connections. The plant can be fully automatic with frequency of regeneration dictated by pre-determined quantity of water passing through or by presence of hardness indicated by test. Adjustment of water quantity is seldom required and chemicals other than salt are not necessary. Paralleling of two interconnected units allows alternate regeneration and therefore continuity of process.

[12]　　Ion-exchange demineralisation. Feed water for modern high pressure plant must be of such quality as to have all salts and dissolved silica acid neutralised.[4] With generation of steam, salts should remain as sediment and condensate virtually becomes distilled water.

[13]　　Much progress in development of methods of water treatment is due to evolution of insoluble artificial resins for the process of ion-exchange in order to render water to a degree of purity required for modern plant. In the demineralisation process water is passed through such beds of granulated exchangers in series, to achieve purity of 5-20 p.p.m. total dissolved solids.

[14]　　In the cation exchanger, cations in water (calcium, magnesium, sodium and potassium) are exchanged for hydrogen ions, forming free acids from water dissolved salts. In the second series connected anion exchange container, the above mentioned acid water loses the free acids leaving silica and carbon dioxide. Water is then fully demineralised.

[15]　　Treatment offering full demineralisation is employed in most power stations and also for manufacturing processes requiring optimum purity of water. Complete demineral-

isation of fill and make-up is not necessary for small and medium sized installations; fully treated water or condensate possibly available from associated or adjacent boiler plant and power stations, proves to be most satisfactory for district heating systems.

New Words and Expressions

compound * [kəm'paund]	n.	复合物化合物，抛光剂
scale [skeil]	n.；v.	结水垢
residual hardness		残余硬度
neutralization * [ˌnjuːtrəlaiˈzeiʃən]	n.	中和
phosphate ['fɔsfeit]	n.	磷酸盐
trisodium phosphate		磷酸三钠
calcium ['kælsiəm]	n.	钙
magnesium [mægˈniːzjəm]	n.	镁
soluble ['sɔljubl]	a.	可溶的
hydroxide [haiˈdrɔkaid]	n.	氢氧化物
sodium ['səudjəm]	n.	钠
carbonate ['kɑːbəneit]	n.	碳酸盐
tannin ['tænin]	n.	丹宁酸
amine ['æmiːn]	n.	胺
dosage ['dəusidʒ]	n.	配料
agitator ['ædʒiteitə]	n.	搅拌器
sludge [slʌdʒ]	n.	泥渣
precipitate * [priˈsipifeit]	vt.	沉积，从溶液中分离
solidification * [səˌlidifiˈkeiʃən]	n.	凝固，固化
propensity [prəˈpensiti]	n.	倾向，习性
foam [fəum]	v.	(使) 起泡沫
prime * [praim]	v.	蒸溅
complication [ˌkɔmpliˈkeiʃən]	n.	复杂，困难
smallish [smɔːliʃ]	a.	略小的，不大的
soften * ['sɔːfn]	v.	软化
suit * [sjuːt]	vt.	使合适
ion ['aiən]	n.	离子
charged [tʃɑːdʒd]	a.	带电的
dissociate * [diˈsəuʃieit]	vt.	分离，离解
dissociation [diˌsəuʃiˈeiʃən]	n.	分解，离解
cation ['kætaiən]	n.	阳离子
cathode ['kæθəud]	n.	阴极
resin ['rezin]	n.	树脂

activate * ['æktiveit]	n.	使活性
bicarbonate [bai'kɑːbənit]		碳酸氢盐
saturation * [sætʃə'reiʃən]	n.	饱和
flush * [flʌʃ]	v.	冲刷
brine [brain]	n.	盐水
chloride ['klɔːraid]	n.	氯化物
manganese [mæŋg'niːz]	n.	锰
contaminate [kən'tæmineit]	vt.	污染，弄脏
dislodge * [dis'lədʒ]	vt.	除去，取走，移动
demineralization ['diˌminərəlai'zeiʃən]		去矿化作用，去矿质作用，去盐
sediment ['sedimənt]		沉积物
condensate [kɔnden'seit]	n.	凝结水
distill * [dis'til]	v.	蒸馏，提取
granulate * [grænjuleit]	v.	使粒化，成粒
potassium [pə'tæsjəm]	n.	钾
anion ['æniən]	n.	阴离子

Notes

①Which 指前面的句子所表示的整个概念。

②as 和前面的 are classified 搭配，构成 are classified as，意为："分为……类"。

③being introduced by raw water 是 of such mechanical impurities as …复合介词短语中的宾语补足语。

④to have all salts and dissolved silica acid neutralized

　　have ＋ 宾语 ＋_____ed（作宾补）结构。

Exercises

Reading Comprehension

Ⅰ.Choose the best answer for each of the following.

　1. Boiler compounds can be used to _____ .

　　　A. stabilize hardness agents

　　　B. ensure water of zero hardness

　　　C. make deposits easily removable

　　　D. neutralize residual hardness

　2. Which of the following can not be used as internal treatment agent?

　　　A. Calcium hydroxide　　　　B. Phosphates

　　　C. Sodium hydroxide　　　　D. Magnesium phosphate

3. Which of the following statements is true?

   A. Internal treatment alone is usually recommended for waters of over 5°hardness.

   B. By means of dosage apparatus internal treatment compounds can be introduced to ensure a reasonable degree of quantity control.

   C. Internal treatment is generally used without limits for small systems.

   D. Salts tend to keep density of water unchanged.

4. Ion-exchange is involved in _____ .

   A. external treatment of water

   B. internal treatment of water

   C. base exchange water treatment

   D. regeneration and frequent renewal of material

5. Base exchange is a neutral ion exchange which change _____ .

   A. both the salt content of water and PH value

   B. neither the salt content of water nor PH value

   C. salts of sodium and soft water

   D. calcium and magnesium salts

6. The softening power of the active exchange material is regenerated by _____ .

   A. saturation by calcium and magnesium

   B. flushing with solution of brine

   C. replacing calcium and magnesium chlorides

   D. high concentration of sodium ion in the brine

7. The frequency of generation of the base exchange softener is dictated by _____ .

   A. pre-determined quantity of water passing through

   B. presence of hardness indicated by test

   C. adjustment of water quantity

   D. both A and B

8. The evolution of insoluble artificial resins for the process of ion-exchange contributes to _____ .

   A. the progress of demineralization

   B. the development of methods of water treatment

   C. regeneration of the active exchange material

   D. internal treatment of water

II. Are the following statements true or false?

1. Treatment offering full demineralization can be used for manufacturing processes requiring optimum purity of water.   (   )

2. It is not necessary for feed water to have all salts and dissolved silica acid neutralized.

                                                                              (   )

3. It is important for small and medium sized installations to have complete demineralization of fill and make-up.   (   )

4. The demineralization process enables water to achieve purity of 5-20 p. p. m.　　（ ）

Vocabulary

Ⅰ. Fill in the blanks with some of the words or expressions listed below，changing the form where necessary.

| optimum | neutralize | free of | ensure |
| dictate | classify | saturation | in form of |

1. Dosage apparatus can be used to _____ a reasonable degree of quantity control.

2. Water softened by the base exchange process is _____ calcium and magnesium hardness agents.

3. In feed water for modern high pressure plant processes all salts and dissolved silica acid _____ .

4. Pre-determined quantity of water passing through can _____ the frequency of regeneration.

5. Full demineralization treatment is employed for manufacturing processes which require _____ purity of water.

Ⅱ. Complete each of the following statements with one of the four choices given below.

1. "Boiler compounds" are used to _____ hardness agents
   A. soften　　B. change　　C. replace　　D. stabilize

2. External treatment of water can _____ most water characteristics.
   A. suite　　B. suit　　C. satisfy　　D. provide

3. Ion exchangers _____ into 3 kinds.
   A. are classified　　B. are divided　　C. are cataloged　　D. are separated

4. Because of _____ by calcium and magnesium，the active exchange material becomes ineffective.
   A. evaporation　　B. oxidation　　C. saturation　　D. neutralization

5. In ion-exchange process，molecules of dissolved salts are dissociated _____ free electrically charged ions in liquid solution.
   A. by way of　　B. in form of　　C. by means of　　D. for the sake of

Translation　　　　　　　　　　长难句翻译（Ⅰ）

　　科技英语在表达复杂概念时，由于逻辑严密，科学性强，而常用多重复句(involved sentence)，结构复杂，句子长。翻译时，首先，弄清原句语法结构和逻辑联系，然后，按汉语表达习惯，用短句分层次逐步译出。

　　长句的翻译要根据句子的结构和表述的层次关系和逻辑次序来区别处理，通常用顺序译法、逆序译法、分译法几种。

Ⅰ. 顺序译法

句子虽长，但表述层次关系和逻辑次序与汉语无异时，即用顺译法依次译出且较通顺。

举例：If ventilation is necessary at a known rate, such as in workshops and factories coming under the Factories Act, or in places of public entertainment coming under local authority regulations, mechanical ventilation is required; in which case, so far as the heating system is concerned, the designer has to make a choice as to whether he will install heating equipment to cope with the fabric losses only, or whether he will include this heat in the ventilation air, bringing it in somewhat warmer to allow for this loss.

如果通风所需的风量是已知的，例如，对于编入工厂法规的车间或工厂，或是编入地方管理条例中的公共娱乐场所，则需要采用机械通风。在这种情况下，就采暖系统而言，设计师必须作出选择：安装的采暖设备是仅仅满足补偿围护结构热损失的需要，还是把通风空气中的热量包括进去，使空气更暖和些，以供热损失之用。

Ⅱ．逆序译法

句子长，出现多重复句，表述层次关系和逻辑次序与汉语相反时，要区别不同或相反部分在整个句中的性质和作用以及与上下文的逻辑关系，从而将原句逆序译成汉语。

举例：However, the simplification of assuming the fluid to be inviscid may not be made when analyses of heat convection are undertaken, because the process of convection of heat away from the wall is intimately concerned with thermal conduction and energy transport due to motion in the fluid layers in the immediate vicinity of the wall.

但是，因为从壁面带走热量的对流过程与热传导和壁面直接邻近区内由流体层运动所产生的能量传递有关，所以当进行对流热分析的时候，不能简单化假设流体为非粘性的。
（because 和 when 引起的两个状语从句用逆序译）

Directions：

Translate the following long involved sentences into Chinese.

1. If the ground is of a clayey nature, liable to shrink considerably when it dries out, the foundation must be deep enough to ensure that the condition of the clay will remain reasonably constant.

2. It is clear that in the interests of conservation of energy and economy of installation and running costs for all time, money spent on weather-tightness of windows is a real economy, since uncontrolled ventilation goes on for 24 hours a day, whereas ventilation is necessary only during the occupied period of a matter of a few hours as a rule, and can usually be dealt with by some controlled means, such as the opening of a window.

3. The construction of such a satellite is now believed to be quite realizable, its realization being supported with all the achievements of contemporary science, which have brought into being not only materials capable of withstanding severe stresses involved

and high temperatures developed, but new technological processes as well.

4. In reality, the lines of division between sciences are becoming blurred, and science is again approaching the "unity" that it had two centuries ago——although the accumulated knowledge is enormously greater now, and no one person can hope to comprehend more than a fraction of it.

5. This classification includes all metal-cutting machinery, the action of which is a progressive cutting away of surplus stock—a gradual reduction in size until the finished dimensions are reached——but excludes sheet metal working machinery and metal-forming and forging machines.

6. The law of universal gravitation states that every particle of matter in the universe attracts every other with a force which is directly proportional to the product of their masses and inversely proportional to the square of the distance between them.

Reading Material A

Some Selected Properties of Coal Components

Curiosity about the differences in composition and other properties of the petrographic entities to be found in a coal dates back to the 1920s. A major obstacle to systematic investigation was the size and distribution of the entities. The sizes of exinites and micrinites are usually very small, a few microns, and in many coals they are dispersed. [1] However, the peculiarities of some coals presented opportunities to demonstrate that the different entities present in bituminous coals and lignites have differing compositions and specific gravities. In many American coals vitrinite and fusinite appear in thick lenses, and samples of them, in nearly pure forms, could be obtained with the aid of a microscope. [2] Also, some coals contain segments very rich in exinite or resins. On comparison the compositions and chemical properties of hand-selected petrographic components were found to be different from those of the whole coal. Studies of the properties of isolated exinites date back to 1928, when Zetsche studied a number of exinites. Later Sprunk and co-workers investigated the properties of a number of exinites found in a variety of American coals, and Macrae likewise studied the exinites found in British and other coals.

Post World War II industrial redevelopment in Europe and concern over the dwindling reserves of coking coals (in the United States and elsewhere) revived interest in a more systematic investigation of coal components. [3] The rapid advances made in electronics and analytical instruments provided additional impetus.

It was observed that fractions of different specific gravity obtained from finely pulverized bituminous coals by successive float-and-sink operations had different petrographic compositions. Exinite tended to concentrate in the fraction of least specific gravity, followed by vitrinite, micrinite, and fusinite, in the order of increasing specific gravity. Although the specific gravity of fusinite obtained from various coals did not seem to fluctuate markedly, the same was not found to be true for the other components, especially exinite. Researchers in France, Germany, the Netherlands, and the United States succeeded in obtaining, by trial-and-error procedures, concentrates of exinite, vitrinite, and micrinite from a number of European and American coals and determined their compositions and various other physical and chemical properties.

Intense research activity flourished for a short period of time. The results of the research activity of this period are discussed and an idea of the differences in composition and some physical properties of the petrographic components of a bituminous coal are given. It is seen that there are significant and systematic differences in their hydrogen contents, densities, and reflectances in oil. The refractive index of fusinite bucks the trend; its higher reflectivity obviously stems from a high extinction coefficient. The surface areas obtained may reflect the sizes of the homogeneous domains in the constituents because they correspond to linear dimensions ranging from 2 to 0.4μ. It should be pointed out here that the differences in the properties of the petrographic components become less as the rank of the coal increases and are practically nonexistent in anthracites.

From a practical point of view it was hoped that a petrographic analysis and an easily determinable property of the petrographic components of coal would permit prediction of the parameters useful in coal utilization. Unfortunately, this has not proved possible. The fact that exinites are rich in hydrogen, hydrogenate easily, and oxidize with greater difficulty (under certain conditions), and that fusinites are relatively more inert, was established muchearlier.

Notes

①exinites and micrinites，壳质煤素质和碎片体煤质。
②vitrinite and fusinite，镜煤素质和焦炭煤素质。·
③二战后在欧洲工业的再度发展以及对炼焦煤储量减少的担心，对煤炭组份更加系统的考察的兴趣又重新流行起来了。

Reading Material B

Refuse Incineration-generation of Heat

In the past two decades much discourse and development has taken place in connection with the particular branch of Environmental Engineering dealing with hygienic disposal of waste materials by combustion in such a manner as to fully obviate all pollution caused by garbage and at the same time utilise to the utmost the inherent thermal value of the refuse and of consequent inert products of incineration. This function can achieve to a notable degree the ideal of "total recovery", sometimes collectively but somewhat unprecisely alluded to by the fashionable term "recycling" within context of realisation that world resources are finite and must no longer be wasted. [1]

Furthermore refuse tips are becoming overfilled and are liable to create public nuisance anddue to pollution of ground water and soil, a danger to health. Against this, incineration reduces foul constituents into much smaller bulk volume of completely sterile residue such asash, clinker, metal scrap (for re-cycling) and cleaned sterile flue gases.

There are various other alternative methods for neutralising refuse such as preparation for composting; demand for this end product is comparatively small and little more than 6% of waste materials would be so reduced. The use of pulverised refuse to supplement fuel in coal burning boilers is limited to a degree of selection of the rubbish in question. Centrifugal separation of refuse into its constituent parts to recover useful materials and subsequently convert combustible matter into fuel pellets is at experimental stage, experiencing comparatively little practical application.

On a more realistic basis, in most European and other developed countries major action has been taken to burn refuse with the aim of consequent creation of useful energy where at all feasible especially as quantitatively household waste is rapidly increasing with universal progress of the "affluent society" and the quality of this waste when related to ultimate extraction of thermal energy is becoming higher, mainly because of modern packaging methods of consumer goods as well as due to considerable decrease of inert ash content in household refuse resulting from greater use of oil and gas fuels for domestic heating [2].

Early incineration plants as well as latter installations often reflecting unfortunate locations or short sighted planning outlook related to economes in investment costs, have been erected purely as distracters of waste materials. There was no consideration given to utilising thermal energy released by the combustion process. Such first cost economies on plant, apart from wasting heat and indirectly fossil fuel resources, can have deceptive financial benefits. Reasons are stated as follows: In the course of actual incineration process the requisite combustion temperature for complete destruction of pollutants would be in the region of 850-900℃. The temperature of direct by-products of burnout has to be reduced to 200-300 ℃ to suitelectrostatic precipitators for gas filtration.

Therefore flue gases have to be cooled prior to filtration and if no provision is made to utilise the released thermal energy, this cooling effect is usually achieved in cooling towers with water spray being injected into the hot gas for evaporative cooling. Large quantities of water are required and this is not only wasted but environmental problems can be created by the water becoming polluted and its condense vapour causing unsightly emissions. Furthermore, to cope with the combined volume of cooled flue gas and admixed vapour, the precipitators must belarger than if only combustion flue gases were involved.

The above described method of incineration, commendable as it is for the purpose of sterile disposal of refuse, has no connection with subject matter related to this publication. The intention is to deal with techniques of using steam or hot water boilers in combination with incineration plant to avoid rejection of usable heat and apply it to perform a worthwhile duty thus contributing to conservation of fuels commensurate with neutralisation of environmental fouling by refuse.

Notes

①sometimes …… "recycling"，有时总括地但不甚确切地用流行的术语"再循环"来引证 ……

②where at all …… "affluent society"，在住户废物随着"富足社会"的普遍进步而急剧增多的场合完全可行……

UNIT FIFTEEN

Text   Refrigeration

[1]   Refrigeration was used by ancient civilizations when it was naturally available. The Roman rulers had slaves transport ice and snow from the high mountains to be used to preserve foods and to provide cool beverages in hot weather. Such natural sources of refrigeration were, of course, extremely limited in terms of location, temperatures, and scope. Means of producing refrigeration with machinery, called mechanical refrigeration, began to be developed in the 1850s. Today the refrigeration industry is a vast and essential part of any technological society, with yearly sales of equipment amounting to billions of dollars in the United States alone. ①

Uses of Refrigeration

[2]   It is convenient to classify the applications of refrigeration into the following categories: domestic, commercial, industrial, and air conditioning. Sometimes transportation is listed as a separate category. Domestic refrigeration is used for food preparation and preservation, ice making, and cooling beverages in the household. Commercial refrigeration is used in retail stores, restaurants, and institutions, for purposes the same as those in the household. Industrial refrigeration in the food industry is needed in processing, preparation, and large-scale preservation. This includes use in food chilling and freezing plants, cold storage warehouses, breweries, and dairies, to name a few. Hundreds of other industries use refrigeration; among them are ice making plants, oil refineries, pharmaceuticals. Of course ice skating rinks need refrigeration.

[3]   Refrigeration is also widely used in both comfort air conditioning for people and in industrial air conditioning. Industrial air conditioning is used to create the air temperatures, humidity, and cleanliness required for manufacturing processes. Computers require a controlled environment.

Methods of Refrigeration

[4]   Refrigeration, commonly spoken of as a cooling process is more correctly defined as the removal of heat from a substance to bring it to or keep it at a desirable low temperature, below the temperature of the surroundings. ② The most widespread method of producing mechanical refrigeration is called the vapor compression system. In this system a volatile liquid refrigerant is evaporated in an evaporator; this process results in a removal of heat (cooling) from the substance to be cooled. A compressor and condenser are required to maintain the evaporation process and to recover the refrigerant for reuse.

[5]   Another widely used method is called the absorption refrigeration system. In this process a refrigerant is evaporated (as with the vapor compression system), but the evaporation is maintained by absorbing the refrigerant in another fluid.

[6]   Other refrigeration methods are thermoelectric, steam jet, and air cycle refrigeration. These systems are used only in special applications and their functioning will not be explained here. Thermoelectric refrigeration is still quite expensive; some small tabletop domestic refrigerators are cooled by this method. Steam jet refrigeration is inefficient. Often used on ships in the past, it has been largely replaced by the vapor compression system The air cycle is sometimes used in air conditioning of aircraft cabins. Refrigeration at extremely low temperatures, below about-200°F (-130℃), is called cryogenics. Special systems are used to achieve these conditions. One use of refrigeration at ultralow temperatures is to separate oxygen and nitrogen from air and to liquefy them.

Refrigeration Equipment

[7]   The main equipment components of the vapor compression refrigeration system are the familiar evaporator, compressor, and condenser. The equipment may be separate or of the unitary (also called self-contained) type. Unitary equipment is assembled in the factory. The household refrigerator is a common example of unitary equipment. Obvious advantages of unitary equipment are that it is more compact and less expensive to manufacture if made in large quantities.

[8]   There is a variety of commercial refrigeration equipment; each has a specific function. Reach-in cabinets, walk-in coolers, and display cases are widely used in the food service business. Automatic ice makers, drinking water coolers, and refrigerated vending machines are also commonly encountered equipment.

[9]   Air conditioning includes the heating, cooling, humidifying, dehumidifying, and cleaning (filtering)of air in internal environments. Occasionally it will be necessary to mention some aspects of air conditioning when we deal with the interface between the two subjects. A study of the fundamentals and equipment involved in air conditioning is nevertheless of great value[③] even for those primarily interested in refrigeration.

New Words and Expressions

brewery ['bruəri]	n.	酿酒厂
pharmaceutical [ˌfɑːməˈsjuːtikl]	n.	制药厂
volatile ['vɔlətail]	a.	挥发性的
thermoelectric [ˌθəːməuiˈlektrik]	a.	热电的
cryogenics	n.	低温技术
ultralow ['ʌltrələu]	a.	超低的
liquify * ['kikwifai]	vt.	使液化
dehumidify [diːˈhjuːmidifai]	vt.	除湿
beverage ['bevəridʒ]	n.	饮料
category ['kætigfəri]	n.	种类，部类
warehouse ['wɛəhaus]	n.	仓库，货栈

humidity * 〔hjuː'midəti〕	*n.*	湿度
compression * 〔kəm'preʃən〕	*n.*	压缩
refrigerant 〔ri'fridʒərənt〕	*n.*	冷冻剂
absorption * 〔əb'sɔːpʃən〕	*n.*	吸收（过程）
unitary 〔'juːnitəri〕	*a.*	具有单一特征的
fundamental 〔ˌfʌndə'mentl〕	*a.*	基础的
be replaced by		被代替
in large quantities		大量
a variety of		种种

Notes

①…amounting to 现在分词作后置修饰语。

②…spoken of as…过去分词作状语，修饰全句。

③…be of great value 很有价值，be of value＝be valuable。

Exercises

Reading Comprehension

Ⅰ. Choose the best answer for each of the following.

1. The fact that the Roman rulers had slaves transport ice and snow from the high mountains indicates that _____ .

   A. ice and snow could be used to preserve food.

   B. they used ice and snow to provide cool drinks.

   C. refrigeration available naturally was used by our ancestors.

   D. natural sources of refrigeration were easily obtained.

2. Mechanical refrigeration began to be developed _____ .

   A. in ancient times   B. in Rome

   C. in the 1850s   D. in the United States

3. People usually classify the applications of refrigeration into the following categories except _____ .

   A. industrial   B. commercial

   C. transportation   D. domestic

4. The food industry needs industrial refrigeration in _____ .

   A. preservation   B. large-scale preservation

   C. retail stores   D. institutions

5. Refrigeration is also used in industrial air conditioning to create _____ .

   A. a controlled environment

B. required cleanliness and humidity

C. required air temperature

D. Both B and C

II. Are the following statements true or false?

1. Refrigeration is defined as the eradication of heat from a substance to bring it to or keep it at a satisfying low temperature. ( )

2. The process that in the vapor compression system a volatile liquid refrigerant is evaporated in an evaporator results in a removal of heat from the substance to be cooled. ( )

3. In the absorption refrigeration system, a refrigerant is evaporated in the evaporation which is maintained by absorbing the refrigerant in another substance. ( )

4. Other refrigeration methods, such as steam jet, air cycle and thermoelectric refrigeration, are also widely used in various applications. ( )

5. A variety of commercial refrigeration equipment, such as reach-in cabinets, walk-in coolers and display cases, is widely used in the food service business, and each has a specific function. ( )

Vocabulary

I . Fill in the blanks with some of the words listed below, changing the form where necessary.

| liquefy | evaporation | assemble | interface |
| internal | variety | classify | component |

1. In the _____ process, a volatile liquid refrigerant is evaporated to remove heat from the substance to be cooled.

2. Scientists sometimes use refrigeration at ultralow temperature to separate oxygen and nitrogen from air and to _____ them.

3. After the production of different components, unitary equipment is _____ in the factory for the advantages of being compact and less expensive.

4. It is in _____ environment that air conditioning includes, the heating, cooling, humidifying, dehumidifying and cleaning of air.

5. The fundamental study of both subjects is quite necessary when the _____ between the two subjects is dealt with.

II. Complete each of the following statements with one of the four choices given below.

1. The separation of oxygen and nitrogen from air and the liquefaction of them are done by _____ a ultralow temperature.

A. cooling B. refrigeration C. refrigerator D. refrigerant

2. Although it is easy to _____ the applications of refrigeration into several categories, the understanding of different categories really takes time.

A. evaluate   B. grade   C. classify   D. group

3. He just knew that there was a _____ of new books about the subject he majored in.

   A. diverseness   B. variety   C. diversity   D. multiplity

4. There are some obvious advantages of _____ equipment that it is less expensive to manufacture if made in large quantities.

   A. unified   B. unitary   C. united   D. unique

5. All the students got to know the main equipment _____ of the vapor compression refrigeration system after studying the subject of refrigeration.

   A. constituent   B. factor   C. ingredient   D. component.

Translation   长难句翻译（Ⅱ）

Ⅲ. 分译法

英语长句，有些句子结构需要用分译处理。有些句子成分与其他部分关系松弛，具有意义上的相对独立性，也需要分出来译成分句。分译时要保持原文内容和逻辑意义的一致性和连贯性，使译文简明、通顺。

举例：① It might be thought that，with so many assumptions and "rule of thumb" estimates，heat losses were little better than guesswork；but in practice they appear to give a satisfactory basis，partly no doubt due to the fact ② that all areas within the building are treated in alike manner and should therefore be consistent，and secondly due to the fly-wheel effect of the structure itself ③ which，even with a lightly constructed building，still has floor slabs，partitions，furniture，etc. to absorb and emit heat and so avoid violent fluctuations.

可能会有这样一种想法：有这么多设想和凭经验的估算，热损失比猜测的结果好不了多少。然而在实际上，它们似乎提供了一个令人满意的依据。毫无疑问，原因之一是由于这样一个实际情况：建筑物内所有的区域都用同样的方式处理，因而得到的结果总是一致的。另一个原因是由于建筑结构本身的调节作用。因为建筑即使是轻型构造的建筑，也依然有楼板、隔墙和附属设备等在进行吸热和放热，因而避免了热损失的剧烈波动。

①It might be thought that，分译出来，是由于句子结构的需要。

②that 引起的同位语，分译出来，符合汉语表达习惯。

③which 引起的定语从句，分译出来，表示原因，更体现了原文内容和逻辑意义的一致性和连贯性，简明，通顺。

Ⅳ. 多种译法的综合运用

英语长句是由多重复句组成，有多种多层次的并列和主从关系。因此，在汉译时，要根据原文的语法关系和逻辑联系，运用顺序译法、逆序译法、合译法、分译法等技巧来综合处理。英语长句的汉译，往往需要多种译法的综合运用。

举例：①Human beings are endowed with a temperature sense ②which enables them to tell at least roughly whether two objects will be in thermal equilibrium ③when they are placed together.

人类具有感知温度的能力；当两个物体摆在一起时，它至少能使人们大体上判断出它们是否处于温度平衡状态。

①句子开头用顺序译。②Which 引起的定语从句分译。③When 引起的状语从句用逆序译。

Directions：

Translate the following sentences into Chinese.

1. As a general rule internal treatment alone, for waters of much more than 5 (UK) (70p. p. m.)

   hardness is not recommended because system and make-up quantities and water composition may become critical and precipitated sludge and salts are liable to increase density of water

   and solidification of sludge with consequent propensity to foaming and priming in steam plant and circulation complications.

2. The advantages of forced circulation greatly outweigh the consideration of cost, which is usually a minor item compared with the overall capital and running cost of the installation, although the cost of pump or pumps and the cost of power for running have to be allowed for.

3. This method of establishing final steam temperature differs from the desuperheater method which has been quite generally used in the past, in which water is mixed with steam already superheated, to reduce its temperature; or the method of passing a portion of the superheated steam through coils submerged in the steam drum to reduce the temperature.

4. Unlike the natural circulation system which depends on the difference between the densities of the water in the downcomers and the riser tubes, the forced-circulation system depends on a pressure differential produced by a pump which forces the water on its way through the boiler tubes, at a rate which is sufficient for effective heat transfer and for protecting the boiler from steam lock.

5. Steam from the evaporator flows upward to the steam drum where it leaves in a saturated state and continues upward to the superheater, where it is superheated by absorbing an additional amount of heat from the sedium in the intermediate circuit before it finally flows to the throttle valves of the steam turbine.

Reading Material A

Refrigerant Evaporators

Several types of evaporators can be used in multistage systems. A tubular, direct expansion evaporator returns oil easily and requires the smallest refrigerant charge. Where direct expansion is impractical, a flooded system or a recirculated system may be used, but these methods compound oil return problems.

Some problems that can become more acute in low-temperature systems than in high-temperature systems include oil transport properties, loss of capacity caused by static head from the depth of the pool of liquid refrigerant in the evaporator, deterioration of refrigerant boiling heat transfer coefficients, and higher specific volumes for the vapor.

The effect of pressure losses in the evaporator and suction piping is more acute in low-temperature systems because of the large change in saturation temperatures and specific volume in relation to pressure changes at these conditions. Systems that operate near zero absolute pressure are particularly affected by pressure loss. For example, with R-12 and R-22 at 140 kPa suction and 27 ℃ liquid feed temperature, a 7 kPa loss increases the volume flow rate by about 5%. At 35 kPa suction and-7 ℃ liquid feed temperature, a 7 kPa loss increases the volume flow rate by about 25%.

The depth of the pool of boiling refrigerant in a flooded evaporator causes a liquid head or static pressure that is exerted on the lower part of the heat transfer surface. Therefore, the saturation temperature at this surface is higher than the pressure in the suction line, which is not affected by the static head. Although tubular dry expanded evaporators do not have appreciable static liquid head, gas pressure drops from the inlet to the outlet of the evaporator create a velocity head that causes a similar condition.

The liquid depth penalty for the evaporator can be eliminated if the pool of liquid is below the heat transfer surface and a refrigerant pump sprays the liquid over the surface. Of course, the pump energy is an additional heat load to the system, and more refrigerant must be used to provide the Net Positive Suction Head (NPSH) required by the pump. The pump is also an additional item to be maintained.

Another type of low-temperature evaporator is the flash cooler in which liquid refrigerant is cooled by boiling off some vapor. The remaining cold liquid can then be pumped from the flash cooler to the evaporator. There it is either top or bottom fed at a rate greater than the evaporation rate to ensure wetting of the entire evaporator surface for maximum heat transfer without an appreciable static head penalty. This liquid overfeed system is frequently used in large refrigerated warehouses with many evaporators.

Another less frequently used system pumps the liquid refrigerant as a secondary coolant from the flash cooler at low temperature. As the coolant passes through a secondary cooler, or coil, heat transfers to it from the material being cooled. The liquid temperature rises to develop a temperature range, but because pressure is maintained sufficiently above saturation by the liquid pump, the coolant does not evaporate until it returns via a restriction to the flash cooler. Sufficient refrigerant must be circulated to accommodate the temperature range. The flash cooler in this system is an accumulator receiver similar to that used in a liquid overfeed system, except that no excess refrigerant is fed to the remote heat transfer surface.

In both types of liquid recirculation systems, the cold liquid can be moved by mechanical pumps or by pressure from the compressor discharge.

Reading Material B

Corrosion Prevention

Corrosion prevention requires choosing proper materials and inhibitors, routine testing for pH, and eliminating contaminants. Because of potentially corrosive calcium chloride and sodium chloride salt brine secondary coolant systems are widely used, test and adjust the brine solution monthly. [1] To replenish salt brines in a system, a concentrated solution may be better than a crystalline form, because it is easier to handle and mix.

A refrigerating salt brine should not be allowed to change from an alkaline to an acid condition. Acids rapidly corrode the metals ordinarily used in refrigeration and ice-making systems. Calcium chloride usually contains sufficient alkali to render the freshly prepared brine slightly alkaline. When any brine is exposed to air, it gradually absorbs carbon dioxide and oxygen, which neutralize the alkalinity and eventually make the salt brine slightly acid. Dilute salt brines dissolve oxygen more readily and generally are more corrosive than concentrated brines. One of the best preventive measures is to make a closed rather than open system, using a regulated inert gas over the surface of a closed expansion tank. However, many systems, such as icemaking tanks, brine spray unit coolers, and brine-spray-type carcass chill rooms, cannot be closed.

The degree of alkalinity or acidity of a salt brine or other secondary coolant can be expressed in pH value. In the pH scale, pH 7 represents the neutral point; values from 7 down represent increasing acidity, whereas values greater than 7 represent increasing alkalinity. A salt brine pH of 7.5 for a sodium or calcium chloride system is ideal, since it is safer to have a slightly alkaline rather than a slightly acid brine. Various chemical and electronic pH indicators are available. Every salt brine system operator should use an indicator regularly.

If a salt brine is acid, the pH can be raised by adding caustic soda that has been dissolved in warm water. If a salt brine is alkaline (indicating ammonia leakage into the brine), carbonic gas or chromic, acetic, or hydrochloric acid should be added. Ammonia leakage must be stopped immediately so that the brine can be neutralized.

In addition to controlling the pH, an inhibitor should be used. Generally, sodium dichromate is the most effective and economical for salt brine systems. The dichromate has a bright orange color, a granular form, and readily dissolves in warm water. Since it dissolves very slowly in cold brine, it should be dissolved in warm water and added to the brine far enough ahead of the pump so that only a dilute solution reaches the pump. The quantities recommended are: $2kg/m^3$ of calcium chloride brine, and $3.2 \ kg/m^3$ of sodium chloride brine.

Adding sodium dichromate to the salt brine does not make it noncorrosive immediately. The process is affected by many factors, including water quality, specific gravity of the brine, amount of surface and kind of material exposed in the system, age, and temperature. Corrosion stops only when protective chromate film has built up on the surface of the zinc and other electrically positive metals exposed to the brine. No simple test is available to determine the chromate concentration. Since the protection afforded by the sodium dichromate treatment depends greatly on maintaining the proper chromate concentration in the brine, brine samples should be analyzed annually. The proper concentration for calcium chloride brine is $0.13 \ g/L$ (as $Na_2Cr_2 \cdot 2H_2O$); for sodium chloride brine, it is $0.21 \ g/L$ (as $Na_2Cr_2O \cdot 2H_2O$)

Notes

①因可能引起腐蚀的氯化钙和氯化盐溶液被次级冷却系统广泛应用，故每个月要检测和调整盐溶液。

UNIT SIXTEEN

Text   Thermocouple Thermometry

[1]   Because of their many advantages, thermocouples have long been used extensively in both scientific research and industrial thermometry. They are inherently simple, consisting usually of two wires, a stable reference junction, and a potentiometer system. [1] More complex thermocouple systems may consist of many separate junctions or thermopiles, but the basic principles and instrumentation remain unchanged. They may be large (to allow mechanical and corrosion protection) or small (to provide rapid response time and small heat capacity). Small wires used in cryogenic systems are very fragile and flexible; the large wires used in furnaces are usually encased and are therefore rigid.

[2]   With careful design, thermometer encapsulations can withstand many types of corrosive atmospheres. Thermocouples can be used over a wide range of temperatures, from liquid helium (-270℃) to high-temperature furnaces (2200℃) However, different alloys are necessary for the extremes in temperatures. Many of the thermocouple combinations give a nearly linear output in a wide range of temperatures. This property leads to calibration and instrumentation methods that are both more simple and more accurate. Unlike the resistance thermometers, thermocouples have no self-heating effect. This is very important in precise calorimetry and in cryogenic research.

[3]   The number of potential thermocouple combinations is virtually infinite, but fortunately there has been a large amount of standardization. This standardization of types and thermometric values has led to the widespread availability, at reasonable cost, of largely interchangeable material from several different alloy manufacturers and many different instrumentation companies. [2]

[4]   And last, but not least, thermocouple systems are easy to instrument: portable potentiometers, laboratory galvanometers, recording potentiometers, and digital multimeters are all commonly used. The need for a stable reference junction may be negated for most applications by the insertion of a temperature-compensated junction; this is the most common industrial practice.

[5]   In 1821 Thomas Johann Seebeck discovered the existence of thermoelectric currents while experimenting on bismuth-copper and bismuth-antimony circuits. He showed that when the junctions of dissimilar metals are heated to different temperatures a net thermoelectric emf is generated. If the wires form a closed circuit, then a thermoelectric current is induced. Withina few years. Becquerel had demonstrated that a platinum-palladium couple could be used to measure temperature. About a decade later Jean Peltier discovered an unusual thermal effect when small, externally imposed currents were directed through the junctions of different thermocouple wires. When current flowed across a junction in one di-

rection, the junction was cooled; when the current flow was reversed, the same junction heated. With the aid of the newly developed theories of thermodynamics, William Thomson (later Lord Kelvin) was able to show that the two effects were related. He also derived the fundamental equations used to this day. ③Theories of thermoelectricity have since become quite refined and complex (though they are unnecessary for using thermocouples in practical applications) A classic for a modern discussion was written by MacDonald and a very thorough, but elementary, review has been prepared by Pollack for the American Society for Testing and Materials.

[6] One of the earliest combinations to have widespread usage was copper vs. constantan, now referred to as Type T. Another standard material with a long history is Chromel vs. Alumel, which is now one of the materials that comply with the standard values of Type K. The most commonly used high-temperature combinations have been platinum vs. platinum-rhodium alloys, Types S, R, and B. The platinum group is referred to as noble metal combinations; the others are called base metal types. In recent years several new materials have been developed and widely accepted. They include the tungsten-rheniums for very high temperatures, the gold-irons for cryogenic ranges, and Nicrosil vs. Visil for intermediate and moderately high temperatures.

[7] The fundamental principles necessary for understanding elementary thermoelectric circuits can be expressed in the following three laws that derive from the fundamental equations.

[8] "Law of homogeneous metals—a thermoelectric current cannot be sustained in a circuit of a single homogenous material, however varying in cross-section, by the application of heat alone."

[9] Therefore at least two different materials are required for a thermoelectric circuit. It should be noted that physical or chemical imperfections cause a material to be effectively inhomogeneous.

[10] "Law of intermediate metals—the algebraic sum of the thermoelectromotive forces [voltages] in a circuit composed of any number of dissimilar materials is zero if all of the circuit is at a uniform temperature."

[11] A third inhomogenous material can always be added to a circuit as long as it is in an isothermal region. Because of this law, one consequence is that the method of joining thermocouple wires, e.g., soldering, welding, clamping, mercury contact, etc., does not affect the thermoelectric output if the junction is isothermal. Another consequence is that if the thermoelectric voltages of two materials are known relative to a reference material, their voltages to each other may be determined additively. ④

[12] "Law of intermediate temperatures-if two dissimilar homogeneous metals produce a thermal emf of E_1, when the junctions are at temperatures T_1 and T_2, and a thermal emf of E_2, when the junctions are at T_2 and T_3, the emf generated when the junctions are at T_1 and T_3, will be E_1+E_2."

[13]   One result of this law is that thermocouples calibrated for one reference temperature can easily be corrected for another reference temperature. Another convenience resulting from this law is the availability of using extension wires without disturbing the resultant thermoelectric voltage.

New Words and Expressions

thermocouple *	['θə:məuˌkʌpəl]	n.	热电偶
thermometry *	[θə'mɔmətri]	n.	测温技术，温度测量
potentiometer *	[pəˌtenʃi'ɔmitə]	n.	电位差计
thermopile *	['θə:məupail]	n.	热电堆
cryogenic *	[ˌkraiəu'dʒenik]	a.	低温的
fragile	['frædʒail]	a.	脆
encase *	[in'keis]	vt.	装（包）在…内
encapsulation *	[en'kæpsəleiʃən]	n.	封装
helium	['hi:ljəm]	n.	氦
extreme	[iks'tri:m]	n.	极限值，极端状态
calibration *	['kælibreiʃən]	n.	标定
instrumentation	[ˌinstrumen'teiʃən]	n.	检测仪表
calorimetry *	[ˌkælə'rimitri]	n.	热计量
availability	[əveilə'biliti]	n.	可得性
instrument	['instrumənt]	v.	装备仪表
galvanometer	[ˌgælvə'nɔmitə]	n.	检流计
digital multimeter			数字万用表
negate *	[ni'geit]	v.	取消
insertion	[in'sə:ʃən]	n.	插入
temperature-compensated			温度补偿的
thermoelectric *	[ˌθə:məui'lektrik]	a.	热电的
bismuth-copper	['bizməθ'-kɔpə]		铋——铜
bismuth-antimony	['bizməθ-əen'timəni]		铋——锑
platinum-palladium	['plætinəm-pə'leidjəm]		铂——钯
induce *	[in'dju:s]	vt.	引起，诱发
refined	[ri'faind]	a.	严密的
copper vs. constantan	['kɔp-'və:səs-'kɔnstəntæn]		铜——康铜
chromel vs. Alumel	[krəuml-'və:səs-æljuməl]		镍铬——镍铝
platinum vs. platimum-rhodium			
['plætinəm-'və:ses'plætinəm-'rəudjəm]			铂－－铂铑
tungsten-rhenium	['tnŋstən-'ri:niəm]		钨——铼
Nicrosil vs. visil			镍铬硅——钒硅

143

homogeneous ＊	[ˌhɔməuˈdʒiːnjəs]	a.	均质的
cross-section			断面
sustain [səsˈtein]		vt.	维持，持续
algebraic sum	[ˌældʒiˈbreiik]		代数和
thermoelectromotive	[ˈθəːməuiˌlektrəˈməutiv]		热电势
isothermal ＊	[ˌaisəuˈθəːməl]	a.	等温的
solder [ˈsɔldə]		v.	钎焊
clamp [klæmp]		v.	紧固
additively [ˈæditivli]		ad.	相加地
resultant ＊	[riˈzʌltənt]	a.	总的
last but not least			最后但不是最不重要的

Notes

①consisting usually of two wires, a stable reference junction, and a petentiometer system.
现在分词短语作状语，表示进一步补充说明。
②at reasonable cost，作状语，插入 availability of … 词组中间，引起分离现象。
③used to this day   沿用至今。
④relative to reference material，形容词短语作定语修饰 thermoelectric
voltages of two materials，这是一种修饰语与被修饰语的分离现象。

Exercises

Reading Comprehension

Ⅰ.Choose the best answer for each of the following.
　1. Usually thermocouples consist of _____ .
　　　A. some wires and many separate junctions
　　　B. thermopiles and potentiometer systems
　　　C. two wires，a stable reference junction and a potentiometer system
　　　D. cryogenic systems and large wires
　2. Thermocouples are believed to _____ .
　　　A. be used only for high-temperature furnaces
　　　B. have no self-heating effect
　　　C. lead to calibration and instrumentation methods
　　　D. be of no importance in precise calorimetry
　3. The widespread availability of interchangeable material results from _____ .
　　　A. alloy manufacturers
　　　B. different instrumentation companies

C. standardization of types and thermometric values

D. potential thermocouple combinations

4. The most common industrial practice of thermocouple systems is _____ .

A. the insertion of a temperature-compensated junction

B. the use of a stable reference junction

C. no need for a stable reference junction

D. the use of portable potentiometers and galvanometers

5. Which of the following is not commonly used in thermocouple systems?

A. Resistance thermometers

B. Digital multimeters

C. Portable potentiometers

D. Laboratory galvanometers

II. Are the following statements true or false?

1. The existence of thermoelectric currents was first discovered by Jean Peltier and Willian Thomson.   ( )

2. The most commonly used high-temperature combinations are platinum vs. platinum-rhodium alloys.   ( )

3. The fundamental principles for understanding elementary thermoelectric circuits are expressed by law of intermediate metals law of intermediate temperatures.   ( )

4. Because of law of intermediate metal, the method of joining thermocouple wires does not affect the thermoelectric output, if all of the circuit is at a uniform temperature.

( )

5. One result of law of intermediate temperatures is that thermocouples calibrated for one reference temperature can easily be corrected for another reference temperature.

( )

Vocabulary

I. Fill in the blanks with some of the words or expressions listed below, changing the form where necessary.

induce	negate	homogenous	comply with
availability		reverse	derive from isothermal

1. The standardization of types and thermometric values offers the wide-spread _____ of largely interchangeable material from alloy manufactures and instrumentation companies.

2. For most applications people may _____ the need for a stable reference junction if a temperature-compensated junction is inserted.

3. When the current flowed across a junction in one direction, the junction was heated; when the current flow _____ , the same junction was cooled.

4. A thermoelectric current _____ after the wires form a closed circuit.

5. The three laws _____ the fundamental equations can express the fundamental principles necessary for understanding elementary thermoelectric circuits.

II. Complete each of the following statements with one of the four choices given below.

1. The application of heat alone cannot sustain a thermoelectric current in a circuit of a single _____ material.

A. homologous   B. homological   C. homogeneous   D. homogenous

2. The method of soldering, welding, clamping does not affect the thermoelectric output provided that the junction is _____ .

A. isothermal   B. isotropic   C. isotonic   D. isomorphic

3. Copper vs. constantan is one of the earliest combinations to have widespread usage and now _____ as Type T.

A. is preferred   B. is used   C. is found   D. is referred

4. If continuous indication or recording of flow rate is necessary, the venturi can combined with permanently mounted meters, recorders, or similar _____ .

A. instrument   B. instrumentation   C. encapsulation   D. calibration

5. Design and construction can vary in detail, depending upon the limits to which the boiler is built to _____ mandatory standards, dimensions and materials' specifications.

A. cope with   B. deal with   C. comply with   D. meet with

Translation

Directions:

Translate the following long involved sentences into Chinese.

1. In pursuance of this aim the author has considered it desirable to quote extensively from the works of the mathematicians of bygone days, for in that way alone can a just appraisal of the great difficulties under which they laboured be made.

2. Although such a rotor is of comparatively small diameter, its peripheral speed may be as high as 13000m/min; these two factors account for its proportions and form _____ with its shaft it often consists of a single steel forging which may be four or five times as long as its diameter.

3. The structure design itself includes two different tasks, the design of the structure, in which the sizes and locations of the main members are settled, and the analysis of this structure by mathematical or graphical methods or both, to work out how the loads pass through the structure with the particular members chosen.

4. The reason that a neutral body is attracted by a charged body is that, although the neutral body is neutral within itself, it is not neutral with respect to the charged body, and the two bodies act as if oppositely charged when brought near each other.

5. It should be also noted that the earth's influence is directive only and the compass is not pulled towards one part of the earth, since both ends of a small magnet are practically at the same distance from the earth's magnetic poles.

6. The development of rockets has made possible the achievement of speeds of several thousand miles per hour; and what is more important, it has brought within reach of these rockets heights far beyond those which can be reached by aeroplanes, and where there is little or no air resistance, and so it is much easier both to obtain and to maintain such speed.

Reading Material A

Venturi Mater

We now direct attention to venturi meters and standard flow tubes. [1] The venturi meter utilizes the basic engineering principle of Bernoulli. Fluid passing through the reduced area of the venturi throat increases in velocity, creating a pressure differential between the inlet and throat areas. After passing through the throat, the flow area is gradually increased, which decreases the velocity and allows pressure recovery. The differential pressure across the throat of the venturi can be read directly or easily translated into actual flow in gallons perminute by use of various types of differential pressure meters and capacity curves. Meter accuracy and reliability are based on Bernoulli's theorem, which provides the relationship between pressure differentials and velocity changes in various flow conditions. A properly calibrated venturi can provide accurate measurements within $\pm 0.5\%$ in all sizes.

A venturi will maintain its accuracy over an extremely long period of time. The venturi is a "self-cleaning" device. Its internal configuration, which permits smooth flow and efficient pressure recovery, eliminates erosion and resists clogging by foreign matter. As an example, hydronic system water is usually dirty, containing particles of foreign matter. Other devices using small orifices, spring loading, or glass readouts in bypass arrangements are not self-cleaning and can be adversely affected by clogging or corrosive action. Such a loss of accuracyover years of continuous operation can seriously affect the system, and maintenance efforts may be required later.

Maintenance of a venturi is virtually unnecessary. Venturis have no moving parts, no springs to fatigue, no glass to break or strain. They will remain in a piping system throughout its life, always available for quick meter attachment and ready measurement. [2] Venturis are also versatile, because they can provide permanent stations with fixed meters, or portable meters which can be carried to a number of stations. A variety of meter types can be supplied, depending on the application. Also the wide range of sizes and beta ratio permits the designer to select the venturi that will exactly suit the needs of system.

A significant advantage of the venturi is its low pressure loss, particularly compared to other devices. For example, a venturi with a 0.6 beta ratio has a pressure loss of only 15% of actual pressure differential compared to 50% with a flow nozzle and 63% with an orifice plate. In addition, pressure recovery is smooth and gradual within a minimum length of pipe after the fluid has passed through the throat area.

A typical flow measurement system can use one of more venturis as primary measuring devices; one or more meters which translate the pressure differential into actual flow rates; and associated fittings, hoses, or piping. A venturi can be installed at each point in any line where the flow rate should be checked. Two pressure taps are built into each venturi, one at a point near the narrowest part of the throat and one upstream. Each pressure tap includes a quick disconnect coupling and valve so that when portable meters are used they can be moved quickly from one venturi to another. If continuous indication or recording of flow rate is necessary, the venturi can be combined with permanently mounted meters, recorders, totalizers, or similar instrumentation.

To provide for various flow rates in each pipe size, venturis are available in several different beta ratios in each size. The beta ratio is a mathematical relationship between the inner diameter of the throat and the pipe. One should study the manufacturer's capacity curve. Each separate beta ratio has its own capacity or flow curve.

Notes

①现将注意力集中到文丘利流量计和标准流量管。
②文丘利流量计在整个使用期间装在管道系统上，它总是适合于快速装接和易于计量。

Reading Material B

Pitot Measurements of Dust

Observations are first made with the pitot tube to confirm the suitability of the chosen sampling position and to determine the values of the pitot pressure differences at the sampling points.

A probe holder is fitted on the pitot tube which is inserted into the flue, the by-pass or equalising valve at the inclined gauge being open and turned so that the impact hole faces upstream. [1] The by-pass valve is closed and the gauge read to establish the order of magnitude of the pitot pressure difference. As a precaution against blowing over the gauge liquid, the gauge should be set to the 0-500 N/m² range, but for the normal range of flue gas velocities the gauge readings will lie on the range 0-125 N/m². The zero setting of the gauge, which is different for each range, should be readjusted with the by-pass valve open. The levelling and the zero setting of the inclined gauge should be checked before every reading because under field conditions its mounting may easily be disturbed.

It will be found that the gauge reading is not constant but hovers irregularly about an average position to which the liquid level returns between fluctuations. The gauge should be watched for 10-30 s before reading the average position. It may sometimes be necessary to damp the fluctuations by inserting a length of fine-bore capillary tubing in the total head side but this will not usually be required for the ellipsoidal nose pitot tube described in Appendix 2. The fluctuations should not be damped out altogether (they can be as much as $\pm$ 30%) because the response of the gauge might then become inconveniently slow.

After the magnitude of the pitot pressure difference has been found and the appropriate range of the inclined gauge has been selected, the pitot tube should be used to establish whether the direction of flow is adequately parallel to the axis of the flue. The direction of flow may be inclined at an angle to the axis of the flue, for example after a bend, or it may be spiralling about the axis, for example after a cyclone-type gas cleaner.[2] The first may be detected by tilting the pitot head at various angles to the axis of the flue (after temporarily withdrawing the probe holder from the access socket) If the pitot pressure difference increases by more than a third on tilting through an angle of 20°, the flow is insufficiently parallel to the axis and another sampling position should be chosen. The presence of spin may be detected by placing the pitot head near the wall and turning the pitot tube (held in the probe holder) about its axis. If the flue gases are spinning, the pitot pressure difference will show a maximum when the head is inclined at an angle to the axis of the flue. Spin is also indicated if the pitot pressure difference (with the head parallel to the axis) is zero or negative at the centre of the flue but increases as the walls are approached.

In all subsequent measurements the pitot head should be aligned parallel with the axis of the flue, even though a higher reading is obtained if it is tilted.

A traverse should be carried out along each line of insertion to see whether there are any dead spaces (zero pitot pressure difference) or regions of reversed flow (a positive reading when the pitot head is directed downstream) It is sufficient to take 'snap' readings of the inclined gauge at ten or so equally-spaced points across the flue (for example every 100 mm in a 1 m diameter flue) It is not necessary to take accurate readings or record them but merely to note whether they change systematically from one side of the flue to the other and that there is no dead space nor a reversed flow. The operation will take only a few minutes. It is important to note that there is no reason to reject a sampling position when there is a considerable variation of the flue gas velocity across the flue so long as the traverse has shown a systematic change.

Notes

①取样探头的支托固定在插入烟道的毕托管上，在倾斜计上的旁通或均压阀开着或者开到脉冲总压孔朝向上游。

②气流方向可能对烟道轴线有一倾斜角，如在弯管后方，或者会围绕轴线呈螺旋形前进，如在 旋风式除尘器后方。

Appendix I　Vocabulary

154

155

Appendix Ⅱ   Translations for Reference

第 1 单元

利用天然气的新领域

新技术的发展使开拓燃气新的应用领域成为可能。在燃气工业史上，一次又一次的技术革新为燃气使用的几个主要方面带来了重要的变化。最为明显的变化就是把燃气的主要用途从用于照明转为厨房烹饪，又从烹饪转向取暖。在 25 年期间，亦即本文所研究的这段时期，在新的技术发展的基础上有可能开发天然气的一些新用途，从而有可能对燃气的需求产生明显的影响。变化着的经济、技术和社会需求究竟会怎样形成天然气新的应用领域？对这个问题，很难、甚至不可能作出任何明确的预言。然而，确认目前的研究领域和技术趋势从而提供未来的某种可能性却是可以做到的。

在今后 25 年中，人们也许主要关注四种技术：燃料电池，联合循环发电，用作汽车燃料的压缩天然气，变燃气为汽油或变燃气为中间馏份的转化加工。燃料电池和联合循环发电能提供高效而不污染环境的电能，很具有吸引力。压缩天然气和变燃气为合成燃料的转化加工，也许使燃气在某些国家运输部门的能源供应上占一重要席位。

燃料电池技术在 80 年代中期仍处于研究和示范阶段。简单地说，燃料电池是用天然气为进料，通过一种逆向电解产生电能（不必燃烧天然气）；天然气中的氢通过电化学作用与氧化合，产生电和可用的热。燃料电池的优点之一就是能迅速增大或减小能量，以满足负载的需要，净洁度和能源效率 50%（与现代水平的常规发电约 40% 相比）。在德国、日本和美国研究工作仍在进行。据一些主要的工业厂家认为，其性能会相当可靠，能确保实用型电池的工程开发。用于工业和商业上的小型现场用的燃料电池被认为是最有可能开发的途径。

利用天然气联合循环发电的方法，已进入开发和商业化的高级阶段。由燃气驱动的涡轮机和蒸汽轮机联合，并利用从烟气回收的热量，可使发电时的转化效率提高。这一点对相当广泛的用户来说很具有经济上的吸引力。在美国，燃气用于联合循环已在工业联合发电上颇受欢迎，其经济性主要取决于燃气和电力在工业上的相对价格。但是也同样取决于向联合发电厂为公共电网提供的过剩电能所支付的费用水准。正如其他所有的新技术一样，联合循环将扩大到多大范围？在动力生产部门，燃气如果会取代其他燃料的话，又会在多大程度上取代？这一切都是很难给出具体数字的。

压缩天然气作为一种汽车燃料并非新技术。早在 20 世纪 30 年代就在意大利形成了。用压缩天然气驱动的汽车已在意大利、新西兰等国行驶，并在荷兰、加拿大和美国的实验汽车队中使用。在世界范围内，由压缩天然气驱动的汽车有 300,000 到 400,000 辆之多。压缩天然气作汽车燃料在经济上的好处主要取决于相应的燃料价格和燃料税收政策。正是这些因素而非技术革新最终决定市场的大小。在现存的税收政策下和目前所假定的燃料价格的情况下，不能预计有很大的增长。

由两个主要的跨国石油公司获得专利的用天然气生产合成液体燃料（汽油、煤油或粗柴油）的加工过程，在技术上已经可行。在经济合作和发展组织（OECD）的范围内，近期内并未存在使这些技术进一步商业化的发展前景。但是，在马来西亚提出了把燃气转化为粗柴油的转化工程项目。总的来说，这些技术作为开发利用偏远地区储气构造的手段，最为合适，否则那些资源也许只能白白地埋在地底下。对于大部分石油燃料产品都靠国外进口的国家来说，这些技术更具有吸引力。在大多数经济合作和发展组织的成员国里，除了新西兰这一明显的例外，燃气储量与已经开发的或潜在的市场比较接近，这就意味着燃气随时有可供选择的销路。这也许会在经济合作和发展组织范围内限制了使用这些技术的项目的可能性。然而，在发展中国家，这些技术也许会为开发能源和进行技术转让提供一个有益的机遇。

第 2 单元

反应动力学

如有足够时间允许建立平衡，则热力平衡常数 K 表示在给定条件下一定的反应向右进行的程度。小 K 值意味着向生成物的转化很小。大 K 值表明了大的平衡转化量。放热反应有自发性倾向。这样，碳在含氧气氛中可望自发氧化，实际情况也确实如此。但是，氧化的速度在环境条件下通常很慢，以致可认为是零。在高温下，氧化速度增快，所释放出来的热有助于进一步提高温度，从而又进一步增加氧化速度。最终温度稳定在某一数值上。这个数值由氧化系统的热损失率和向碳输送的反应用氧的速率来确定。

在另一方面，只有从外部热源向反应系统供给吸热的热量而使温度升高时，吸热反应才能以较快的速度进行。因此，吸热反应不可能认为是自发的，也不可能有上述那种自供热反应。石墨的蒸气气化就是一个很好的例子。在石墨的蒸气气化中，反应是高度吸热的，并表明平衡常数在室内温度下很小，以致在这一温度下碳向一氧化碳的平衡转化量实际上为零。然而，随着温度增高，热力平衡常数很快增大，而反应的吸热几乎保持不变。很明显，温度的增高至少从两个方面使碳向 CO 的转化更容易：有利于较大的平衡转化；随温度增高而增大转化速度。

这种讨论不可避免地得出这样的结论：热力学平衡常数与所给定反应的动力学有关。此外，既然我们主要是讨论气相和固相之间的相互作用，扩散效应必须加以考虑。因此，当碳在含氧气氛中燃烧时，在碳氧化之前，氧必须扩散到碳界面上。在氧从空气扩散到这种界面过程中，由于来自界面的气体混合物中氧的耗尽，在靠近界面处有氮气聚集的趋向。因此，扩散到界面的氧和从界面扩散出来的一氧化碳和二氧化碳必须找到各自通过未反应过的和"滞止的"氮分子膜的路径。稳定膜对反应物和生成物的扩散形成阻力，这种膜被气体和固体之间的较高的相对速度所减薄。在极限范围内，气体的高相对速度冲刷滞止膜的厚度（即阻力），使其在外形表面趋近于零，但是它不可能影响反应固体微孔结构中碰到的类似膜阻力。

为了研究包含在煤和其他碳氢化合物的蒸气和氢气气化中的各种反应，进行了大量动力学考察，并且出版了大量的文献。大多数作者持这种观点：在煤的蒸气和氢气气化中，初始反应速度比后来的残炭的转化速度明显地要快得多。Johnson 假定整个气化过程有三个顺序阶段：（1）脱去挥发分；（2）甲烷快速形成；（3）低气化速率。三个阶段的反应是独立的。他进一步假设：碳以两种形式出现，一种称作"基"碳，另一种是挥发性物质中的碳。挥发性碳只能通过高温分解才释放出来，与发生反应的气体介质无关。在脱挥发分作用完成后，基碳仍留在煤炭里。接着这种碳或在甲烷快速形成阶段气化，或在低速气化阶段被气化。

当在高压下有含氢气体存在时，发生脱挥发分作用。这时含有挥发物的煤或煤炭，除了热高温分解反应外，还呈现出对甲烷形成的高度活性。以良好时间分辩率进行的研究表明：甲烷快速形成速度至少比脱挥发分作用慢一个数量级。这可以解释为甲烷快速形成发生在脱挥发分作用之后。

在瞬态的高活性期间，碳气化为甲烷的数量随氢气分压的增高而显著地增加。证据表明：在足够高的氢分压条件下，在脱挥发分作用期间，未释放出来的全部碳实际上能够通过此过程很快被气化为甲烷。

脱挥发分反应在大约 700°F 的温度下开始，随着温度达到 1300°F，其速度持续提高。在 1300°F 温度下，速度被认为基本上是瞬时性的。这些速率实际上是由温度，压力和脱挥发分过程中的气体组成所决定的。在脱挥发分作用和甲烷快速形成阶段完成以后，碳以很低的速度气化。这种残炭气化的新的缓慢速度由温度、压力、气体组成、碳转化和先前的历程所决定，特别是根据温度来决定的。

第 3 单元

工业通风原理

通风的目的是为了使建筑物内的空气保持某种规定状态及其清洁度，即保持温度、空气速度和浓度。

归根结底，达此目的解决办法是：把污浊的空气从建筑物排出（抽气通风），而通常将特殊处理的干净空气引入屋内取而代之（进气通风）。

从本质上讲，这可归结为进入建筑物的空气和现存空气之间的热量和质量传输。如果由于内部热量的过度产生，建筑物内的空气温度趋向于超过规定的标准，将较冷的空气引入，并和室内空气混合，使空气温度（由于热传输）保持为标准值。如果有害气体或蒸气释放出来，则用清洁空气冲淡，使浓度保持在规定的极限范围之内。

质量传递和热量传递往往同时发生。例如，对流热的产生常常伴随着各种气体和高度分散的灰尘的释放。通风可由风机作用（机械通风），或由内部气柱和外部气柱的密度之差作用，也可以是由风的作用（自然通风）。

通风可以是全面的，或是局部的。局部抽气通风旨在从污染源处排除被污染的空气，防止污杂物散布到整个建筑物。将尽可能多的污杂物以这种方式排除，以使只是最小量的污染空气要用送入的空气冲淡。局部排风实际上不是真正的通风。

因此，局部通风限制了散布的范围。这种方法辅助以固定屏板，或空气幕。污染物通过抽走污染空气而得以排除。这可以与把污杂物驱向抽气口的空气射流相结合。

如果把空气引入建筑物，则室内就形成某种超压。在稳定状态下，当通过专设的通风孔或建筑物外表上不规则的裂缝而排出的空气总量和引入屋内的空气总量相等时，便保持一定的压力。从建筑物抽排空气也会产生同样情况。这时，建筑物内形成负压（稀薄），导致通过空隙从外部和相邻房间吸入空气来取代抽走的空气。

在某些情况下，这种空气有不利的影响。例如，如果外部冷空气进入有大量水蒸气生成的建筑物，则在与屋内的热而湿润的空气混合时会产生薄雾。如果从外部流入，或从相邻房间流入的空气能满足卫生要求，那么可以利用自然通风取代全面的机械通风。

通风实质上是控制建筑物内换气的一门科学。

在解决通风课题时，会出现以下问题：（1）单位时间内应该有多大量的空气供入建筑物内？（2）进入的空气应该具有何种特征？空气的预先处理是否有必要（加热、冷却、除湿、调节、除尘）？（3）进风口和排风口应该如何布局？（4）应该如何设计限定换气率的各种要素？

为了解决全面通风问题，必须了解单位时间内进入建筑物空气中污染物的量。了解污染物在建筑物内是如何散布的，同时通风怎样影响其分布等问题也是很重要的。

把空气从污染物浓度高的区域排出去可大大减少通风所需的空气量。例如，在铸铁车间上部一氧化碳可能是 $0.04g/m^3$，而在工作区就不应超过允许的标准 $0.02g/m^3$。这种浓度分层现象是靠在地面上供给新鲜空气，并从高处抽走污浊空气来保持的。假定在靠近天花板供入新鲜空气，当它下沉时，会打乱浓度分层现象，并与污浊空气混合，且以同样多的换气量，使工作区的一氧化碳的浓度为 $0.03g/m^3$。为了获得 $0.02g/m^3$ 的浓度，必须增加约 1.5 倍的通风空气量。因此，预测通风空气量与通风的配置有直接关系。

为了计算和设计喷淋式的局部通风，必须了解射流的性质，控制射流速度、温度、浓度和几何尺寸等变化的规律。为了使工作区空气符合卫生规定的参数，首先要掌握空气初始参数，然后选择喷嘴形式，使其生成满足上述要求的射流。

第 4 单元

相似性与实验方法

由于空气的自然和强制对流及其循环流动，建筑物内空气处于运动状态。从而使各种蒸气、气体、热量和微尘得以传递和散布开来。

速度和浓度场不是相互独立的。因此，这两者被看成是不同性质而又相互关联过程的集合体。而相互关联的过程受到质量和能量守恒通用定律的支配。解决这些问题的初始方程式是下列微分方程：（1）连续方程；（2）运动方程；（3）传热或传质方程；（4）固体物质和流体之间边界上的热交换方程。

这些微分方程可应用于范围很广的各种现象，例如大气层空气的运动，河流中水的运动，等等。为了对问题进行限定，并单值地规定其过程，对于那些稳定状态的现象必须阐明临界条件，亦即所需要的函数值，这些数值事先知道并足以求微分方程的唯一解。

在大多数情况下，数学分析的应用对解决复杂的技术问题被局限于问题的公式化，即列出微分方程式并确定边界条件，因为解这些方程式在大多数情况下仍然是不切实际的。由于通风现象极为复杂，不可能有分析解。因此，在解决通风问题时，人们往往必须求助于实验和测试。

有时候，必要的实验可以在实际条件下进行。在其他情况下，就得在模型上对现象进行研究。为了通过模型来研究通风，人们必须再现往往同时作用的空气动力的、热力的和分子的过程，以便确定保证通风有效性的实际参数是什么，即确定空气的速度、温度和气体浓度。

实验室模型试验法比原型真实条件下的研究考察具有更多的优越性，即在开发阶段有可能进行装置研究；有可能对某些特定因素在独立于所有其他制约整个现象的因素情况下所产生的影响进行系统的研究；使得对那些在自然环境实地观察中弄不明白的快速变化的各种现象的研究成为可能。此外，实验室的模型研究比现场研究的费用少。在原型或模型上进行实验时，人们研究特殊现象，然后将研究结果进行一般化，以便找到计算其他有关情况的根据。

只有是将单项测试结果推广到类似的情况才是合理的。在实际条件下，怎样将单项试验的研究结果推广到其他条件中去？如何将模型实验结果转用于实际条件？这均是相似论讲授的内容。人们可区分几何相似、力学相似和热相似。

众所周知，几何相似是与不同几何形状体中角度相等和相关边的比例有关。

力学相似可理解为现象的运动学或动力学相似。运动学相似的先决条件是两股流的速度与加速度之间的成比例关系。力学相似以产生相似运动的各种力的相似性为前提。

在热相似中，温度和热流仍然是相似的。

相似理论指出：

1. 彼此类似现象具有完全相同的相似准则（无量纲数组）。

2. 表征某一现象的某些变量之间的任何关系，可表示为相似准则之间的关系。

3. 对于那些相似的现象，边界条件相似，并且相似准则在数值上完全相同。

相似理论表明：在测试中有必要去测量所有那些包含在相似准则中的量，而且将测试结果通过无量纲量或数组来进行处理。

单项测试的数据可以扩展到类似的现象，即，其他具有类似边界条件的现象，只要由边界条件中的量组成的无量纲数组（相似准则）在数字上完全相同。当热源、湿源、有害蒸气、气体和灰尘出现而需换气时，模型方法可以研究机械的、自然的或联合的全面通风和局部通风。

当有必要对不同的通风系统作出对比评价和对防风屋顶间隔的空气动力特征描述时，以及当在很多其他情况下，分析解法特别困难时，得求助于模拟方法。在研究如何解决通风中人们所面临的非常复杂的各种问题时，模拟是一种可靠的方法。

模拟通风现象的工作介质可以是空气和水。这两者都有自己的长处和不足，用空气的模化技术比较简单。

第5单元

自然通风及其应用范围

由于风和室内外空气密度差的结果，建筑物里产生自然换气。如不加以控制，这样的自然渗入是不规则的。如果设计出一种配置能在多变的室外条件下保持所希望的室内空气状态，这种过程才能合理地称作"通风"。

温度差和风速能引起大量的空气传输。例如，测定结果表明：在平炉车间或轧钢厂，自然换气量可达约 0.2 亿每小时公斤。在锻工车间，炼铁厂和其他高温车间里，空气传输量也许会有数兆公斤每小时。

利用机械方式使如此大量空气流动需要消耗大量的能源。自然通风的最大的经济上的重要意义，就在于它不必消耗机械能即可产生大量换气。

需要解释自然通风的益处和证实其应用的合理性的时代早已过去。证据很简单而且富有说服力，都是通过机械通风和自然通风对比后得出的。在高温车间里，主要着重于机械通风，而把自然换气视为不重要而根本不予考虑。在所有的测试中发现，自然换气的体积超过机械通风量的很多倍。这表明，尽管全面机械通风的装置大，且运行费用高，但其作用是微不足道的。在这些情况下，机械通风最好是以空气幕和局部送排风的形式作为对自然通风的一种补充。

每年的高温季节几乎每个工业部门都可以利用自然通风。只有少数几种工业企业，因为技术上的原因，要对空气作预处理，无法利用自然通风。在单跨车间，户外空气通过墙脚的通气孔进入屋内，而车间里的污浊空气通过屋顶天窗排出。在多跨车间，单单用墙上的通风孔是不够的，因为在远离外墙的工作区的通风，需要通过屋顶凸窗之间的空隙从屋顶引入更多的空气。在这种布置方式中，需要利用这些空隙获得良好的进气，并交替安置冷热跨。户外空气通过冷跨的屋顶开口处进入建筑物，然后分散到相邻的热跨中去。冬季自然通风需确定，室内过量的热足以对预计空气量进行加热，并且除了屋顶凸窗的开口以外，还有一系列的进冷空气的通气孔（高出地面5至7m）。计算这些通气孔的高度时，要确保进入的空气从此高度降到工作区时通过与室内暖空气混合而被加热。

自然换气首先适用于有大量热量释放的高温车间，即高炉，平炉，轧钢车间，锻工车间，铸造车间，热处理车间，锅炉房，发动机间等。正如上文所提及的，全面自然通风与局部机械通风相互结合，在这些情况下常常是特别有用。

自然通风的有效程度取决于很多因素。这些因素不仅在规划建筑物时而且在使用建筑物时都必须加以考虑。

成功地控制工业房屋自然通风所依靠的主要因素是热源的布局和位置，建筑物的设计（跨数、屋顶的式样和形状），墙和屋顶凸窗通风口的安排等。若建筑师和工程师共同协作，并在设计阶段除了考虑必须满足工业企业的大量而又复杂的要求以外，还要重视自然通风问题，这样才能获得令人满意的解决方法。

很多现存的工业厂房早在厂房设计阶段就提供了自然通风，并且自使用以来一直是令人满意的。另一方面，在房屋设计时没有充分重视自然通风的情况很多。这种忽视正在付出昂贵的代价。

为了阐明自然通风的问题，我们首先讨论在单跨和多跨建筑物里热源对由它产生的气流的影响。而且也要考虑风对建筑物的影响和由此而形成的压力分布。

鉴于这些现象的理论研究的极端复杂性，最好是借助两维和三维模型，利用空气或水作工作介质进行实验研究。

第 6 单元

粉尘的形成

工业上产生大量粉尘的工艺过程有：破碎（选矿）、制粉、喷砂，或将散料从一个输送带转到另一个输送带的运输过程。在下述一些机加工时也会产生粉尘：粗磨、细磨或抛光，打亚麻、清棉花和铸工车间中的脱模等。在喷漆时，粉尘是由溶剂和颜料的微滴形成的。在酸洗、镀铬和电解的过程中，会产生"气泡"，也就是那种充满氢气的球状液体薄壳。在空气流上升时，薄壳破裂，形成的极为细小的颗粒，其组成大多数是酸洗槽的酸性溶液。

空气中的含尘量，以可用单位体积中粉尘的重量（mg/m^3）来表征，或者以每 cm^3 中所含的颗粒数来表示。为了给粉尘下一完整的定义，这两个量都必须知道。

根据苏联工业厂房设计的卫生标准，工作场所空气中的无毒粉尘含量，对于含有百分之十以上石英的粉尘或石棉粉尘，不得超过 $2mg/m^3$，对于其他的无毒粉尘，最大限量是 $10mg/m^3$。

粉尘对工作人员的健康是有害的。举例来说，大家都知道，长期吸入大量含有二氧化硅（SiO_2）或石棉的粉尘会分别导致矽肺病和石棉肺病。含有二氧化硅的石英砂与河砂在铸造工厂被用作型砂和砂芯，并用于铸件的喷砂，还作为生产陶器、玻璃和瓷器的主要原材料。

从排气孔和通风设施排放出来的工业粉尘造成厂区周围及生活区的大气污染。在大气中，粉尘吸收大量阳光，在城区由于尘粒充当水蒸气凝结的核而产生烟雾。此外，在一定条件下可能会因某些粉尘而造成火灾与爆炸的危险。

通常，工业粉尘是由不同物质颗粒构成的混和物，有时，由某特种物质占主体。各种类型的粉尘在物理性质上也有所不同，即：颗粒的大小、密度、形状、密实度、电荷、吸附能力，可燃性和爆炸性。

在工业条件下，粉尘云团中颗粒的大小很不一样，从零点几 μ 到 100μ 以上。尘粒大小的分布取决于粉尘的起源、机械加工形式和暴露程度等。

粉尘颗粒可有三种基本形状，亦即：层片状、纤维状和颗粒状。通常，工业粉尘是这三种形状的混合体，还有大量介于三者之间的粉尘。粉尘颗粒大小、形状、密度和电荷是至关重要的性质，它们决定了室内粉尘颗粒的特点。这些性质在技术上，以及在卫生方面都是很重要的。从技术方面看，这些特性影响到在尘源处对粉尘的收集以及从空气中除去粉尘。大颗粒的粉尘很快沉降。几十微米大小的重颗粒不会进入人的呼吸器官。轻的、纤维状的、针状的粉尘，还有冷凝而成的松散絮凝状的粉尘都可以在空气中长时间悬浮，缓慢沉降。

一般认为，可以吸入肺里的粉尘大部分可达到 $5\mu m$。最大可达 $10\mu m$。较大的粉尘颗粒沉积在上呼吸道的粘膜上（鼻腔和喉咙）。尺寸小于 $5\mu m$ 的颗粒对肺部细胞的影响是最危险的。

当代卫生界权威人士并不认为，$0.5\sim0.25\mu m$ 或再小的粉尘颗粒相对地无害。有理由相信，如果这些颗粒不滞留在鼻腔里，则它们将深入肺细胞。

调查结果表明，在工业厂房空气中占主体的是 $10\mu m$ 以下的颗粒，有 $40\%\sim90\%$ 小于 $2\mu m$。无机矿物质和金属粉尘中小于 $2\mu m$ 的颗粒的百分比要大于有机动植物粉尘中这类颗粒的百分比。

尺寸小于 $0.1\mu m$ 的颗粒受到不规则的布朗运动的影响。这类颗粒要么以曲折路线非常缓慢地沉降（颗粒半径为 $0.1—0.05\mu m$），要么就根本不沉降（半径为 $0.001\mu m$ 或更小的），参加空气分子的运动，全方位扩散。尘团中颗粒尺寸分布随时发生变化。各种不同因素都会使颗粒凝聚，从而迅速沉降。颗粒的凝聚速度取决于它们的均匀性，形状及电荷。如果其他情况相同，则对于较大尺寸的颗粒来讲，凝聚更快。在多分散性系统中比在均匀系统中凝聚得要快，因为较大颗粒可以充当较小颗粒凝聚的核心。分散度高的粉尘含有带电荷的颗粒，有些带正电荷，同一物质的另一些颗粒带负电荷。具有相同电荷的颗粒相互排斥，但感应作用经常将相斥转变成相吸，带有相反电荷的颗粒更易凝聚。

每个粉尘微粒被所吸附的空气层所包围，其分压力在颗粒表面较大，然后迅速降到周围空气的压力。由于这个原因，有些细小的粉尘在长时间存放后不会结块，而像液体一样流动。

被吸附的空气体积可能是吸附空气的粉尘体积的很多倍。举例说，一升的烟灰可能有 $950cm^3$ 被吸附的空气，在常温和常压下，仅 $50cm^3$ 的烟灰所吸附的空气将占 2.50 升。由此可知，烟灰颗粒周围的空气受到更大的压缩。这样被空气覆盖的粉尘颗粒只显示出很小的凝聚倾向。

粉尘按尺寸分类是通过一套从 $42\mu m$ 以上的网筛进行筛选而完成的。不同粒级的重量百分比是对筛余物进行称重而决定的。小于 $42\mu m$ 的细小粉尘粒在空气淘选器中处理，这种淘选器可用来确定个别粒级的重量百分数，还可根据其沉降速度对这些粒级进行分类。

第7单元

空气喷淋

空气喷淋是向人吹的局部气流。与任务是在整个建筑物内保持规定的空气条件的全面通风不同，局部气流（如空气喷淋）的目的是在建筑物内的一块或几块地方创造一种特殊的空气条件。例如，在固定的工作地点，或是人们长时聚集的地方，也可能是休息场所。因此，其用意是，通过气流的作用，在一个限定空间内保持特定的条件。这些条件必须满足规定的卫生与生理要求。

空气喷淋应该用于以下地方：

1. 如果不可能通过全面通风来获得所需效果，像锅炉房、发动机房、发电站和联合热电站上的一些控制岗位；

2. 当所需要的条件虽然可以通过全面通风达到，但却必需以极高的费用使用大量空气。例如，在大型的干燥室里只有几个工人工作，在这样的情况下，空气喷淋的作用从技术角度来看也是合宜的，因为任何全面降低气温的做法都会大量损失干燥设备的热能，从而增加燃料的消耗。

在很多情况下，在强辐射的条件下作业，而全面通风不能维持所需要的温度与湿度，从而保持自然的热量调整（人体与周围介质之间的正常传热），此时用空气喷淋可改善条件。这种方式适用于冶金和重型机械工厂（靠近炉子、滚轧机、气锤、压力锻机等处需设空气喷淋），以及玻璃制品厂，印染厂和面包房等地。

当通过窗扉进入的自然风不足以供给某些特殊工作场所的需要时（在锻造、铸造和热处理车间等），空气喷淋还被应用于许多设有自然通风的工场。

当自然送风不能进行预处理（加热、冷却等）时，空气喷淋显得特别重要。喷淋用的空气预处理费用低，喷淋所需空气量仅是整个自然换气量的一小部分。

最后，在室外气温高的地区的热车间里，当全面通风（自然的或机械的）使室内气温仍然高于室外温度3-5℃时，空气喷淋可以用预先冷却的室外空气在工作区提供舒适的条件。

值得指出的是，在全面机械通风的情况下，送风必须直接指向工作场所，亦即供气应符合任何局部通风的要求。所以，进风口的位置与形状，气流的速度和温度等必须遵守在工作区为达到所需环境条件的要求（即：规定的空气温度和速度分布以及污染物的浓度）。

人们可以用空气喷淋来改变工作区空气的速度、温度和湿度，以及空气中杂质的浓度。

在其他参数不变的情况下改变速度最为简单。这可以通过使建筑物内的空气流动的风扇来完成。

工作区空气的温度、湿度和浓度可以通过从室外供气来改变，如果必要的话，室外空气要进行预处理。

空气的运动可以增进人体热量的散失，这对在辐射热的条件下作业尤为重要。热量的散失还可以通过低温送风（与室内周围温度相比而言）来强化，有时还可以靠喷水来降温。水滴落在物体和衣服的外露部分，然后蒸发，产生附加降温。为热车间设计空气喷淋时，首先要力求通过自然通风来降低空气的温度。

对高温车间设计空气喷淋时，尤其要尽量通过自然通风来降低空气温度。

对在辐射热的条件下作业来讲，需考虑下列因素：

a、在固定地点的辐射强度，作业地点不固定，则以经常工作的地方为准；

b、在工作区不同地段连续暴露在辐射下的时间和中断的时间（辐射和所做工作的性质）；

c、是否人体的某些特殊部位连续暴露在辐射之下，是否由于改变作业位置，整个身体表面依次被照射。

如同在生产条件下所进行的大量考察所确立的那样，有热辐射的工作场所必须做到：

1. 首先在工人遭受辐射时间最长的区域布置空气喷浴，即使这里的辐射强度低于别的地方（两个因素都要考虑到，即热辐射的辐照量和强度）。

2. 如果人体的上半部（胸部、脖颈和头部）受到辐射时，要考虑到人体能够承受的热负荷最低。因此，人体的这些部位要首先置于空气射流之下。

气流要正对着人体受辐射时间长的部位，虽然气流也要尽量散布到人体的其他部位。

在选择射流的方向时，如果进风口设置在热源，例如，炉口附近，则必须考虑到烟、火焰、火花，甚至热空气会被卷吸入射流的可能性。因此，射流方向应该是先入射到工作场所，然后再遇到热源与污物源，这样可将污物吹离作业地点。同时，还必须注意到，不要把杂质吹向邻近的工作区。

在夏季，空气的冷却对于空气喷淋的效果来讲是非常重要的。最便宜的冷却方法是用在封闭回路中循环的水将空气加湿。

在作业点，射流的宽度应为 $1.0\sim1.2m$，当射流需担负更大的面积的情况例外。

第 8 单元

舒适与不舒适

环境工程师和建筑师的目标之一就是要确保建筑中的舒适条件。在一个不舒适的环境中，只能使身体的局部或是临时地获得热舒适。长时间的连续不断的热舒适感是不可能有的。我们只能将舒适这一概念理解为无不适之感而已；这似乎是一个令人沮丧的定义，但是，它毕竟代表了一种现实的要求。

人在特别热或特别冷的时候，会有到一种全面的热不舒适感觉。另外，还有一些使人局部不舒适的潜在原因，如脚冷或有穿堂风。

要想达到舒适，就必须将这些不舒适的方式与环境的物理变量联系起来，以便制定出这些变量的允许范围。惯用的作法是通过人的热感觉来衡量总体的热不舒适感。

至于其他形式的不舒适是不可能简单地以总体热感觉的尺度为根据来确定的。很可能出现热中性状态，既不想提高温度，也不想降低温度，但由于环境中的某些不均匀性人们仍是不舒适。例如：有穿堂风或辐射不对称。发现一个人是否舒适最直接的办法是问他。在一般情况下询问的主题是让他确定自己是否舒适或者温度条件是否可以接受。可以预计，不同的人可能在不同的外界影响作用下变得不舒适，因此，如果把一些声称不舒适的人按照受到刺激的程度按比例标记下来，我们就可以画出一条这种状态的曲线。这是一种理想的表达方式，因为这一信息的终端用户可以确定哪些不舒适因素使哪一部分人不舒适，从而考虑控制这些不舒适因素所需的费用。

在实际工作中，我们怎样才能获得这么准确的表达方式呢？通过实验室研究，对可能引起不舒适的刺激因素的控制与测量，可以达到任何所要求的精确程度。比如，这种刺激可能是辐射不对称，可以将一个受验者依次置于几种不同的辐射不对称的条件下，而其他的环境状态保持不变。在这样的情况下问他是否舒适。在足够多的受验者经过不同程度的辐射不对称实验以后，这一条曲线的形状就被画出来了。

这一实验的范例为许多人能够在舒适的环境下工作提供了基础，但是也存在着一些不足。受验者在做出舒适与不舒适判断的时候，实验室里的周围环境是他所不熟悉的，受到刺激的时间也是有限的。尔后，这一实验的成果可能被运用到在正常环境中工作的一群人身上。这样就忽略了一个事实，即：一个人所做出判断在很大程度上要依赖于先后环境变化。比如，直晒阳光所产生的辐射不对称的程度远远超过使人们不满意的辐射取暖装置，但是，人们却寻找阳光，喜欢阳光。人们抱怨，现代化的办公室普遍存在穿堂风问题。但是，即便是轻轻走路，所产生的通过身体的气流速度也要大于1m/s，这常常被认为是穿堂风很严重的情况，但是：没有人抱怨自己走路所产生的风有什么不舒服。对于刺激的反应取决于周围的整体环境和人的思想准备。

一个典型的例子就是量级分布效应。当一个观察者经历了一个分布域的刺激量之后，如果让他将这些刺激量在等级尺度上评定，他趋向于把刺激量从分布域的中间放到评定尺度的中间几级，以此来评定刺激量的大小。这一点在噪声接受能力实验中清楚地表现出来。暴露在一声级分布域的受验者倾向于将可接受与不可接受的界线放在他们所听到噪声分布域的中间位置。所以，经常暴露在强噪声下的人比暴露在弱噪声下的人明显地能承受更大的噪声。量级分布效应不能仅适用于由实验者所提供的刺激量分布域。人们根据自己的一般经验，各有自己的标准，将新刺激量与此标准进行比较。因此，舒适与不舒适这些词的含义是没有绝对评价的，是相对个人的经验与期望而言的。加吉等（1967年）把一些年轻人放入48℃的环境试验室中，这些人把这种环境评定为稍微不舒适。有一点怀疑，同样的环境在办公室内也许会被认为是不可忍受的。然而，受验者知道自己是在生理实验室里，期望着出汗，并不强烈反对这种体验。

然而，他们的舒适评价显然不能转用于不同境况。可接受的标准是由人们所习惯的刺激量的分布域来确定的。波尔顿（1977年）指出：这意味着，提供一个能够使人们普遍接受的环境这一目标将永远可望而不可及。如果人们根据自身的经验对（环境的）可接受性做出判断，那么，随着综合水准的降低，最大可接受性水准也会随之降低。如果一个地区总的噪声水准降低了，那么，不能被接受的噪声水准也会随之降低。因此，任何时候，那个最高的噪声总是太闹了。空调工程师们经常听到抱怨，随着空调工程技术水平的提高，人们的期望值也在不断上升，所以，人们的不满程度将总是不变。

第9单元

蒸气采暖与高压热水采暖

蒸气采暖

蒸气生产：在此还要概要说明的是：当热量加给部分充满全封闭容器中的水，达到沸点时，进一步补充热量，便引起物态的变化，使水变成蒸气。在这一过程中所包含的热量，在大气压下是 2258kJ/kg，与使水从 0℃升到沸点时的 420kj/kg 相比是相当大的。

蒸气在封闭容器中无法外泄，热量的进一步加入会引起压力上升。防止压力超过容器强度的办法是由安全阀提供的。压力上升时，温度也上升。这样，更多的热量是以液体和蒸气的显热形式进入水中的，当压力上升时潜热下降。

蒸气用于采暖包括冷凝过程，在此过程中，潜热被采暖系统的散热表面取去并复原为与蒸气温度相同的水。这种热水或冷凝水必须在它一形成时就排走，否则取暖设备将积水变得毫无用处。然而，冷凝水是在压力下，当释压至大气压时，要经受降温。实际上，冷凝水中部分超出大气压下沸点的热量用来使一部分液体再蒸发为较低压力下的蒸气，这被称作自蒸发蒸气。这种自然蒸发蒸气的用途有多种。但如果它不被有效利用会构成损失，就象冷凝水中余留的热量废弃所造成的损失一样。所以，在实践中冷凝水被收集起来并返回到锅炉里再使用，与此同时，提供了蒸馏水，并节省了水的消耗。

遗憾的是，冷凝水可能带有不凝性气体，如氯、二氧化碳和氧，这些气体易引起冷凝水管线的严重腐蚀。

冷凝水的回流：在取暖设备中冷凝成水后，如果排入下水道，会造成很大的浪费。它可能是燃料费用的 20%。如前所述，在正常情况下冷凝水将回流到锅炉再使用。

在放热设备或散热器的排放点，需要采用一些允许水但不允许蒸气通过的措施。这种器件被称作蒸气疏水器。有各种类型疏水器，依据将冷凝水与蒸气辨别和分离的方法可归如下三大类：1. 机械式的，包括（a）上部开口吊桶，（b）倒置的吊桶，（c）浮球；2. 恒温式的，有各种部件（a）平衡压力，（b）液体膨胀，（c）双金属的；3. 其他类，包括（a）迷宫式，（b）热力式，（c）脉冲式。

疏水器类型的选择由多个因素决定，例如：负荷特点（恒定的或波动的），出口和进口的压力，相关联的恒温器或用汽设备上的其他控制装置，以及疏水器相对液位和冷凝水主管道，等等。

高压热水采暖

高压热水系统之父是帕金斯（Perkins），他的此项专利在 1831 年提出。在他的系统中，管道非常坚固，口径约 22mm，形成一连续的盘管。管的一部分通过锅炉，其余部分放在需取暖的房间，形成加热面。在封闭容器的顶部允许水膨胀。在一个盘管不够的地方，用两个或更多的盘管。当水加热时，水的膨胀压缩容器中的空气，可达到相当高的压力。其原理是，水在系统中承受的压力防止蒸气的形成。此系统目前已废弃，尽管主要在一些教堂和小教堂或许仍然使用。

温度范围：初始的温度越高，很明显在供水和回水之间允许有更大的温降，相应地，单位水质量流的热容量也就越大，规定负荷所需管道尺寸越小。另一方面，压力越高，锅炉和其他设备的费用越大。

压力较低的系统需更多的加热面以满足给定的输出率。然而，对于较小的设备来讲，它也有很多足以补偿的优点。

由于这一原因和其他原因，人们普遍认为，负荷低于 2000 至 3000 千瓦的系统，设计成高压就毫无意义。低于这一负荷的系统，中压最为适宜。随着规模的不断扩大和干管的大大伸长，高压系统才得到它的应用。

与蒸气的比较：封闭系统中处于压力下的热水可以在设计的最大温度值以下的任何温度下运行。用于供暖设施的场合，水的温度可依天气而改变，所以能减少主管道热量损失，但一般要通过较好的控制。对蒸气来说，温度不可能随时改变，或是打开或是关掉。任何想减少流量的尝试都有可能导致在较远的端点积水。（这不包括有更加复杂装置的真空蒸气系统。）

热水系统不需要蒸气疏水器。通过自蒸发蒸气和冷凝水回流的潜在热损失可能达到甚至超过燃料消费的 10%。和其他辅助设备一样，疏水器也需要维修。

铺设热水主干管道可以不考虑标高问题，而蒸气主干管道需要仔细找坡度和排水。还要避免冷凝水管线的腐蚀。

在管道尺寸和造价方面，总的来说，两种系统的差别很小。

第 10 单元

效率再度流行

"Synallagmatic" 这个词是法律用语，定义为"施加相互义务并以彼此的权利和职责为特征"。这个词不是限定"Cogeneration"（联合生产）的，但它指明了正确的方向。"伙伴关系"一词更加适合。"达到互利"最切合导至有效的联产协议的宗旨。Synergism（协合作用）一词亦清楚地包含这个意思。

远在这个名称出现之前，在实践中，cogeneration（联合生产）就以多种形式出现了。据一份美国能源部的主题报告："从广义上讲，联合生产是表示同时生产电能或机械能和有用热能（通常以热液体或气体的形式）的任何一种形式。联产系统包括具有双重目标的发电厂，废热利用系统，某些形式的区域供热系统，和总体能量系统。"

区域供热系统就是热电联产的一例，这时城市电厂或有自备电厂的工业，以蒸汽或热水的形式把热能供应给用户。当一个区域供热系统不包括发电而仅简单地燃烧燃料来供热时，热电联产也就不存在了。

总体能量系统，比如由佛罗里达州，杰克森维尔市的 Regeney Sguare 购物中心运营的系统，能发电、供热、供冷，这种系统主要是针对密集开发区，比如购物中心、医疗综合设施、大学校园、或相当规模的公共机构等。

在美国，传统的能源系统一般仅提供一种产品，或是电能或是热能。引进热电联产后，一种系统设计成提供热能和电能，结果是在燃料和运行效率方面有显著改善。在热电联产操作中，本来也许要被废弃的热能又得以利用。通过节省能源和燃料需求量的方式，使系统明显地比以前更加有效。

热电联产有以下的好处：

●使用燃料的灵活性：各种可能供应的其他燃料均可供使用，而不仅是石油和天然气。

●效率：由于废弃能量的消除或减少，国家能源的自给率得以提高。

●费用优势：使用较少燃料达到多种目的，热电联产既节省能源也节省资金。

●环境的改善：热电联产系统只需较少的燃料产生额定的热能，这意味着相应的燃料燃烧释放污染物的减少。

●节约资源：以较少燃料，获得更多的能量，热电联产节省非再生燃料资源以及开采和运送这些资源的能耗。

●可靠性：在紧急情况下更有可能获得可靠动力，如自然灾害、危害性天气或地区性停电。

过去几十年，热电联产被认为是一种节省能源的手段，上述所有优点也都得到认可，但对热电联产介绍得很少。廉价能源供应的必然结果就是随意浪费能量。

80年代，常规的能源供应不那么容易得到了，也不那么可靠了，价格也贵多了。结果，热电联产在美国开始受到重视，而不再被忽视。节省燃料、降低支出、保护环境、确保可靠的能源供应，已成为重要的目的，而这个目的只有热电联产才能有效地达到。热电联产技术并不是新技术，各种形式的联产可以追溯到19世纪。对此技术的熟悉本身就是一种优势，因为在应用之前，不必再花时间去研究开发它。美国能源部就联产问题所作报告指出："联产是一个有生命力的技术方案，从眼前和长远看，它为美国向能源自给这一目标努力提供了又一种战略。"

有两种基本类型的热电联产系统可采用：上部循环系统：能发电和排出热能用于区域供热或相应功能。（2）下部循环系统：生产工业过程或区域供热用的热能，而一部分热能用来发电。每一种系统有特殊的装备要求。采用何种系统取决于用户的专门要求和情况。

城市电厂通常通过上部循环系统供应区域供热的蒸气或热水。机关团体、购物中心、类似的综合设施以及某些工业部门可能首先需要蒸气用于供热、供冷或工艺过程操作，这些单位最好是采用下部循环系统，利用一小部分蒸气来驱动汽轮机供电。

第11单元

集中供热管网规划

供热管网布局　供热管网布局的形状、设计及造价是与流体特性、供热地区的外形与位置以及用户负荷的地点及集中程度等密切相关的。从锅炉房接出的环状干管其优点是，允许供热点在周边布置，且可灵活分隔次级管网。对某些布局来讲，以锅炉房为起点和终点的单根干管也是可能的。其缺点牵涉到需要高负载循环泵，大口径主干管以及随平衡温度与热负荷带来的一些问题。管网的常规设计，特别是对那些房屋已经存在的情况，除了一些小系统之外，很少能证明环状干管是正确可行的。

一般的做法是采用枝状管线布局，它更加容易适应有卫星城镇的大城市的规划和适合于非常分散的地区。这种布局可能由多组从热源供出和回流的分支管组成，每一对干管在小区内为相关区段提供保证。每个分隔开的回路可拥有自己的循环水泵，其规格依管网范围大小而定。通常的做法是，可加设置几台备用泵或与供水管线连接的泵，以这种方式来保证备用容量。备用泵的大小，最恰当是以夏季家庭用基本热水循环量来确定。

供热干管 现行的做法有时仍要涉及到在可供采用的方案中进行选择，诸如单管、双管、三管及四管系统。除了较少采用的环状干管布局外，单管系统用于把水蒸气当作基本流体分送到广而散的管网中，以致于冷凝回水管线的初期投资和维修开支都非常高，把处理过的水废弃掉反而显得更为经济的场合。单管系统的另一个可供采用的方案是，将主要管网的供水用于各种家庭或市政服务设施和工艺过程中，最终都消耗掉。这种做法在苏联有明显的代表性。单管系统，除了取消回干水管而明显节省外，在西欧的具体条件下，在经济上和技术上是不合适的。

双管系统是最普通和广泛使用的供热形式，它包括一条供出管和一条单独的回流管。对蒸气供热来讲，这种系统也是很常见的，这时冷凝水回流管的直径要比蒸汽干管的小些。

当今，所有型式的热水供热系统均以双管布局为基础，它具有最佳设计和经济优越性，因此大大简化了好多方面的操作。对于城区供热和小区供热管网来讲，只考虑封闭系统，管内应保持清洁，并通过适当的水处理使之无腐蚀。

60年代中期前后，在西欧三管系统极少用于高压热水，这是因为当时普遍采用较低的水温和压力，以及越来越多地采用干管直埋方式，而第三根管子的任务是在非采暖期用来输送家庭用热水，这种做法也就不再流行。虽然这第三根管子在夏季月份只需输送较少量的水，相对来说供热损失也较小，可能会提供一些与此相关的优点，但有些论点是相当迷惑人的。与此相关的原因是：第三根管子的保障及维护费用；在夏季与冬季供水干管隔离开，而其中的水容量很大，从而出现为避免停流而采取防腐处置的问题。双管系统运行的经验证明，因新型干管的有效保温，在夏季使用较大的复合式供水干管，其额外热损失，实际上也可略去不计。采用三管系统时碰到的一个典型技术问题涉及到有效的热水供应失调，结果是在春秋季居室过热。这是因为大型家用热水加热器放水量小，致使复合式回水管的温度过分升高而引起的。

四管式供热系统旨在适应单独的分别设置的主供热系统和家庭用热水管网。集中式换热器安装远离用户，譬如可能在锅炉房内。四管系统将逐渐过时，其不明显的优越性已经被额外的费用所抵消，其中两条家庭用热水管要传送未经处理的自来水，这也可能引起麻烦。

第12单元

管道热膨胀及其补偿

一个极其值得注意的事实是，管子的长度与截面积随着温度的升降而增减，这是因为管材本身具有热膨胀系数。碳钢的膨胀系数为 0.012mm/m ℃，铜为 0.0168mm/m℃。它们的弹性模数分别是：钢为 $E=207\times10^6kN/m^2$，铜为 $E=103\times10^6kN/m^2$。例如：假设输水管的基本温度为 0℃，任何直径的钢管和铜管在加热到 120℃时，各自长度每米线性膨胀量分别为 1.4mm 和 2.016mm。而钢管的单位轴向力要比铜管大 39%。管子直径的变化与轴向伸长相比无实际意义，但由于膨胀或收缩而产生的轴向力是可观的，且能使施加约束力的附件断裂，这种力的大小与管子的尺寸有关。例如：有两条长度相等而直径不等的直管，在两端固定位，加温升到 100℃，对固定点作用的轴向力的总量近似地与各自直径成比例。

重要的是，在管道布线的设计，要以降低轴线应力的方法为这种热的作用提供充分的补偿措施，这种应力是与固定点之间的管长度与工作温度范围直接相关的。

热膨胀力的补偿

就膨胀问题而言，理想的管网应可能有最大限度的自由移动并且伴随有约束力的最小限度。所以，保障补偿和卸掉力的最简单和最经济的方法，就是利用管线方向的改变。如果有些地方直行的管道很长，且无方向改变的布线，则在适当间距内采用预先准备好的折线形变向补偿，这也是可行的。

另一种作法是，在直行管线上的计算间距内安装上特别设计的膨胀环管或"U"型弯。根据设计和可利用空间，在直管段上加膨胀弯头，它具有所谓双补偿"U"型弯头或是马蹄型或"竖琴"环的特点。最后几种名称的补偿器很少用于大型供热管网，它们可作为制造厂标准部件供应，在地下安装时需要完善的结构工程。

地下管道的固定的热位移量在正常的情况下可以被三种形式的膨胀弯所吸收，这就是："U"型弯、"L"型弯和"Z"型弯。在管子 90°转向的情况下常用"L"和"Z"型弯。有关设计固定点之间热膨胀预防措施的原则，实际上对这三种补偿器都是一样的。"U"型弯补偿器通常是由 4 个 90°的弯头和直管构成的，它容许有良好的热位移，且固定点的荷载比其他形状的环管要小。这种形状的膨胀弯对于预制的管中管系统来说是一个标准化模式。

所有热补偿器的安装都是为了调节等量的膨胀和收缩。因此，为了获得补偿器位移长度的充分利用，必须在安装时将补偿器环张开，使伸开量大约等于总计算热位移置的一半。这一工艺可以用"冷拉"或其他机械手段完成。两个固定点之间总伸长量的计算要以常年周围温度和设计运行温度为基础进行，使得在较低和较高温度时的应力和反力可控制在允许的极限以内。预加应力不影响管道的疲劳寿命，因此，在计算管网应力时不起重要作用。

有大量阐述管道设计和应力计算的专门出版物，一些是特别针对有专利的配管和膨胀节。以综合经验为背景的设计数据以及各种图表，都可以从生产厂家的出版物上获得，提供各类管子应力问题的解决方法。

取代上述热膨胀补偿方法并可用于空间有限地方的补偿器是更加昂贵的波纹管或套管式机械型补偿器。市场上有许多种有专利的型号和样品，下列几种型号较为常用：以轴向补偿器为形式的波纹管型膨胀节，为管子沿着轴线方向膨胀移动提供了保证，波纹管内在的移动仅仅是由拉伸和压缩产生的。还有一种铰接式波纹管补偿器，它可以把角运动和横向运动组合起来。铰接式补偿器是由两个补偿单元组成的，由越过每个波纹管的中线销住的定位夹板约束，或者是同样沿长度方向受约束的拉紧的一对波纹管。这样的补偿器适用于接纳很大的管道膨胀量，适合于有角度和横向位移的组合情况。

第 13 单元

经济型烟管锅炉

经济型三回程烟管锅炉

迄今的经验表明：如果由锅炉房集中生产热能，采用按著名的、历史悠久的三回程原理设计的新型全焊钢制经济型锅炉，即可获得最佳成本效益，这几乎没有例外。这种锅炉的最新型号已经发展到具有效率高，经济耐用，紧凑等特点，花钱购买它很值得。它的设计和制造在细节上有所区别，这取决于生产厂家和对锅炉的要求范围，使其符合指令性标准、尺寸和与其造价相适应的材料的技术要求。很多年来，锅炉型号的开发在如下有关方面达到了顶峰：现代精美的制造和现代运营；具有高平均生产效率；按合理有效标准操作和维修具有 25 到 30 年的预期使用寿命。就像所有的产品一样，高质量很少有造价低的现象，买方在最低价的投标之前常常必须三思而行。

在考察特殊用途的三回程烟管锅炉房时，最可取的作法是确保提供按其工况而专门设计的锅炉，工况要处于生产的工质和必要的运行参数范围以内。

蒸气锅炉改用于热水，完全可能在壳体的上部有过大的水容积，且因影响水流的热分布不当而导致循环不良。在热水锅炉中，对回水循环来说重要的是：采用自然水流结构，以便快速混合来均衡可能出现的分层和冷窝，避免由于供回水温度差形成的热冲击。

相反，如果热水锅炉改用于蒸气，大型壳体内的空间同样要引起体积上的变化并产生原来预定用于水的炉室和烟管周围加热区的位移。其结果是导致影响燃烧、循环和热容量的不均衡，特别是在部分负荷运行时。

高压锅炉改为低压运行，用于产生蒸气或由蒸气变为热水，它能引起排烟温度低和循环不良。这是由于在不同压力下和在水容积不平衡时介质的平均操作温度的差别很大而形成的。这种改装也许需要更高的生产成本。

经济型锅炉的效率

普通的新型三回程经济型锅炉在燃烧轻油、重油、天然气和其他燃气及煤时，应该能以同等的高效率生产。此时，锅炉必须适当地安装燃烧器或固体燃料炉排。如果装上匹配的多种燃料燃烧器或某些废料或木材专用的炉排，已经发展为具有高性能的锅炉。

新型三回程烟管锅炉和燃烧系统可望在 75%～100% 的负荷下获得大约 85%～87% 的生产效率；在理想状况下，1/3 到 1/2 负荷时、效率不低于 85%。

三回程烟管锅炉可看作是三回程兰开夏锅炉的最终发展，用第二回程和第三回程构成管束，替代砌筑的烟道。因较高的额定功率与较高的烟气流速相匹配，从而确保更高的效率。按当前的标准，这种经济型锅炉可被认为具有相当大的水容量，有助于储存热量和适应变化无常和断续的热负荷，而不致于丧失功能反应和灵活性。

火管

烟管锅炉第一回程是为燃烧火焰传播和辐射热传递而设计的火管。它构成了锅炉总受热表面的 10%～15%，但却占锅炉输出的大约 45%～55%，因此，这部份受热表面的负荷和随之出现的材料的应力显得很高，这是因为辐射传热的量值基本上是火焰温度的函数，其温度范围为 1000℃。现代炉室的容积通常这样设计，以保持燃烧强度不超过 2.0～2.2 MW/m³，以确保燃烧器有效可控，且使通过炉壁的热散失不要接近于钢板的上限温度。

火管可以作成波纹形的或光滑的。较为传统的波纹形炉室具有更大的传热接触面，但很难保持清洁和维修，从而抵消了它所具有的长处。在最近约 10 年期间，光滑火管得到许多人的赞同，因为它具有较大的刚度，而且烟灰和其他燃烧生成物容易除掉。而且，造价低，更换简单且费用少。

烟管

第一回程以后，烟气进入后烟箱。烟箱通常由水包围（湿背），以改善传热的平衡。然后烟气流经构成第二回程的适量烟管群进入锅炉前部的回程箱，再进入第三回程，将烟气送至尾部排烟口。

烟管对流加热表面上的传热率比火管的辐射传热要低得多。这不仅与温度有关，而且是气体速度和气流特性的函数。因此，可减少烟管，使等体积的烟气速度提高，从而增加传热。这仅在一定的切实可行范围内是可能的。烟气通过量的阻力能引起燃烧器风机过载，并增大动力费用。与此同时，过大的热应力会缩短锅炉的使用寿命。

第 14 单元

锅炉水处理

炉内水处理

市场上有众多的化学药品，有些被称作"锅炉抛光剂"，并被推荐作为"炉内"水软化和其他处理用。它们的作用是稳定硬度剂，防止结水垢或使沉积物易于除掉。这类化学药品还用于外部处理后系统中残余硬度的中和。这种性质的化学药品是以溶解状态，以及近乎恒定的流率供入给水箱或系统中。最常用的化学药品是磷酸盐，磷酸三钠是最知名的化学药品。它与钙盐和镁盐反应产生非溶性磷酸钙和磷酸镁。其他的内部处理药剂是氢氧化钙、碳酸钠、氢氧化钠、丹宁酸和胺。

在投入炉内处理化合物的过程中，能保证控制适量程度的最有效方法是采用定量器，它由一个或多个带有人工或机械驱动的搅拌器的容器和一个定量泵组成。

一般来说，对于硬度超过5°（英国）（70p.p.m）的水，不推荐单独使用炉内处理。这是因为系统和补充水量以及水的成分会变成危险状态，析出的泥渣和盐容易增加水的密度和泥渣的固化度，同时随之在产汽装置内有起泡和蒸溅的倾向，导致水循环困难。

炉内水处理一般限用于小型装置，比如说达到2～3MW，或作为残余处理，以及将pH值提高到某一需求值。

外部水处理

对于各种规模的装置和管网来说，系统中和补充水的外部软化是更加有效和广泛使用的水处理方法，它能适合大多数水质。目前外部处理牵涉到离子交换原理，它能确保有实际硬度为零的水。

离子交换过程可描述如下：溶解的盐分子在液体溶液中离解成自由荷电离子，在力场中离子被相反电荷所吸引，阳离子吸向阴极，阴离子吸向阳极。离子交换剂是非溶解的人造树脂，带有结合的可离解离子的化学基团附着在树脂上。按照活性基团的离解特性，离子交换剂可分为强活性，中等活性和弱活性三类。

阳离子交换水处理

在阳离子交换过程中，含钙盐和镁盐的原水流经由钠盐基活化的阳离子合成树脂床。钙盐和镁盐交换成数量上相当的碳酸氢钠和软水。

这种中性离子交换并不改变水中的含盐量和pH值，从而使自由的和结合的碳酸含量保持不变。由阳离子交换过程所软化的水不含钙和镁硬度剂。碳酸氢钠溶于水，并防止了沉淀。在高于110℃的情况下，碳酸氢钠可能会分解，产生部分结合和全部结合的二氧化碳，作为腐蚀剂释放出来。

当活性材料由于钙和镁的饱和而失效时，通过盐溶液冲洗，使其软化机能得到再生。盐溶液中的高浓度钠离子取代了交换剂中的氯化钙和氯化镁，并使其再活化。氯化钙和氯化镁随盐溶液排入下水道。

对再生没有实际上的限制，交换剂不会耗尽。在原水中带有的诸如含铁量超过0.3mg/L或含锰量超过0.2mg/L的机械杂质的情况下，交换剂可能被污染，从而降低交换能力。如果碰到这种不干净的水，最好采用预过滤器。杂质在再生过程中不可能从交换器床取出，并且交换剂的经常更换将成为必要。

阳离子交换软化器由特殊衬里的钢制圆筒和半满交换剂组成，并配以适当的连接口。这种装置能完全自动化，其再生周率由预定的流通水量，或由测试所得的硬度来决定。很少需要调节水量，除了盐之外，不需要其他化学药品。由两组设备相互并联，可使其交替再生，从而使过程连续进行。

离子交换除矿质作用

现代高压装置的供水的质量应该是所有的盐类和溶解硅酸均要被中和。生产蒸汽时，盐类应保留为沉积物，凝结水实际上变成了蒸馏水。

水处理方法发展的很大进步是由于非溶性人造树脂的演变。离子交换过程使用树脂是为了使得水能达到现代装置所要求的纯度。在脱矿质过程中，水流经串联的颗粒床交换器，以达到总溶解固体为5～20p.p.m的纯度。

在阳离子交换器里，水中的阳离子（钙、镁、钠、钾）与氢离子交换，由水溶的盐生成自由酸。在与阴离子交换容器相连接的第二列中，上述酸水失去了自由酸，剩下硅和二氧化碳。这时，水被完全除盐。

高度软化的处理方法用于大多数电站和需要最佳水纯度的制造工艺。对中小型装置来说，填充水和补给水不必完全软化。全部处理过的水，或从附属和相邻锅炉房，或从电站可以获得的凝结水，证明最适用于区域供热系统。

第 15 单元

制　　冷

当能自然地制冷时，曾为古代文明所利用。罗马统治者让奴隶们从高山上搬运冰、雪，用来保存食物，并在暑热时提供冷饮。当然，这种制冷的自然资源就地点、气温和范围而言是极其有限的。使用机械产生冷量的方式称作机械制冷，是 19 世纪 20 年代开始发展起来的。当今，制冷工业是任何技术社会的庞大而重要的一部分，仅在美国设备年销售额就达到数十亿美元。

1．制冷的用途

制冷的用途可简便地分为下列几类：家用、商用、工业用和空气调节。有时，运输被单独列为一类。家用制冷用于家庭的食物制备和保存，制冰和冰镇饮料。商业制冷多用在零售店、餐厅和公共机关，与家用制冷目的一样。食品工业中的工业制冷用于食品加工与制备，以及大规模的保存。略举几项，它包括在食品冷藏冷冻厂、冷藏库、酿酒厂和乳制品厂中的应用。成百上千的其他工业也使用制冷，其中有制冰厂、炼油厂、制药厂。当然滑冰场需要制冷。

制冷也广泛使用在舒适的民用空调和工业空调。工业空调用来为生产过程创造所需的空气湿度、温度和洁净度。计算机也需要一个可控制的环境。

2．制冷方法

制冷，通常所说的冷却过程，可更加正确地定义为"从一物质中排除热量，使其达到或保持在一理想的低温状态，"低于周围环境温度。"传播最为广泛的机械制冷的方法称为蒸气压缩系统。在此系统中，易挥发的液态制冷剂在一个蒸发器内蒸发，其结果是使热量从被冷却物质排出（冷却）。为了维持蒸发过程和使制冷剂复原再用，需设置压缩机和冷凝器。

另一种广泛使用的方法称为吸收式制冷系统。在制冷过程中制冷剂蒸发（如同在蒸气压缩系统中一样），但这种蒸发是通过在另一种液体中吸收制冷剂来维持的。

其他制冷方法有热电式、蒸气喷射和空气循环制冷。这些系统仅用于特殊用途，它们的工作原理在此不作解释。热电式制冷仍相当昂贵；一些桌置式小型家用冰箱用这种方法制冷。蒸气喷射制冷效率不高，过去常用于船舶，现已大量被蒸气压缩系统所替代。空气循环制冷有时用于机舱空调。以极低的温度制冷，低于大约-200°F（-130℃）被称作低温技术。要用特殊的设备达到这种状态。超低温制冷的一种用途是从空气中分离氧和氮，并使它们液化。

3. 制冷设备

蒸气压缩系统的主要设备组件是熟悉的蒸发器、压缩机和冷凝器。设备可能是分离的或整体式的（也称作整装的）。整体式设备是在工厂组装的。家用冰箱是整体式设备的普通实例。整体式设备明显的优点是更加紧凑，并在大批量生产时较便宜。

商业用制冷设备种类繁多；每种都有其指定的功能。开式冷柜、能进人的大冰箱和展品柜被广泛应用于食品服务业。自动制冰机、饮水冷却器和冷藏销售器也都是常见的设备。

空调包括内部环境空气的加热、降温、加湿、除湿和净化（过滤）。有时当论及两个学科之间的相互关系时，必须提到空调的一些内容。对空调所涉及的原理和设备的研究甚至对那些主要对制冷感兴趣的人来说也是很有价值的。

第 16 单元

热电偶测温

由于热电偶具有很多优点，所以长期以来一直被广泛用于科学研究和工业测温。热电偶结构简单，通常由两根导线，一个稳定的基准接点，一个电位差计组成。更复杂的热电偶系统可由很多单独的接点或热电堆组成，但基本原理和检测仪表不变。它们也许是大型的（有机械保护和防腐蚀），也可能是小型的（提供快速响应时间和热容量小）。用于低温系统的细小导线很脆和易变形。用于炉子内粗导线通常是铠装的，因而坚固。

经精心设计的温度计密封套可经受住很多种腐蚀性环境的考验。热电偶可用于很广的温度范围，从液体氦（−270℃）到高温炉（2200℃）。然而，对各种温度极限值需要有不同的合金。很多热电偶组合在很大的温度范围内产生近似线性的输出量。这种特性导致标定和检测方法更加简单和准确。不象电阻温度计那样，热电偶没有自热效应，在精确的量热和低温研究中这是非常重要的。

可能有的热电偶组合的数量实际上是无限的。但有幸的是，大量的电偶组合已经标准化了。各种型号和测温值的标准使得人们能以合理的价格从若干不同的合金厂家和很多仪器公司那里广泛获得大多能互换的材料。

最后，但并非最不重要的一点是热电偶系统容易装备仪表：便携的电位计、实验室检流计，记录式电位计和数字式万用表等均为通常使用的。对于大多数实际应用来说，插入温度补偿接点可取消所需稳定的基准接点，这是最为普遍的工业实际情况。

1821 年 Thomas Johann Seebeck 在铋—铜和铋—锑电路上做实验时发现了热电电流的存在。他证明：当非相同的金属的连接点加热到不同的温度时，产生净热电电动势。如果导线形成一个闭路回路，就感应出热电电流。几年之内，Bequerel 实验证明铂—钯偶能用于测量温度。大约 10 年后，Jean Peltier 发现：当外部施加的小电流通过不同的热偶导线接点时，产生一种异常的热效应。当电流在一个方向通过一连接点时，该连接点冷却下来；而当电流流向相反方向时，该连接点被加热。借助于最新发展的热力学理论，Willian Thomson

（后来被封为开尔文爵士）能证明这两种效应是相互联系的。他又推导了一些沿用至今的基本公式。从此以后，温差电学理论已相当严密和复杂（虽然热偶的实际应用并不需要这些理论）。一部现代研究的经典著作是由 Mac-Donald 写出的。Pollack 为美国测试和材料协会（ASTM）作了一个非常全面的基础性的评论。

最早的而又广泛应用的电偶组合之一是铜—康铜，现称之为 T 型。另一种长期使用的标准材料是镍铬合金—镍铝合金，现为符合 K 型标准值的材料之一。最为普遍应用的高温电偶组合是铂—铂铑合金，即 S 型、R 型和 B 型。铂系被称为贵金属组合，其余的被称作贱金属型。近几年来，若干新材料已开发出来，而且被广泛接受，包括适用于高温的钨—铼，适用于低温范围的金—铁，适用于中间和中等高温的镍铬硅—钒硅。

了解基础热电回路所需要的基本原理可以由基本方程式推导出的下述三个定律得到解释。

1. 均质导体定律——在单一均质材料回路中，即使断面变化，单靠加热不能产生热电电流。

因此，对热电回路来说，至少需要两种不同的材料。应该指出，物理和化学上的缺陷会使材料实际上不均匀。

2. 中间导体定律——如果全部回路处在均匀温度下，在不同材料组成的回路中的热电势（电压）代数和为零。

第三种非均质材料只要处于等温范围之内，总是可被加进一回路中去的。鉴于此定律，结果是：如果连接处等温，连接热力偶导线的方法，如钎焊，焊接，紧固，水银连接等等，都不影响热电输出量。另一结果是，如果两种材料相对于某一基准材料的热电电压已知，则其彼此之间的电压可相加而得。

3. 中间温度定律——当连接点温度为 T_1 和 T_2 时，假定两个不相同的均质导体热电动势为 E_1；当连接点温度为 T_2 和 T_3 时，假定热电动热势为 E_2。当连接点温度为 T_1 和 T_3 时，所产生的电动势将是 E_1+E_2。该定律的结果之一是，为某一基准温度而标定的热电偶能很容易地为另一个基准温度进行校正。这一定律带来的另一方便之处，就是有可能利用延伸导线而不干扰合成的热电电压。

Appendix III　Key to Exercises

UNIT ONE

Reading Comprehension

I 1. D 2. C 3. B 4. D 5. A

II 1. T 2. F 3. F 4. T 5. T

Vocabulary

I 1. impact 2. feedstock 3. warrant 4. quantify 5. operation

II 1. B 2. B 3. A 4. C 5. D

Translation

I . 1. 这些灯的燃料是动物油脂。

2. 功之大小等于力和距离之乘积。

3. 土木工程师不能免试口试。

4. 适应自然环境的建筑物更受欢迎。

5. 我会很高兴尽最大努力作好那方面工作。①传热面；②大块混凝土温度升度；③防水膜；④水灰比强度定律；⑤排气通风机；⑥通风调节装置；⑦排气冷凝器；⑧排气煤气采暖器；⑨近似计算；⑩污水处理。

UNIT TWO

Reading Comprehension

I 1. B 2. D 3. C 4. B 5. B

II 1. T 2. F 3. T 4. T 5. F

Vocabulary

I 1. be oxidized 2. gasification 3. is diffused 4. evolve 5. facilitate

II 1. A 2. C 3. B 4. D 5. B

Translation

1. 磁铁是怎样给我们指示方向的呢？

2. 在注重强度的工地，如果水泥现场存放时间过长，就应该对水泥进行测试。

3. 眼睛生来就是借助光来判别物体形状的，光的明暗表现出物体的形状。

4. 生活中充满活力的种种表现与其他经历溶合就会成为画家的丰富的表现力。

5. 就象任何一个产品一样，质量高而又造价低是不常见的。因此，买主千万不要轻意去购买这种最廉价的推销品。

6. 没有什么地方比家好。

UNIT THREE
Reading Comprehension
   I 1. D 2. A 3. C 4. B 5. D 6. A

   II 1. T 2. F 3. T 4. F

Vocabulary
   I 1. vitiate 2. exhausting 3. is diluted 4. be dispersed 5. ventilation

   II 1. C 2. A 3. C 4. B 5. D

Translation
   I. 1. 样品里的缺陷，即使有的话，可用超声波检出。

     2. 单跨结构通常用于较小的厂房，而多跨结构则用于较大的厂房。

     3. 该旅馆的设计采用了高低层结合的方式。

     4. 在 24 小时内，它的强度等于普通波特兰水泥 30 天所达到的强度。

     5. 这块锻件是六英寸长，八英寸宽，二英寸厚。

     6. 当电流在一个方向通过一连接点时，该连接点冷却下来，而当电流向相反方向时，该连接点被加热。

   II. 1. 只要用得适当，这种锅炉非常有效率。（省译 it）

     2. 听说你对计算机很了解。（省译 it，that）

     3. 这些支点所产生的反作用力是向上的。（省译 the，which，in，an，direction）

     4. 这些年轻人把照顾邻居老人当作份内的事。（省译 it，that）

     5. 由此可见，不是所有的物质都能导电。（省译 it，that）

     6. 正是采用了空调设备才大大地克服了内廊式没有穿堂风的缺点。（省译 it，that，its）

UNIT FOUR
Reading comprehension
   I 1. B 2. D 3. C 4. D 5. D

   II 1. T 2. F 3. F 4. T 5. T

Vocabulary
   I 1. turn to 2. are applicable 3. is confined

     4. have resort to 5. are confronted

   II 1. B 2. B 3. A 4. C 5. D

Translation

1. 未必全对。

2. 不是全部数据都错了。

3. 不是两种计算都不正确。

4. 李教授在该书中的结论不是每个都很科学。

5. 不是每件事都能干好。

6. 设计师不都总是和材料打交道。

7. 我确信，没有传导对流传热就不可能发生。

8. 据认为大多数塑料不容易传热和导电。

9. 这个方案不是因为它简单才放在首位，它已被广泛接受。

10. 他动身比我早不是因为他想第一个到达那儿。

UNIT FIVE

Reading comprehension

Ⅰ 1. C 2. B 3. A 4. C 5. D

Ⅱ 1. F 2. T 3. T 4. F 5. T

Vocabulary

Ⅰ 1. hapharzard 2. natural ventilation 3. justified
4. take account of 5. alternately

Ⅱ 1. A 2. C 3. B 4. A 5. D

Translation

1. 那天发现一个<u>类似</u>飞碟的奇怪现象。

2. 轻质混凝土主要是最近 20 年来<u>发展起来</u>的。

3. 他们<u>用</u>动物作实验。

4. 水银的<u>重量</u>约为水的十三倍。

5. 众所周知，重的东西比轻的东西<u>稳定性</u>大些。

6. 如果时间允许，应该对孔洞进行适当的<u>设计</u>。

7. 我们帮助了他们<u>摆脱</u>重重困难。

8. <u>直到可得到</u>廉价的煤，因而<u>可得到</u>廉价水泥之后，才可能<u>出现</u>优质坚固而耐久的混凝土。

UNIT SIX

Reading comprehension

Ⅰ 1. C 2. D 3. A 4. C 5. D

Ⅱ 1. F 2. T 3. F 4. F 5. T

Vocabulary

Ⅰ 1. graduations 2. particles 3. conveyor

4. respectively 5. Adverse

Ⅱ 1. D 2. A 3. C 4. B 5. D

Translation

1. 瓶子里没有水。

2. 土壤试验贯穿建筑工程始终。

3. 铜的导电性比其他材料强。

4. 我们把电子计算机应用于工业设计。

5. 计算准确，迅速是电子计算机的主要特点。

6. 以室内产生过量的热足以对预计量的空气加热为前提，冬天使用自然通风。

7. 在确定通孔高度时，确保通风孔将室内暖空气通过混合对进气加热。

8. 液体环流的形成是由于液体内引流和能量传递的结合。能量传递产生于液体运动本身；而液体运动由人工 方式形成或重流形成。

UNIT SEVEN

Reading comprehension

Ⅰ 1. B 2. C 3. D 4. A 5. B

Ⅱ 1. F 2. T 3. T 4. F 5. T

Vocabulary

Ⅰ 1. parameters 2. air current 3. ameliorate

4. congregate 5. hygienic

Ⅱ 1. B 2. D 3. A 4. C 5. D

Translation

Ⅰ 1. 该实验介绍了一个其重要性要予以特别强调的事实。

2. 然后必须增加空气温度以便产生更为适合的相对湿度。该相对湿度通过加温形成，或通过与尚未冷却的空气混合而成。

3. 工业通风可视为三部分组成：工业环境控制系统、工业排气设施系统和工业干燥系统。

4. 空调科学可解释为提供和保持理想的室内大气环境不受外部环境影响的一门科学。

5. 通风的估量与通风设计方案有直接联系。

Ⅱ 1. 一般说来，送至火焰上的氧气并非全部耗尽。

2. 一份好的说明书将扩展和明确图纸说明，规定材料和技术质量，确定施工范围，详细说明直接承包者的职责。

3. 从设备的单位小时运行费来考虑，使用热泵比使用具有独立采暖设施的制冷系统更为合算。

4. 液体靠重力作用从泵中流出并仅靠大气压力作用而上升，但大气压力不可能将水提升高度超过 30 英尺。

5. 我们看见现代建筑物都或多或少装有空调，这几乎成了惯例。

UNIT EIGHT

Reading comprehension

Ⅰ 1. B 2. A 3. D 4. D 5. C

Ⅱ 1. F 2. T 3. F 4. F 5. F

Vocabulary

Ⅰ 1. lack 2. trade 3. Draught

4. category 5. receding

Ⅱ 1. A 2. C 3. D 4. B 5. A

Translation

1. 几乎所有的国家采用米制。

2. 铁是通过高炉冶炼从矿石中提取的。

3. 在口语中，"功"和"功率"常被混淆或相互代用。

4. 电为人类所熟悉已有几千年了。

5. 气体通常被看作是可压缩的，而液体则是不可压缩的。

6. 已经注意到采取防腐新措施。

7. 现代工业使用大量蒸气来产生动力。

8. 燃料中储藏的可用能量通过称为燃烧的过程转为热能。

UNIT NINE

Reading comprehension

Ⅰ 1. B 2. C 3. A 4. C 5. A

Ⅱ 1. T 2. F 3. F 4. T 5. F

Vocabulary

Ⅰ 1. corrosion 2. remainder 3. latent

4. obsolete 5. reverted

Ⅱ 1. B 2. A 3. C 4. A 5. D

Translation

1. 现已公认，除非有运动，否则就不做功。

2. 据估计，新型晶体管的开关时间缩短为三分之一。

3. 据推测，太阳比地球大 33 万倍。

4. 众所周知，高度越高，则那里空气越少，压力越低。

5. 对流器的外部由钢板构成，而内部则用砖砌成。转换器斜装在对流器一侧。

6. 前一章节的描述仍然非常过于简化。碳分子结构和最后的燃烧不是集中在非常接近理想表面，控制碳分子 结构的反作用，由于某种原因，而被延误了。

7. 就近开采的骨料必须进行筛分，洗去粘土或泥沙，并且按正确的比例重新组合。

8. 完成全部勘探以后，再进行实地钻井。把天然气或原油打出地面，并将它堵住。就让这口井保持这种状态，直到需要天然气或原油时才打开。

UNIT TEN

Reading comprehension

I 1. T 2. F 3. F 4. T 5. T

II 1. D 2. A 3. D 4. D 5. D

Vocabulary

I 1. denotes 2. discharged 3. depletable 4. implementation 5. Viable

II 1. B 2. A 3. C 4. D 5. B

Translation

1. 太阳是地球的 33 万倍那么大。

2. 氧原子的重量是氢原子的 16 倍。

3. 水银是水重的 14 倍。

4. 波束宽度为原来的两倍。

5. 当时估计，剩余的煤储量是已开采量的两倍。

6. 煤产量比 1990 年增加了两倍。

7. 温度升高 100℃，半导体的电导率就增加了五十倍。

8. 这两个城市之间年电话往来量增加到（原来的）7 倍。

9. 将增音机间距减少一半，能使带宽增加到（原来的）4 倍。

10. 氮分子和氧分子的质量比氢分子分别大 13 倍和 15 倍。

UNIT ELEVEL

Reading comprehension

I 1. D 2. C 3. A 4. A 5. B

II 1. F 2. T 3. F 4. T 5. F

Vocabulary

I 1. standby 2. practice 3. bulk

   4. optimum 5. modulation

Ⅱ 1.D 2.A 3.C 4.B 5.D

Translation

1. 预计到 2000 年，世界石油年产量将下降百分之三十五。

2. 煤的含氧量每增加百分之一，其热值下降百分之一点七左右。

3. 压力将减少到原来数值的四分之一。

4. AB 线比 CD 线短一半。

5. 该机器的输出功率比输入小二分之一。

6. 电压降低为原来的五分之一。

7. 新设备的误差率为原来的七分之一。

8. 测试表明，放射性可降低到原来的十分之一到百分之一。

9. 和老式打字机相比，主要的优点是重量减为原来的四分之一。

10. 人体内金属污染物的磁场通常约为地球磁场的百万分之一。

UNIT TWELVE

Reading comprehension

Ⅰ 1.A 2.D 3.B 4.B 5.D

Ⅱ 1.T 2.T 3.F 4.F 5.F

Vocabulary

Ⅰ 1. inserted 2. elasticity 3. advantage

4. leaner 5. coefficient

Ⅱ 1.B 2.D 3.C 4.B 5.A

Translation

1. 煤提供的能量是千百万年前的植物储存的太阳能。

2. 为我们提供全部热量的太阳是一个极好的能源。

3. 空气从压力高的地方流向压力低的地方。

4. 穿过大气层时所损失的太阳能大约等于在地球表面上所接收的太阳能。

5. 作为煤的主要成分的碳，已与空气中的氧化合成二氧化碳。

6. 钢的含碳量如低于 0.2%，就是一种延展性好的软钢产品。

7. 分子运动的速率取决于分子所具有的能量。

8. 在存放电子计算机的房间里不能有一点灰尘。

9. 必须指出污染是我们必须解决的迫切问题。

10. 核裂变发生时放出大量的能。

UNIT THIRTEEN

Reading comprehension

Ⅰ 1. D 2. A 3. D 4. B 5. C

Ⅱ 1. T 2. F 3. T 4. F 5. T

Vocabulary

Ⅰ 1. is counteracted 2. commensurate with 3. cost-effectiveness

4. excessive 5. replacement

Ⅱ 1. C 2. A 3. B 4. D 5. A

Translation

1. 燃料是一种物质，在适当温度下能够燃烧并放出热量。
2. 射电望远镜有巨大的抛物形天线，使用这种天线我们可收集来自外层空间的无线电波。
3. 微粒灰尘能反射蓝光，但粗粒灰尘却不能。
4. 与氧结合的过程就是氧化，燃烧就是其中的一种。
5. 固体二氧化碳的温度低，这使得它很适用于冷冻。
6. 离子的运动就是那些得到或失去电子的原子运动，这种运动，多半发生在化学溶液中。
7. 固体燃料，如煤和木材，只能在表面燃烧，因为表面接触空气。
8. 电灯里不能氧气，因为金属丝在氧气里会烧毁。
9. 铜的阻力很小，所以广泛用于电力传输。
10. 尽管电子计算机有很多优点，但是它们不能进行创造性工作，也不能代替人。

UNIT FOVRTEEN

Reading comprehension

Ⅰ 1. B 2. D 3. B 4. A 5. B

6. B 7. D 8. B

Ⅱ 1. T 2. F 3. F 4. T

Vocabulary

Ⅰ 1. ensure 2. free of 3. are neutralized

4. dictate 5. optimum

Ⅱ 1. D 2. B 3. A 4. C 5. B

Translation

1. 如果地基是粘土性的，干燥后会显著收缩，那么，基础就必须有足够的深度，以使粘土的状态保持适当稳定。
2. 很清楚，为了节能和节约设备费、永久运行费，对窗户加防风雨措施是经济实惠的，因为非控制性的通风一天 24 小时都在进行。而通常每天和使用房间的几个小时里才需要通风，在这种情况下，常用一些可控制的 通风方法，如开窗通风。

3. 现代科学的一切成就不仅提供了承受高温高压的材料，而且也提供了新技术工艺，依靠现代科学的这些成就，我们相信完全可以制造这样的人造卫星。

4. 虽然现在积累起来的知识很多，而且任何个人也只可望了解其中一小部分，但事实上，各学科之间界线 却变得模糊不清，科学再次近似于两百年前那样的"单一整体"。

5. 这类机器包括所有的金属切削机床。其作用在于能连续切削多余的备料，即尺寸逐渐缩小，直到符合规定的大小为止。但这类机器不包括金属板加工机，金属成形机和锻压机。

6. 万有引力定律表明，宇宙中每种物质的粒子都对其他物质的粒子产生引力。这种引力与特质粒子质量的乘积成正比，与它们之间的距离的平方成反比。

UNIT FIFTEEN

Reading comprehension

Ⅰ 1. C 2. C 3. C 4. B 5. D

Ⅱ 1. F 2. T 3. F 4. F 5. T

Vocabulary

Ⅰ 1. evaporation 2. liquefy 3. assembled

4. internal 5. interfere

Ⅱ 1. A 2. C 3. B 4. B 5. D

Translation

1. 由于系统和补充量以及水的成分会变成危险状态，析出的泥渣和盐容易增加水的密度和泥渣的固化度，同时随之在产气装置内有起泡和蒸溅的倾向，导致水循环困难。所以，一般来说，对于硬度超过5℃（英国）（70P.P.m）的水，不推荐单独使用炉内处理。

2. 尽管必须考虑泵的价钱和运行动力费用，但强制循环的益处大大超过费用的重要性。而这一费用与总投资和设备运费相比，只不过是个小数。

3. 这种建立蒸气最终温度的方法与过去曾被广泛采用的过热降温器的方法不同。在过热降温器中，水与过热 蒸气混合，使得蒸气温度降低。它也不同于使一部分过热蒸气通过浸没在蒸气包中的盘管来降低温度的方法。

4. 自然循环系统依靠上升管与下降管中水的密度差进行循环。与此不同，强制循环系统依靠水泵所产生的压 力差而形成。这一压差使水以满足有效传热和防止锅炉产生汽塞的流速流过锅炉管束。

5. 来自蒸发器的蒸气行至蒸气呈含饱和状态的蒸气包，随后继续上行到过热器中·在最后流至汽轮机的节流阀前，蒸气在过热器中通过吸收在中间环路内钠的附加热量而达到过热状态。

UNIT SIXTEEN

Reading comprehension

Ⅰ 1. C 2. B 3. C 4. C 5. A

Ⅱ 1. F 2. T 3. T 4. F 5. T

Vocabulary

Ⅰ 1. availability 2. negate 3. was reversed

4. is induced 5. deriving from

Ⅱ 1. D 2. A 3. D 4. B 5. C

Translation

1. 为达此目的,作者认为理想的办法是从过去的数学家著作中大量摘引。因为唯有此法才能对他们经历的巨大困难作出正确的评价。

2. 虽然这样的转子直径较小,但其圆周速度可达13000m/min。这两个因素又可解释转子的尺寸比例与形状。转子与转子轴常常是一个整体钢锻件,其长度可能为转子直径的4至5倍。

3. 结构设计本身包括两项不同任务:一是结构设计,确定主要构件的尺寸和位置;二是用数学方法或图解方法,或两者兼用进行结构分析,以便在构件选定后计算出各荷载通过结构的情况。

4. 虽然中性物体本身是不带电的,但对于带电体来说,它并非中性。当两个物体彼此接近时,就会产生极性相反的电荷作用。这就是中性物体被带电体吸引的原因。

5. 还应当指出,由于一个小指南针的两端与地球的两极之间的距离几乎相等,因此指南针不会被拉向地球的某一边,地磁的影响只是指向而已。

6. 火箭技术的进展已使速度可达几千英里每小时,而更为重要的是,这种进展已使火箭能达到远远超过飞机所能达到的高度。在这样的高度上,很少或根本没有空气阻力,因而很容易达到并保持火箭的那种高速度。

图书在版编目（CIP）数据

建筑类专业英语. 暖通与燃气. 第二册/向阳主编. —北京：
中国建筑工业出版社，1997（2022.2重印）
高等学校试用教材
ISBN 978-7-112-03036-1

Ⅰ. 建… Ⅱ. 向… Ⅲ.①建筑学－英语－高等学校－
教材②采暖－英语－高等学校－教材③通风－英语－高等学
校－教材④燃料气－英语－高等学校－教材 Ⅳ. H31

中国版本图书馆 CIP 数据核字（2005）第 156721 号

本书按国家教委颁布的《大学英语专业阅读阶段教学基本要求》规定组织编写的专业英语教材。本册包括通风、供热、燃气工程、锅炉设备、制冷工程、热工仪表等概述性的内容及新技术的发展概况。全书安排 16 个单元，每单元除正课文外，还有两篇阅读材料，均配有必要的注释。正课文还配有词汇表和练习，书后附有总词汇表、参考译文和练习答案，语言难度大于第一册，还对科技英语翻译技巧作了简要说明，并增加例句和翻译练习题。本书可供本专业学生三年级下学期使用，也可作有关专业人员自学英语之用。

高等学校试用教材

建筑类专业英语

暖通与燃气

第二册

向　阳　　　　　主编

钱申贤　夏　岩

陈素红　胡　昱　　　编

钱申贤　　　　　主审

*

中国建筑工业出版社出版、发行（北京海淀三里河路 9 号）

各地新华书店、建筑书店经销

天津翔远印刷有限公司印刷

*

开本：787×1092 毫米　1/16　印张：12¼　字数：301 千字
1997 年 5 月第一版　　2022 年 2 月第二十次印刷
定价：**48.00** 元
ISBN 978-7-112-03036-1
（38361）